The Phenomenology of Revelation in Heidegger, Marion, and Ricoeur

Studies in the Thought of Paul Ricoeur

Series Editors

Greg S. Johnson, Pacific Lutheran University/Oxford University (ELAC), and Dan R. Stiver, Hardin-Simmons University

Studies in the Thought of Paul Ricoeur, a series in conjunction with the Society for Ricoeur Studies, aims to generate research on Ricoeur, about whom interest is rapidly growing both nationally (United States and Canada) and internationally. Broadly construed, the series has three interrelated themes. First, we develop the historical connections to and in Ricoeur's thought. Second, we extend Ricoeur's dialogue with contemporary thinkers representing a variety of disciplines. Third, we utilize Ricoeur to address future prospects in philosophy and other fields that respond to emerging issues of importance. The series approaches these themes from the belief that Ricoeur's thought is not just suited to theoretical exchanges, but can and does matter for how we actually engage in the many dimensions that constitute lived existence.

Recent Titles in the Series

The Phenomenology of Revelation in Heidegger, Marion, and Ricoeur, by Adam J. Graves

Reading Religious Ritual with Ricoeur: Between Fragility and Hope, by Christina M. Gschwandtner

Reading Scripture with Paul Ricoeur, edited by Joseph A. Edelheit and James F Moore

Paul Ricoeur and the Hope of Higher Education: The Just University, edited by Daniel Boscaljon and Jeffrey F. Keuss

Paul Ricoeur and the Lived Body, by Roger W. H. Savage

A Companion to Ricoeur's The Symbolism of Evil, by Scott Davidson

Narrative Medicine in Hospice Care: Identity, Practice, and Ethics though the Lens of Paul Ricoeur, by Tara Flanagan

The Phenomenology of Revelation in Heidegger, Marion, and Ricoeur

Adam J. Graves

LEXINGTON BOOKS
Lanham • Boulder • New York • London

Published by Lexington Books
An imprint of The Rowman & Littlefield Publishing Group, Inc.
4501 Forbes Boulevard, Suite 200, Lanham, Maryland 20706
www.rowman.com

86-90 Paul Street, London EC2A 4NE, United Kingdom

Copyright © 2021 The Rowman & Littlefield Publishing Group, Inc.

All rights reserved. No part of this book may be reproduced in any form or by any electronic or mechanical means, including information storage and retrieval systems, without written permission from the publisher, except by a reviewer who may quote passages in a review.

British Library Cataloguing in Publication Information Available

Library of Congress Cataloging-in-Publication Data

Names: Graves, Adam J., 1977- author.
Title: The phenomenology of revelation in Heidegger, Marion, and Ricoeur / Adam J. Graves.
Description: Lanham : Lexington Books, 2021. | Series: Studies in the thought of Paul Ricoeur | Includes bibliographical references and index. | Summary: "Adam Graves presents a new framework for understanding the importance of the concept of revelation in the development of phenomenology while also charting a path towards a more fruitful understanding of the relationship between reason and revelation, one that is rooted in a deeper appreciation of the complexities of our linguistic inheritance"-- Provided by publisher.
Identifiers: LCCN 2021022725 (print) | LCCN 2021022726 (ebook) | ISBN 9781793640574 (cloth) | ISBN 9781793640598 (paperback) | ISBN 9781793640581 (ebook)
Subjects: LCSH: Phenomenology. | Revelation. | Ricœur, Paul. | Heidegger, Martin, 1889-1976. | Marion, Jean-Luc, 1946-
Classification: LCC B829.5 .G694 2021 (print) | LCC B829.5 (ebook) | DDC 142/.7–dc23
LC record available at https://lccn.loc.gov/2021022725
LC ebook record available at https://lccn.loc.gov/2021022726

∞™ The paper used in this publication meets the minimum requirements of American National Standard for Information Sciences—Permanence of Paper for Printed Library Materials, ANSI/NISO Z39.48-1992.

The eye—it cannot choose but see;
We cannot bid the ear be still;
Our bodies feel, where'er they be,
Against, or with our will.
Nor less I deem that there are Powers
Which of themselves our minds impress;
That we can feed this mind of ours
In a wise passiveness.
Think you, 'mid all this mighty sum
Of things for ever speaking,
That nothing of itself will come,
But we must still be seeking?

William Wordsworth, *"Expostulation and Reply"*

Contents

Preface	ix
Acknowledgments	xv
List of Abbreviations	xix
Introduction	xxi
Chapter 1: Retracing the Turn: Revelation and the Two Faces of Phenomenology	1
Chapter 2: Phenomenology, Theology, and Counter-Contamination in Early Heidegger	23
Chapter 3: Marion's Radical Revelation: Givenness and the Anonymous Call	77
Chapter 4: Ricoeur's Hermeneutic Phenomenology of Revelation: The World Reconfigured	145
Conclusion: Language, Reception, Contingency	197
Epilogue: In the Beginning Was the Word	205
Bibliography	207
Index	215
About the Author	223

Preface

More years than I care to admit have passed since I first began to formulate the ideas and arguments contained in the chapters that follow. Although I am fortunate that scholarly interest in the subject has only grown over that period of time, I cannot feign surprise. For the concept of revelation has long played a critical role in phenomenological discourse, and in the wake of the so-called theological turn in phenomenology questions about the precise nature of that role have become all the more urgent. Nonetheless, the subject has still received relatively little attention in the scholarly literature. This book tries to rectify that situation by offering a general framework for understanding the core problems and issues associated with the phenomenology of revelation. I develop this framework through a series of close readings which, when viewed collectively, essentially stage a dialogue or debate between three of its central figures—Martin Heidegger, Jean-Luc Marion, and Paul Ricoeur. Remarkably little has been written specifically about Ricoeur's contribution to the theological turn. By placing Ricoeur into an imaginary dialogue with Marion (arguable the theological turn's leading figure), I hope to fill that lacuna as well.

It probably goes without saying that there is no such thing as *the* phenomenology of revelation. However, I will argue that despite their many differences, phenomenologist have generally adopted one of two basic approaches. Some have adopted a "radical" approach to revelation that seeks to disclose—either through a radicalization of the phenomenological reduction or a return to facticity, Being, etc.—a purely heterological experience of revelation, one that is not only *anterior* to objectivity and theoretical reflection but, crucially, *prior* to all forms of linguistic mediation as well.[1] Others have adopted a "hermeneutical" approach, which characterizes revelation in terms of an eruptive event that unfolds *in front of* concrete texts—texts which are themselves recognized as invariably situated within a particular historic-linguistic milieu.[2] One might say, then, that both strands conceive of revelation as taking place *before* the text, but that radical phenomenologists understand the preposition in its temporal sense (i.e., "anterior to"), whereas hermeneutical phenomenologists take it in the spatial sense (i.e., "*in front of*"). In the course of my analysis, I show that the essential difference between these two approaches concerns the relation between revelation and language, and that this, in turn, reflects contrasting attitudes toward historical, linguistic, and textual mediation in post-Husserlian continental philosophy more broadly.

I have done my best to present the various phenomenological accounts of revelation in their own terms—that is to say, in terms of the broader philosophical projects to which they belong (whether that be Heidegger's fundamental ontology, Marion's phenomenology of givenness, or Ricoeur's hermeneutical phenomenology). That means, among other things, that I have sought to clarify their respective philosophical concerns and the commitments that have motivated their divergent, if not diametrically opposed, attitudes toward revelation. However, my objective is not simply to juxtapose them, to lay them side by side, or to compare them with the disinterested eye of an intellectual historian. One might say that I have a horse in the race. One of my central claims is that the radical conception of revelation—which, I believe, is implicit in early Heidegger and explicit in Marion's philosophical work—is motivated by a misguided desire to satisfy a hopeless standard of philosophical rigor by integrating revelation into a phenomenological project that could claim to be presuppositionless. In attempting to escape the charge of "theological biases" or "contamination," proponents of the radical approach have tended to overcompensate, ultimately attributing the formal character of revealability (i.e., the phenomenological *possibility* of revelation) to the actual *event* of Revelation itself. This results in conception of revelation that has been stripped of the concrete, material content that phenomenology was initially mean to describe. I characterize this misstep as a kind of "counter-contamination" resulting from the illegitimate influence of certain methodological pressures upon the material character of revelation itself. I also contend that the hermeneutical approach adopted by Ricoeur is more or less immune to these kinds of pressures, and so it yields a conception of revelation that is capable of capturing and accommodated the richness of the phenomenon's literary, figurative, and linguistic content. But it does so at the price of having to renounce the title of "presuppositionless philosophy" (a cornerstone of the phenomenological method as it was originally conceived by the movement's founder, Edmund Husserl). Therefore, the principal challenge facing the hermeneutical approach to revelation is whether it can provide a coherent account of what it means to do phenomenology in the absence of this kind of foundation. Ricoeur's work, I argue, lays the groundwork for such an account, and I offer my own thoughts about how this might be further developed in my conclusion.

Before launching into a detailed analysis of revelation in Heidegger, Marion and Ricoeur, I set the stage in my Introduction by considering, in admittedly broad terms, the history of revelation in enlightenment thought—a history which proves to be indispensable for understanding the distinctive role revelation comes to play in twentieth-century continental philosophy. Over the course of the enlightenment, the earlier scholastic conceptions of the relationship between reason and revelation began to harden into a diametrical opposition. A common goal among enlightenment thinkers (whether rationalist, empiricist, Kantian, or post-Kantian) was to render revelation superfluous as means of knowledge by demonstrating that so-called revealed truths could be more reliably attained through the unaided use of human reasoning. However, beginning in the late nineteenth century, continental philosophers became increasingly suspicious of the enlightenment's overly sanguine attitude toward human reason and of the kind of subjectivity underwriting this attitude. In certain phenomenological circles, revelation came to serve as the "logical" (that is to say, the historically appropriate) foil for the enlightenment's narrow conception of philosophical reason. So, whereas enlightenment figures generally sought to *reduce* revelation to reason, the phenomenologists discussed in this book have generally turned to revelation in order to upend a narrow enlightenment conception of reason and thereby *expand* the scope of philosophical understanding. As the "other" of enlightenment reason, revelation poses, in a way that only it can, a critical question about what is (or is not) a legitimate object of phenomenological investigation and, thus, about the limits of philosophy itself.

In fact, debate over the so-called theological turn in French phenomenology has been largely animated by this very question. However, in Chapter 1, I suggest that the general issues raised by revelation (and by religious phenomena more generally) had been present nearly from the inception of the phenomenological movement. The theological turn, therefore, should really be viewed as a theological "re-turn." I claim that in order to understand why the phenomenology of revelation eventually developed along two separate tracks—that is to say, along radical and hermeneutical lines—one must revisit works from that earlier period, especially the works of Heidegger in the nineteen twenties. Moreover, I also contend that the conflict between the two phenomenological attitudes toward revelation is connected to, if not prefigured by, certain debates within theological discussions of revelation.

In Chapter 2, I turn to a more detailed reading of the early Heidegger. In the past couple of decades, it has become increasingly clear that Heidegger's effort to uncover "factical life experience" during the postwar period was tied to his interest in the eschatological experience of the early Christian community. While most commentators (including Derrida, de Vries, and Caputo) have focused on the manner in which this early theological interest taints or "contaminates" his later fundamental ontology, I contend that the reverse is equally true—namely, that Heidegger's preoccupation with ontological questions led to a process of formalization that served to minimized and attenuate the concrete historical content of revelation itself. This process of counter-contamination is evidenced not only by the privilege he finally grants to the formal possibility of revelation (i.e., *Offenbarkeit*) over and above any actual revelation (*Offenbarung*), but also by the way that his conception of the former shapes his understanding of the latter.

In Chapter 3, I turn to a phenomenologist who first gained international attention for his efforts to rehabilitate the concept of God by means of a critique of Heideggerian ontology, namely, Jean-Luc Marion. Though Marion's appeal to revelation could be considered part of his critique of limitations of Heidegger's ontology, I argue that Marion's project paradoxically recapitulates the Heideggerian schema outlined in Chapter 2. In an effort to preempt the charge that his phenomenology is contaminated by theological presuppositions, Marion imposes the formalism of "revealability" onto "Revelation" itself. In characterizing revelation as a givenness that both exceeds and precedes linguistic determination, he thereby deprives revelation of its determinate content. I support this claim by way of a careful reading of his principle philosophical works, culminating in a discussion of his conception of the pure call.

In Chapter 4, I turn to an alternative phenomenological approach (that of Paul Ricoeur) which fuses phenomenological reflection with the hermeneutics of concrete texts. I argue that Ricoeur's theory of revelation is based on a unique synthesis of the phenomenological notion of 'world' and a hermeneutical theory of textual mediation. He articulates an idea of revelation as the surplus of meanings which unfolds itself *in front of* concrete texts that are always already situated within a specific historic-linguistic milieu. I argue that this hermeneutical alternative constitutes an important, yet often ignored, counterpoint to the previous two conceptions of revelation that have in fact dominated current phenomenological discussions.

In my conclusion, I once again revisit the old, enlightenment dichotomy of reason and revelation in order to see how it might be addressed from the vantage point of a philosophy that has absorbed lessons from both radical and hermeneutic strands of phenomenology. I suggest that a nuanced conception of the phenomenon of language allows us to dig beneath the surface of this opposition and to see both the craving for speculation and the calling to faith as part of a unique linguistic inheritance. In the end, the phenomenology of revelation is perhaps best seen as an attempt to respond to the solicitations implicit within a complex linguistic heritage which encompasses, in a mutually productive tension, both critique and conviction, reason and revelation.

NOTES

1. "Radical" in the sense most faithful to the word's etymology—as "pertaining to a root or roots," pertaining to that which is "fundamental," "original," or "primary." (*The Compact Edition of The Oxford English Dictionary*, Vol. II. New York: Oxford University Press, 1971, 2403).

2. Whereas the term "radical phenomenology" is not widely used, the term "hermeneutical phenomenology" is well established. Don Ihde's *Hermeneutic Phenomenology: The Philosophy of Paul Ricoeur*—the first major study of Ricoeur's work to appear in English—was largely responsible for solidifying this term's place within common philosophical parlance in the early nineteen seventies. Though my use of the term is consistent with Ihde's, it takes on a more determinate meaning when fleshed out in terms of the specific issues and problems raised by the phenomenon of revelation.

Acknowledgments

I want to thank my colleagues, mentors, and friends for their many contributions to this work, without laying any of its inevitable shortcomings at their doorstep. I am grateful to Richard Kearney and Emmanuel Falque for their friendship, warm hospitality, and spirited conversations—whether at the top of a snowcapped mountain or seated around a table at Le Doucet café, these have provided much insight and inspiration. In fact, had it not been for my recent involvement with the International Network in the Philosophy of Religion and the community of scholars that Emmanuel gathers every other summer at the *Institut Catholique de Paris*, I would have found it more difficult to summon the motivation necessary to carry this work to completion. I also want to thank the *Fonds Ricoeur*, which provided numerous opportunities for carrying out research at its archive at the *Institut Protestant de Théologie* in Paris and for sharing the fruits of that labor with its supportive and intellectually stimulating community of scholars. Among its many members, organizers, and participants to whom I am indebted, I would especially like to thank Marc Boss, Azadeh Thiriez-Arjangi, Johann Michel, Geoffrey Dierckxsens, Maureen Junker-Kenny, and Olivier Villemot. Thomas Carlson and Scott Davidson organized conferences and sessions at the AAR and elsewhere which gave me important opportunities to test my ideas early on. Conference organizers at the Katholieke Universiteit Leuven, the Society of Ricoeur Studies, Jagiellonian University in Kraków, and the National Research University of Moscow provided similar occasions at various stages along the way. Some of my earliest, and thus most outstanding, debts are owed to the community of scholars in the greater Philadelphia region, including Villanova, Swarthmore, and especially the University of Pennsylvania. I want to thank Jack Caputo, Mark Wallace, and Stephen Dunning for their insights and for providing feedback on early versions of some of the chapters.

I also want to thank Paul Guyer, Joel Weinsheimer, and the late Wilhelm Halbfass. I have especially fond memories discussing the paradoxes of the gift with my mentor and friend, Jean-Michel Rabaté.

Over the years, I have gained both pleasure and insight from less formal exchanges with Andrew Norman, Gabriel Grinsteiner, Eddis Miller, and Carl Raschke, as well as my students and colleagues at Metropolitan State University of Denver. Thanks must also go to the *Studies in the Thought of Paul Ricoeur* series editors, Dan Stiver and Greg S. Johnson, Lexington Books staff editor Jana Hodges-Kluck, Sydney Wedbush, and a particularly helpful anonymous reader.

I am forever grateful to my parents, Jim and Julie Graves, for having given me the encouragement and support to pursue my passions, even when they carried me in directions that might have seemed unintelligible to them; to my sons, Devan and Dhilan, whose frequent interruptions pleasantly redirected my attention away from books and back toward the mysterious world of everyday life (the world that philosophy should principally endeavor to understand); and, above all, to my astonishingly gifted wife, Suchitra Mattai, without whose constant inspiration, example, and love I might never have learned how to hear, let alone heed, the call in the first place.

Quotes republished with permission of John Wiley & Sons-Books, from *The Religious*, edited by John Caputo, 2002; permission conveyed through Copyright Clearance Center, Inc.

Epigraph from *The Unthought Debt: Heidegger and the Hebraic Heritage* by Marlène Zarader, translated by Bettina Bergo. Copyright © 1999 by Editions du Seuil. English translation © 2006 by the Board of Trustees of the Leland Stanford Junior University. All rights reserved.

Extracts from *Being and Time*, by Martin Heidegger, trans. J. Maquarrie and E. Robinson are © SCM Press Ltd, 1962. Used by permission. right@hymnsam.co.uk.

Extracts from *Being and Time* by Martin Heidegger. Translated by John Macquarrie and Edward Robinson. Copyright © 1962 by Harper & Row, Publishers, Incorporated. Used by permission of HarperCollins Publishers.

"Description Without Place," and "Nudity in the Colonies" from THE COLLECTED POEMS OF WALLACE STEVENS by Wallace Stevens, copyright © 1954 by Wallace Stevens and copyright renewed 1982 by Holly Stevens. Used by permission of Alfred A. Knopf, an imprint of the Knopf Doubleday Publishing Group, a division of Penguin Random House LLC. All rights reserved.

Excerpts from *The Collected Poems* by Wallace Stevens, 2006. Used by permission of Faber and Faber Ltd.

Excerpts from Jean-Luc Marion, *God without Being: Hors-Texte*. Translated by Thomas Carlson. Chicago: University of Chicago Press, 1991.

Epigraph republished with permission of Princeton University Press, from *Philosophical Fragments*, Søren Kierkegaard, Johannes Climacus trans., 1984; permission conveyed through Copyright Clearance Center, Inc.

Epigraph republished with permission of University of Chicago Press, from *Living Up to Death*, Paul Ricoeur, 2009; permission conveyed through Copyright Clearance Center, Inc.

List of Abbreviations

BG Jean-Luc Marion, *Being Given: Toward a Phenomenology of Givenness*. Translated by Jeffrey Kosky. Stanford, CA: Stanford University Press, 2002.
BT Martin Heidegger, *Being and Time*. Translated by Macquarrie and Robinson. New York: Harper & Row, 1962.
CI Paul Ricoeur, *The Conflict of Interpretations: Essays in Hermeneutics*. Translated and edited by D. Ihde. Evanston, IL: Northwestern University Press, 1974.
EBI Paul Ricoeur, *Essays on Biblical Interpretation*, edited by L. Mudge. Philadelphia: Fortress Press, 1980.
FS Paul Ricoeur, *Figuring the Sacred: Religion, Narrative, and Imagination*, edited by M. Wallace and translated by D. Pellauer. Minneapolis: Fortress Press, 1995.
GWB Jean-Luc Marion, *God without Being: Hors-Texte*. Translated by Thomas Carlson. Chicago: University of Chicago Press, 1991.
HH Paul Ricoeur, *Hermeneutics and the Human Sciences: Essays on Language, Action and Interpretation*, edited and translated by J. Thompson. Cambridge: Cambridge University Press, 1981.
OA Paul Ricoeur, *Oneself as Another*. Translation by K. Blamey. Chicago: University of Chicago Press, 1992.
PT Martin Heidegger, "Phenomenology and Theology." In *The Religious*, edited by John Caputo. Oxford, UK: Blackwell Publishers, 2002.
RG Jean-Luc Marion, *Reduction and Givenness: Investigations of Husserl, Heidegger, and Phenomenology*. Translated by Thomas Carlson. Evanston, IL: Northwestern University Press, 1998.

RM Paul Ricoeur, *The Rule of Metaphor. Multi-Disciplinary Studies of the Creation of Meaning in Language*. Translated by R. Czerny and K. McLaughlin. London and Henley: Routledge and Kegan Paul, 1978.

TA Paul Ricoeur, *From Text to Action. Essays in Hermeneutics II*. Translated by K. Blamey and J. Thompson. London: The Athlone Press, 1991.

TB Paul Ricoeur and André LaCocque, *Thinking Biblically: Exegetical and Hermeneutical Studies*. Translated by D. Pellauer. Chicago: University of Chicago Press, 1998.

TN Paul Ricoeur, *Time and Narrative. Vol. III*. Translated by K. McLaughlin and D. Pellauer. Chicago: University of Chicago Press, 1984.

Introduction

A BATTLE CRY: REASON, REVELATION, AND THE 'THEOLOGICAL TURN'

Reason and Revelation

No single theological concept poses a greater challenge to philosophy than that of revelation. Unlike the concept of faith—which in principle, if not always in practice, wears humility as a badge of honor, pitching its tent just beyond the fortress of philosophical knowledge—the very idea of revelation implies a claim to disclose truth, and it therefore allegedly confronts philosophy on its own turf. And unlike the concept of God—whose contested nature and existence has offered philosophy a ceaseless spring of argument and counter argument—revelation need not immediately appeal to human reason in order to justify itself. Revelation, one might say, is its own justification. In this respect, it is an affront to reason, an anathema to philosophy (or, at the very least, to a certain influential conception of philosophy). Revealed truth and rational truth are not merely *different*. They appear to be utterly *opposed*, destined from birth to face off as mortal enemies, caught in an endless, take-no-prisoners battle wherein each seeks to reduce the other to itself, to monopolize truth by capturing and colonizing the other's terrain.

Of course, this combat metaphor only captures one dimension of the relationship between reason and revelation, and one might very well suspect that it overexaggerates the antagonism between them. But even when one tries to avoid using it, or opts to portray the relationship in less oppositional terms, one nevertheless find oneself having to broker a truce between two potentially hostile parties whose tempers have been worn thin by centuries of battle.[1] Whatever progress has been made over the years towards negotiating a lasting peace has not only taken place against the backdrop of a precarious cease-fire, it has often come at the cost of having to partition the territory into two distinct, autonomous zones. Aquinas, whose thought will be discussed at greater length in the following chapter, was among the first to have rigorously drawn out the borders demarcating rational truths (the domain of *theologia philosophiae*) from the so-called revealed truths that remain wholly inaccessible to the natural light of reason (the domain of *theologia sacrae doctinae*). But he also introduced the idea of *revelabilia*—a broader and more inclusive category which refers to *all* that God has revealed, whether by natural or supernatural means—and so one might say that he also sought to normalize diplomatic relations between the two domains of truth. For Aquinas, of course, there was little doubt about the hierarchical relationship between these domains and the respective sciences corresponding to them: philosophy was to be subordinate to theology. Nevertheless, the fact that both reason and revelation could serve as sources of divine knowledge effectively guaranteed a sort of rational commerce between these two distinct ways of knowing.[2]

At the height of the German Enlightenment this essentially scholastic distinction found its way into modern philosophical discourse by way of another well-known distinction—namely, Leibniz's demarcation between necessary truths of reason, on the one hand, and contingent truths of fact or experience, on the other. While the opposite of a necessary truth implies a contradiction (and thus an impossibility), the opposite of a contingent truth remains entirely possible (at least, in principle). This philosophical theory of two truths provided a number of eighteenth-century enlightenment thinkers with a handy epistemological framework for determining the meaning, scope, and legitimacy of revelation, a framework that often accommodated, but also served to modify the Thomistic conception. Thus, for example, Gotthold Lessing observed in his influential 1777 essay "On the Proof of the Spirit and of Power" that revelation, insofar as it concerns historical events which cannot be directly inferred through reason but can only be known on the basis of human testimony, must be situated squarely within the class of merely contingent truths. This observation effectively stripped revelation of its claim to express eternal or necessary truths.[3] For to draw a necessary truth out of historically contingent fact would require one to cross what Lessing characterized as the "ugly, broad ditch" separating these two epistemic classes. No matter how earnestly he tried, Lessing found that he simply could not bring himself to make the leap: "accidental truths of history can never become the proof of necessary truths of reason."[4] And Lessing was not alone. A growing reticence towards making this leap of faith was common among his enlightened contemporaries. By the time Kierkegaard came along and boldly declared that "eternal happiness" can indeed be "built on historical knowledge," it was already more than obvious that the Dane's declaration was merely an exception that proved the rule: modern philosophy had largely come to see revelation as a historical relic that could never supersede the self-evident and eternal truths of reason. At best, it could provide an alternative means of arriving at these truths for those who may not have the fortune of philosophizing for themselves. This view both reflected and sharpened the underlying dualism of the scholastic formula. But as with all reflections, the reflected image was totally reversed—in other words, the scholastic distinction was maintained, but the hierarchical relationship between the two terms had been inverted.

Nonetheless, it is important to note that the border between the eternal truths of reason and the historical truths of revelation remained relatively unstable, as it was continually renegotiated and redrawn throughout the eighteenth and nineteenth centuries. With the enlightenment's glorification of humanity's rational capacities, there arose a widespread conviction that the "soul" of the Christian religion—its core teachings, and especially its moral ones—could be only "saved" if one could demonstrate that the historical contents of revelation somehow coincided, or were at least compatible, with the conclusions of autonomous reason. So began the often tedious and sometimes dubious hermeneutic task of sorting out those elements of revelation that are merely historical, merely contingent, from those that are consistent with the universal and purely rational—sorting out the merely "positive" religion from the true, "rational" one.[5] One of the most notable examples of this pervasive enlightenment operation is found in Kant's essay on *Religion Within the Boundaries of Mere Reason*, which sought "to hold the fragments of [. . .] revelation, as a *historical* system, up to moral concepts [or the principles of practical reason, in order to] see whether it does not lead back to the pure rational system of religion."[6] Although Kant executed this procedure with remarkable sophistication, the project itself was neither entirely new, nor unique.[7] Almost exactly one century before, Locke had declared in his essay on *The Reasonableness of Christianity* that "God, out of the infiniteness of his mercy [. . .] gave [humanity] reason, and with it a law, that could not be otherwise than what reason should dictate, unless we should think that a reasonable creature, should have an unreasonable law."[8] Although Locke maintained that this law must be consistent with reason, he nevertheless insisted that it could not have been supplied by reason alone, that is to say, without the aid of divine revelation, since "some parts of that truth lie too deep for our natural powers easily to reach [. . .] without some light from above to direct them."[9] As if to anticipate the more radical claims of later enlightenment thinkers, who would assert that these moral truths could be entirely derived from, and thus reduced to, the principles of reason alone, Locke offered a kind of psychological observation that cautioned against such reductivist tendencies: "When truths are once known to us, though by tradition, we are apt to be favorable to our own parts, and ascribe to our own understandings the discovery of what, in reality, we borrowed from others."[10] But Locke's cautionary tale would be tossed to the wind in the century that followed, as the Deistic views expounded by the likes of John Toland and Matthew Tindal began to gain favor among Europe's intellectual elite. Even Rousseau, the onetime Catholic convert, would come to reject all types of "particular" revelation (i.e., those based on historical texts or testimony) in favor of what he, speaking through the voice of his fictional Savoyard Vicar, referred to as "general" revelation (i.e., a revelation which could be understood solely on the basis of one's own "natural lights," or the universal faculty of reason).

But modern philosophy never fully put the idea of particular revelation to rest, even if its contents were made to rest upon a procrustean bed of reason, lopping off anything that might protrude beyond the edge of theoretical or practical reason. In fact, the belief that particular revelation was in some sense irreducible to the colder, more clear-eyed conclusions of enlightenment thought proved to be remarkably persistent. And if one listened closely, one could periodically hear echoes of Locke's earlier insistence that revelation contributed something to human understanding and society beyond what was obtainable through the natural lights alone. Even Kant, who was perhaps the staunchest advocate for the autonomy of reason, managed to preserve some function (albeit a severely truncated one) for particular revelation—for it formed the implicit basis of an *ecclesiastical* community that could, in turn, serve as a vehicle for bringing about what he referred to as the "true church."[11] It is also worth recalling that Hegel, who famously argued that "the rational alone is real," nevertheless believed that revealed religion not only contained the same content (*Inhalt*) as philosophy, but that philosophy itself could only achieve absolute knowledge by first passing through the picture thinking (*Vorstellung*) of religion. Thus, within the Hegelian system the relationship between reason and revelation assumed all of the ambiguities of the notoriously enigmatic *Aufhebung*: reason does no more to abolish or supersede revelation than it does to preserve it. But perhaps Lessing himself offers the most telling sign of modernity's lingering ambivalence toward revelation in his essay on *The Education of the Human Race*, exclaiming on one page that "revelation gives *nothing* to the human race which human reason could *not* arrive at on its own"[12] and, on another page, that revelation provides insights which "human reason would *never* have reached on its own."[13] Lessing and his contemporaries may have refused to leap directly from the contingencies of historical revelation into the eternal truths of reason, but that explicit refusal was apparently not enough to prevent them from occasionally falling into the "ugly, broad ditch" separating the two.

The above is hardly an exhaustive summary of the relation between reason and revelation in modern thought. I have been quite deliberately cruising at ten thousand feet, an ideal altitude for surveying the most prominent features of the intellectual landscape. Only from this height—from this level of generality—can one catch a glimpse of the sinuous contours of the trenches below and begin to make out where (and how) the battle lines have been drawn and redrawn over time. I have tried to show how the enlightenment clarified and indeed sharpened the scholastic distinction between reason and revelation by assigning them to two, heterogeneous epistemic realms, and how philosophy sought to secure its epistemic status by inverting the traditional hierarchy between these realms. One can also see that, to some extent, revelation's increasing identification with the contingencies of history and human testimony made it the quintessential 'other' of enlightenment reason. It appears as though the kind of autonomy and transparency which philosophy had claimed for itself could only be defined and maintained when juxtaposed against the backdrop of its proper epistemic 'other,' as though the eternal truths of reason could only ever shine against the supposedly opaque and impenetrable surface of revelation and its contingent truths. But the fact that this other was occasionally viewed as a *supplement* to reason, as an expedient or necessary means for arriving at certain eternal truths, whether moral or metaphysical in nature, suggests an enduring ambivalence toward and fascination with the revealed content itself. This ambivalence reflects an all-too-obvious fact: rational truth, once defined in contradistinction to revealed truth, could not do away with its other without doing away with itself. Every soldier needs an adversary.

Phenomenology and Revelation

Today, one of philosophical frontlines in this centuries-old battle between reason and revelation is located within (or shall we say *upon*?) the field of phenomenology. Or so I will contend in this book. Though the battle wages on, the stakes of the conflict have changed considerably over the past century or so. The factors that have shaped these new circumstances are much too complex to treat exhaustively here (though I will return to them again in the following chapter). For the time being, I simply want to call attention to two basic shifts that have occurred in the intellectual terrain, one theological and the other philosophical. On the theological front, we can see a gradual shift away from an emphasis upon the propositional content of revelation towards a more dynamic and significantly less dogmatic (or doctrinal) conception of revelation. Though the theological concept of revelation has never been fully divested of its textual and historical content, that content has become more intimately connected with an experience of God through faith rather than a set of statements comprising a doctrine. (I'll have more to say about this shift in the following chapter.) On the philosophical front, we have witnessed a steady collapse in the enlightenment's unmitigated optimism concerning the faculty of reason and the form of rational subjectivity to which it belongs.[14] Taken together, these two factors have proven rather decisive: Whereas the enlightenment controversy concerned the extent to which the content of revelation might be *reducible* to reason, today the controversy occupying phenomenological circles concerns the extent to which the scope of philosophical discourse might be *broadened* so as to accommodate or include revelation or, at the very least, a philosophical figure of revelation.

It is important to note that the growing effort to challenge the classical enlightenment notion of reason and the desire to broaden the scope of philosophical inquiry are really two sides of the same coin. Heidegger, Marion, and Ricoeur have, each in their own way, sought to undermine the enlightenment's claim that reason is autonomous and wholly transparent to itself. They have contested the once pervasive idea that the limits of reality, being, or human experience are determined by the conditions that the modern rational subject imposes upon the world and our cognition of it. Now, if revelation represents the "other" of reason, then it is hardly surprising that each of these figures has turned to the phenomenon of revelation in the course of challenging the pretensions of reason. As the old adage goes, "the enemy of my enemy is my friend." And so the claim of revelation has quite naturally been employed as a way of challenging, limiting or upending the narrow claims of reason. This appeal to the category of revelation would not have been possible, perhaps not even desirable, were it not for the general loosening of the theological conception of revelation from its strictly doctrinal interpretation, which had occurred over the course of the previous century. But as the idea of revelation became more closely associated with a particular quality of *experience*, or a particular kind of *phenomenon*, rather than a mere collection of dogmatic propositions, the stage was set for its philosophical reevaluation.

And phenomenology, the philosophical method first developed by Edmund Husserl around the turn of the last century, proved to be the perfect vehicle for carrying out this new effort. Husserl's phenomenology claimed to offer a purely descriptive and non-reductive science of things as they appear within the subjective stream of conscious life. As Dermot Moran put it, phenomenology is at its core nothing more than "the careful description of what appears to consciousness precisely in the manner of its appearing."[15] This is not to say that Husserl was only, let alone primarily, interested in 'states of consciousness' or in empirical 'mental processes' as this was conceived by the psychologists of his day.[16] (Were that the case, it would be impossible for phenomenology to see past the conditions imposed upon the given by the subject.) On the contrary, phenomenology as envisaged by Husserl aims at uncovering matters themselves, and so it is concerned not just with appearances but primarily with the essence (*Wesen*) or *eidos* of appearances, with what appears *as such*. But the issue is complicated, since Husserl's founding insight was to have recognized that consciousness represented a privileged field (or domain) for this investigation into the essence of things. In a rudimental sense, all that is or may be known can only be known '*within*' consciousness. So, paradoxically, if one is to achieve rigorous, scientific knowledge of things as they are in themselves, one will first need to pay careful attention to the manner in which they give themselves to consciousness. This is what distinguishes phenomenology from other positive sciences, such as physics, biology, or psychology. Those sciences operate on the basis of certain basic presuppositions (typically related to an uncritical adoption of what Husserl called the 'natural attitude') about their respective objects, presuppositions which are not based upon our actual concrete consciousness of those objects themselves and, which, moreover, could never even be justified within the frameworks of those particular sciences. In order to obtain genuine scientific knowledge of things as they are in themselves, Husserl believed that one must begin by *excluding* everything that is not immanent to consciousness, by bracketing all such "positings" or presuppositions—including all natural, empirical, metaphysical, and, yes, *even* theological assumptions about the nature of reality.[17] But if Husserl's so-called phenomenological *epochē* (or bracketing) also requires the suspension of theological presuppositions, one might wonder how it could possibly serve as the best method for developing a philosophical account of revelation. The answer, of course, has to do with the manner in which the phenomenological *epochē* serves to open up an entirely new domain of philosophical investigation, one that, in principle, neutralizes the biases that had resulted in the enlightenment's subordination of revelation to reason (or the subordination of religious phenomena to the phenomena of the rational and empirical sciences).[18] In other words, phenomenology effectively leveled the playing field, and opened the door to a new generation of thinkers who were eager to expand the scope of philosophical discourse so as to accommodate the phenomenon of revelation—including the likes of Jean-Luc Marion, Paul Ricoeur, Michel Henry, Claude Romano, Emmanuel Falque, Richard Kearney, Jean-Louis Chrétien, Hent de Vries, John Caputo, Kevin Hart, etc.

Given what might be called the "scientific" temperament of Husserl himself, it is hardly surprising that the proliferation of religious motifs in contemporary phenomenology has spawned a great deal of debate.[19] While some have greeted what is now commonly referred to as "the theological turn" with enthusiasm—viewing it not only as a new manner of approaching theological issues, but also as the fulfillment of Husserl's original aim, namely, a pure description of the full range of phenomena—others have looked upon it with a great deal of suspicion, calling into question both its methodological moves as well as its underlying motives.

This tension within the phenomenological movement came to a head in the early nineteen nineties, when the *Centre de recherches phénoménologiques et herméneutiques* (CRPH), in association with the Husserl Archive in Paris, held a two-year seminar devoted to the theme of "Phenomenology and Hermeneutics of Religion," which culminated with a daylong symposium where key representatives of the so-called theological turn—including Paul Ricoeur, Jean-Louis Chrétien, Michel Henry, and Jean-Luc Marion—presented their phenomenological research.[20] These events attested to both the strength and breadth of what appeared to be an emerging field of philosophical inquiry—one which not only redeployed phenomenological modes of analysis in order to shed new light upon the nature of religious experience, faith, prayer, revelation, etc., but one that often claimed to fulfill the original aims of the phenomenological enterprise itself by expanding its methods so as to allow phenomena to "show themselves" as they are given "in and of themselves."

In 1991, while this seminar was still in progress, Dominique Janicaud's highly critical essay, "The Theological Turn of French Phenomenology," exploded on the phenomenological scene. Janicaud's essay began as a review, written at the behest of the International Institute of Philosophy, that would serve as a sort of *post scriptum* to Vincent Descombes's classic, *Modern French Philosophy*,[21] updating readers on philosophical developments that had transpired since 1975.[22] What he produced instead was a scathing critique of what, in his view, constituted the single most distinguishing feature in the development of phenomenology over the past thirty years—namely, "the opening [*ouverture*] to the invisible, to the Other [*Autre*], to a pure givenness [*donation*], or to an 'ache-revelation.'"[23] Janicaud was willing to acknowledge the value and legitimacy of addressing issue of otherness, or "the paradoxical revelation of Transcendence [. . .] at the heart of phenomenality."[24] After all, the great discovery that led to Husserl's theory of intentionality was that consciousness is always a consciousness "of something that is [irreducibly] other than self," that consciousness is by its very nature opened toward the other, toward something which transcends it.[25] But this opening, Janicaud insisted, is invariably woven into the very fabric of experience and must be sought therein. As the study of appearances, phenomenology can—and indeed *must*—interrogate the inherent exteriority and excessiveness of experience from within the very horizon of immanence. Janicaud lamented that many of the recent theologically inclined phenomenologists have abandoned this interrogation of the visible in favor of a blind and imprudent affirmation of radical transcendence: "Between the unconditional affirmation of Transcendence and the patient interrogation of the visible, the incompatibility cries out; we must choose. But are we going to do so with the head or with the heart—arbitrarily or not?" Throughout his essay, Janicaud insisted that the majority of the proponents of the theological turn had simply chosen with the heart—affirming, without any concern for the "phenomenological order," a pure form of transcendence, and then identifying this pure transcendence with none other than God (and a specifically biblical God at that).[26]

The same year that saw the publication of Janicaud's polemical essay also witnessed a passionate exchange between Jean-Luc Marion, the so-called architect of the theological turn, and the editors of the *Revue de métaphysique de morale*.[27] The exchange centered around the then-recent publication of Marion's *Reduction and Givenness*, a detailed study of the work of Husserl and Heidegger that culminated with the proposal for a new and radical reformulation of the phenomenological reduction. Marion had insisted that the original aim of phenomenology (as expressed in Husserl's "principles of all principles"[28]) was to allow phenomena to *give* themselves as they are in themselves, that is to say, without imposing any prejudices or subjective conditions upon the given. However, according to Marion, the rigor of Husserl's own analysis was compromised by his unchecked commitment to an epistemological quest for scientific certitude that led him to "reduce" and thus restrict phenomena to the horizon of objectivity. Though Heidegger's return to the question of being removed this unwarranted restriction, Marion argued that it too was flawed since it reduced the given to the horizon of Being. Marion himself proposed a third formulation of the phenomenological reduction—namely, a reduction to givenness *as such*, beyond any horizon of expectation, whether this horizon be determined by epistemological (objectivity) or ontological (Being) interests. But the editors of the *Revue de métaphysique de morale* remained suspicious of both Marion's general intentions and his specific methodological proposals. Can phenomenology as a descriptive method really do without a horizon? Can one legitimately claim to describe a phenomenon which, by definition, defies all description? Then again, does not Marion's own concept of 'givenness' itself already imply a new, albeit more extensive, horizon? These are just some of the questions posed by the editors of *Revue de métaphysique de morale*.

The philosophical legitimacy of this emerging theological or quasi-theological brand of phenomenology may very well be disputed. One may wonder whether it transgresses the boundaries of phenomenology by abandoning the original intentions and the methodological exigencies of the movement's founder. One may ask whether its new and peculiar reinterpretation of key phenomenological principles—such as horizon, reduction, intentionality, world, etc.—signals the culmination of the phenomenological enterprise (as Marion, Chrétien and others have claimed) or whether it signals a departure from and deterioration of phenomenology as such (as Janicaud has argued). What *cannot* be disputed, however, is the significance of this 'turn' as a purely historical event. The fact that this event has taken place, that some of the most visible and influential figures in the contemporary phenomenological arena have endorsed this new theological trend, and that this, in turn, has contributed to the broader resurgence of interest in religion which has recently swept across the academy—these facts can hardly be contested.[29]

If, as some have claimed, phenomenology has remained the most powerful and enduring force on the Parisian philosophical scene since its initial reception in the middle of the last century,[30] then the phenomenological appropriation of the category of revelation may be said to represent—for better or worse—the single most significant event in recent French philosophy. How did this event come to pass? What concrete challenge has it raised, and what paths have phenomenologist taken in order to meet those challenges? How has this event altered the phenomenological enterprise itself—its methods, its objectives, and its own self-understanding? How has it altered or informed our understanding of the nature of revelation, or perhaps even of the nature of philosophical reason? In the chapters that follow, I present a conceptual framework for understanding the nature and complexity of this event, clarifying its various trajectories and measuring its impact. This framework is developed through a careful analysis of key texts by three of the most influential phenomenological figures—Heidegger, Marion, and Ricoeur. After charting the progress and the pitfalls each thinker has encountered along the way, I try to make some suggestions about what the phenomenology of revelation may reasonably hope to accomplish. But before we direct our attention toward these key texts, I want to take a step back in order to situate the current theological turn in its wider historical context, beginning with the early decades of the phenomenological movement, and to consider how the philosophical issues considered in the following chapters relate to earlier theological discussions of revelation.

NOTES

1. Emmanuel Falque makes this point eloquently in the introduction to *Crossing the Rubicon: The Borderlands of Philosophy and Theology*. Although Falque states that "the controversy between philosophy and theology is not primarily a matter of war," battle, invasion, or conquest remains the dominant trope throughout the work. Emmanuel Falque, *Crossing the Rubicon: The Borderlands of Philosophy and Theology*, trans. Reuben Shank (New York: Fordham University Press, 2016), 16.

2. Etienne Gilson, *The Christian Philosophy of St. Thomas Aquinas*, trans. L. K. Shook (Notre Dame, IN: University of Notre Dame Press, 2006), 10–11 and 93.

3. Gottheld Lessing, *Lessing's Theological Writings*, trans. Henry Chadwick (Stanford, CA: Stanford University Press, 1957).

4. Lessing, *Lessing's Theological Writings*, 53.

5. By "positive" I simply mean that which is historical and thus contingent in nature, rather than necessary or universal.

6. Immanuel Kant, *Religion within the Boundaries of Mere Reason, and Other Writings*, eds. Allen Wood and George di Giovanni (New York: Cambridge University Press, 1998), 40.

7. One could point to any number of similar projects: Think, for instance, of Rousseau's Savoyard Vicor, who rejected all types of particular revelation based on historical texts and human testimony, and embraced only what he—along with the positive Deists—referred to as "general" revelation, i.e., a revelation which could be understood on the basis of one's own "natural lights," one's universal faculty of reason, or upon natural knowledge.

8. John Locke, *The Reasonableness of Christianity*, ed. I. T. Ramsey (Stanford, CA: Stanford University Press, 1958), 75.

9. Ibid., 65.

10. Ibid.

11. Kant, *Religion within the Boundaries of Mere Reason*, 6:115–116.

12. Lessing, "The Education of the Human Race" in *Lessing's Theological Writings*, 83.

13. Ibid., 95.

14. Of course, exceptions to this optimism could be found even during the enlightenment period. But these exceptions (Hamman, for instance) are now generally associated with the so-called counter-enlightenment. Talk of the "limits of reason" among enlightenment figures *proper* (Kant *et al.*) should not be conflated with this counter-enlightenment, even though the relationship between them is clearly more complicated than the mere qualification (i.e., the word "counter") suggests. Moreover, in spite of oft-quoted claim that Kant restricted the use of reason in order to make room for faith, his essay on religion (and, more generally, the role of the postulates within his practical philosophy) clearly demonstrate that the so-called limits of reason (taken in its theoretical and practical forms) ultimately circumscribed the limits of religion: hence the essay's title, *Religion within the Boundaries of Reason*. Religion, for Kant, is grounded in practical reasoning, and not vice versa.

15. Dermot Moran, *Husserl: Founder of Phenomenology* (Malden, MA: Polity Press, 2005), 1.

16. For a clear account of Husserl's understanding of the difference between phenomenology (as a science of transcendental consciousness) and psychology (as the science of empirical consciousness), see Dan Zahavi's *Husserl's Phenomenology* (Stanford, CA: Stanford University Press, 2003), 7–13.

17. In section 58 of *Idea I*, Husserl includes, within the transcendental reduction, a reduction of that mode of transcendence that pertains exclusively to God: transcendence of the world. Edmund Husserl, *Ideas Pertaining to a Pure Phenomenology and to a Phenomenological Philosophy: First Book*, trans. F. Kersten (Boston: Kluwer Academic Publishers, 1982).

18. Edmund Husserl, *Cartesian Meditations: An Introduction to Phenomenology*, trans. Dorion Cairns (London: Kluwer Academic Publishers, 1997), 65.

19. Dominique Janicaud, "The Theological Turn of French Phenomenology," in *Phenomenology and the "Theological Turn,"* trans. Bernard Prusak (New York: Fordham University Press, 2000), 16–106. An exchange on this topic between Jean-Luc Marion and the editors of *Revue de métaphysique et de morale* was also published the same year: *Revue de métaphysique et de morale* 1 (1991). In addition to these published disputes, a number of conferences have focused on the issue, such as the debate between Marion and Derrida held at Villanova University in September of 2007.

20. See Jean-François Courtine's "Phenomenology and Hermeneutics of Religion" in *Phenomenology and the "Theological Turn,"* trans. Bernard Prusak (New York: Fordham University Press, 2000), 121.

21. Vincent Descombes, *Modern French Philosophy*, trans. L. Scott-Fox and J. Harding (New York: Cambridge University Press, 1980).

22. Janicaud, "The Theological Turn," 16.

23. Ibid., 17.

24. Ibid., 23.

25. As Janicaud eagerly observed, this insight could be recognized and accommodated by even the most atheistic of phenomenologists, such as Sartre, whose first essay on phenomenology was in fact devoted to establishing this very point. "The Theological Turn," 18. See also: "Intentionality: A Fundamental Idea of Husserl's Phenomenology" (trans. Joseph Fell), *Journal of the British Society for Phenomenology* 1–2 (1970): 4–5.

26. Janicaud adds: "There is no respect for the phenomenological order; it is manipulated as an ever-elastic apparatus, even when it is claimed to be strict." Janicaud, "The Theological Turn," 26 and 65.

27. John Caputo, *The Religious* (Malden, MA: Blackwell Publishers, 2002), 8.

28. Husserl, *Ideas I*, §24, 44–45.

29. As Emmanuel Falque observes, "The relation between philosophy and theology in France has recently shifted. To deny this would be to act in bad faith or in such great blindness that we would seem to be guided by nothing but ignorance of that which has transpired." Falque, *Crossing the Rubicon*, 16.

30. Jeffrey Kosky, "Translator's Preface: The Phenomenology of Religion: New Possibilities for Philosophy and for Religion," in *Phenomenology and the Theological Turn*, ed. Janicaud (New York: Fordham University Press, 2000), 108.

Chapter 1

Retracing the Turn

Revelation and the Two Faces of Phenomenology

THE THEOLOGICAL RETURNS

On February 14, 1928, Heidegger stood before his colleagues at the University of Marburg to deliver what would be his final lecture before returning—triumphantly, as it were—to Freiburg, where he was to take over as the successor to his former mentor, Edmund Husserl. The topic Heidegger chose for his parting address was "Phenomenology and Theology."[1] This choice might have bewildered some of more rigid disciples of Husserl, the founder of the phenomenological movement, but it would not have taken his Marburg colleagues by surprise. After all, Heidegger's roughly five years in Marburg had been filled with intense but often congenial conversations with its world-renowned theological faculty, and particularly with Rudolph Bultmann. His interest in theology actually extended much further back: theology was his first course of study during his early student-days at the University of Freiburg, and as a young boy he seemed almost destined to enter the priesthood. (He apparently would have, were it not for an extended period of poor health, which prevented him from embarking down that path).[2] As a young professor, he had spent several semesters lecturing on such subjects as Paul's *Epistles* and Augustine's *Confessions*, and he had also prepared, though never taught, a course on medieval mysticism. By the time he arrived in protestant Marburg, he had already cultivated a serious interest in various aspects of Luther's thought and was quite eager to make the most of his newfound proximity to such a distinguished faculty of protestant theology.

Heidegger's 1928 lecture not only marks the culmination of nearly two decades of intellectual and profoundly personal reflection on the nature of Christian faith and revelation, but it also offers a snapshot of his thought during one of its most verdant periods, the years immediately surrounding the publication of his magnum opus, *Being and Time*. Both that work and his lecture were the products of a prolonged engagement with questions concerning the nature and scope of phenomenology itself, and it is clear that these methodological concerns often overlapped with theological ones. The more we learn about the evolution of Heidegger's thought, the clearer it becomes that key features of the fundamental ontology of Dasein presented in *Being and Time* were deeply influenced by his earlier explorations of theology and his phenomenology of religious life: the distinction between chronological time and *kairological* time foreshadows the later analysis of history (*Historie*) and historicity (*Geschichtlichkeit*) in Division Two; the "being-wakefulness" of faith anticipates the later authentic resoluteness of Dasein; anxiety regarding the *parousia* bears a striking resemblance to the existential anxiety involved in being-towards-death; and the characterization of the process whereby primal Christian experience becomes concealed through Greek conceptuality prefigures Heidegger's later description of the history of the forgetfulness of Being—the all-important *Seinsvergessenheit*.[3] As these examples show, the phenomena of religion and of revelation were not just special topics to which Heidegger would occasionally apply his phenomenological method; rather, they were central to his elucidation of phenomenology itself, providing the very foundations upon which his fundamental ontology would eventually be built.[4]

Today, of course, the so-called theological turn in phenomenology is typically associated with a group of predominantly French philosophers who gained notoriety in the final decades of the twentieth century—figures such as Michel Henry, Jean-Louis Chrétien, and perhaps especially Jean-Luc Marion. However, Heidegger's intellectual formation offers clear indication that the tryst between theology and phenomenology had begun more than a half-century earlier. And if we cast our sights back over the last hundred years or so, we will see that Heidegger was not alone. Nearly from its inception, phenomenology had been appropriated by philosophers, theologians, and scholars of religion who were interested in shedding light on the religious dimensions of human experience. Max Scheler had adopted phenomenology as a means for advancing theological-political ends in his popular writings, while French theologian Jean Héring relied heavily upon Husserlian methodology in his exploration of the ontological relation between the human individual and God.[5] That both of these men were members of the "Göttingen Circle"—one of the first groups devoted to the study of Husserl's method—attests to the fact that a preoccupation with theological concerns was present from the earliest stages of the phenomenological movement.[6] In 1917, Rudolf Otto published his influential *The Idea of the Holy*, which developed this theological strand along an entirely different line. Even though the book displayed no strict fidelity to his philosophical method, Husserl nevertheless gave it a surprisingly positive review, claiming that it marked the "beginnings of a phenomenology of religion."[7] And indeed, the work inspired others, such as Gerardus van der Leeuw and Marcea Eliade, to develop what might be called a "comparative religion" based upon a reinterpretation of certain key Husserlian concepts—most notably, the *epochē*, which is often understood in the field of religious studies as an act of bracketing questions of truth (or suspending presuppositions associated with a modern scientific attitude) in order to consider the inner dynamics of a belief system or to gain access to worldviews belonging to non-Western cultures.[8]

The justifications for this theological and scholarly interest in phenomenology were complex and varied, but they usually centered around a common insight: by reducing phenomena to their mode of appearing *to* consciousness, Husserl's descriptive method treated every intuition, every appearance, as its own "source of legitimacy" (*Rechtsquelle*) of cognition, without demanding that such appearances satisfy or conform to metaphysical conditions, which would otherwise rule out certain kinds of phenomena in advance.[9] On account of this "intuitionism," everything that appears to consciousness—including religious phenomena—could, at least in principle, become a legitimate object of phenomenological description and thus philosophical investigation. In his final Marburg lecture, Heidegger gave this basic epistemological point a characteristically ontological inflection: While certain kinds of religious phenomena only disclose themselves to particular modes of existence (i.e., faith), this should not be taken as a symptom of their illegitimacy but rather as a philosophical challenge to clarify the standards of evidence appropriate to them, without reference to alien forms of justification drawn from other modes of existence. It follows, or so he argued, that "In no case may we delimit the scientific character of theology by using [natural, historical, or psychological] science as the guiding standard of evidence for [theology's] mode of proof or as the measure of rigor of its conceptuality."[10]

Given this pre-history, any attempt to understand the nature and significance of the current "theological turn" (or rather the current theological *re-turn*) must inevitably begin by revisiting that earlier period, if only to get a running start. In the chapters that follow, it will become clear that Heidegger's thought in particular—especially as it unfolds in the decade leading up to the delivery of his final Marburg lecture in 1928—represents the single most important source for understanding the nature and diversity of the more recent interest in the phenomenology of revelation among French philosophers. More specifically, I will argue that the two dominant strains within the phenomenology of revelation can be traced back to two seemingly opposed tendencies in Heidegger's own attitude regarding the relationship between language and the disclosure of being. But before I begin to articulate the differences between these two strains, it is worth exploring the reasons underlying their shared interest in the phenomenon of revelation in the first place. In other words, I want to say something about why revelation *per se* represents a pivotal category when it comes to making sense of the theological "re-turn" in phenomenology.

2. PHENOMENOLOGY OF REVELATION AND THE TRIAL OF REASON

Broadly speaking, each of the philosophers discussed in this book employ phenomenology in a common quest to free revelation from the jaws of an enlightenment project that sought to exclude the possibility of revelation altogether or to reduce the content of revelation to that which accords with principles of moral and metaphysical reason. Phenomenology would not be the first, let alone the only, means of defending revelation against philosophy's reductionist critique—for the same might be said of any number of earlier thinkers and movements.[11] Attempts at "dehellenizing" Christianity are nothing new: Kierkegaard, Pascal, and Luther each sought in his own way to undo the knots that had, over the course of centuries, bound Athens to Jerusalem, philosophy to theology, the God of philosophers to the God of Abraham. What *is* new, however, is that the appeal to the category of revelation within twentieth-century phenomenology is no longer made exclusively in the service of *theology* but, paradoxically, in the service of *philosophy*—or, more precisely, it is made in the service of a philosophical project that seeks to pass beyond the modern enlightenment figure of philosophy. Theologically inclined phenomenologists turn to revelation in the course of challenging the autonomy of the modern subject, the primacy of theoretical and scientific modes of knowledge, and the reduction of all of reality to its naturalistic characterizations.

If one bears in mind the heterogeneity between reason and revelation discussed in the introduction, the justification for this appeal is less difficult to understand. As the 'other' of enlightenment reason, revelation may be said to constitute the ultimate test case or "trial" for a philosophical enterprise that seeks to pierce through the prison walls of enlightenment thought in order to reach the other side—whatever that other side may be.[12] In this sense, one could say that the interest in the phenomenon of revelation within recent phenomenology is by no means accidental. As Jean-François Courtine has observed, the religious phenomenon is not something "toward which [the phenomenologist] would be free to 'turn' or not. Rather, it would affect the central aim of phenomenology itself, considered in terms of its own task and style."[13] It "would lead phenomenology to its limit" and therefore serve as a touchstone "for assessing the pertinence and the rigor of phenomenology's fundamental principles and the methodic procedures that constitute it."[14] Or, as Marion has put it in the published version of his Gifford Lectures, *Givenness and Revelation*: "Doubtless [revelation] is an exception [in the sense of being exceptional] when compared to other phenomena, but an exception confirming the general definition of every phenomenon as that which shows itself only to the extent that it gives itself."[15] The phenomenologist does not take up religious phenomena in the same manner that he or she takes up, for instance, social, historical, or aesthetic phenomena, as if it were a matter of simply applying its method to yet another domain of objects, to one "region" among others. Instead, "revelation, by virtue of the givenness that it alone performs perfectly, would accomplish the essence of phenomenality."[16] Thus, as a phenomenon, it is at once exceptional *and* paradigmatic. Jeffery Kosky also caught sight of the intrinsic connection between the phenomenological project and religious phenomena in his introduction to *The Theological Turn in French Phenomenology*: "the religious phenomenon represents a trial for phenomenology: more than posing a question *for* phenomenology, it poses the question *of* phenomenology itself—of its limits and the criteria it uses to determine phenomenality."[17]

In addressing the issue of revelation, therefore, phenomenology is not simply adopting a theological question that would be foreign or even peripheral to its core concerns. On the contrary, it is actually tackling a question about phenomenology itself, about its ability to live up to its own promise of enabling phenomena to appear as they give themselves out to be, as they are given beyond the limitations of enlightenment reason—and that means independent of scientific or naturalistic presuppositions, the narrow constraints of the principle of sufficient reason, and the conditions of possibility imposed upon them by the modern subject. If phenomenology claims to pass beyond the modes of thought rooted in enlightenment paradigms, its success or failure will depend upon its ability to expose itself to that which lies *beyond* this thought. That it must therefore engage the phenomenon of revelation is, ironically, in perfect keeping with the tradition of modern philosophy (a tradition that has appointed revelation as the long-standing rival of enlightenment rationality). From this perspective, the question about the possibility of revelation was *not* grafted onto phenomenological discourse as if it were a wholly foreign species. Nor was it superimposed upon phenomenology by tacit theological concerns about the mystical, the supernatural or the ineffable—concerns that may in fact be alien to its own philosophical aims and methodological exigencies. In fact, phenomenology's interest in revelation stems from its own root concerns and core problems, and from its effort to explore and express those problems in terms which it has inherited from the broader philosophical tradition. This, of course, by no means precludes the possibility (or, indeed, the *probability*) that its encounter with revelation might occasionally function as a kind of pretext for advancing theological views, or as an opening through which proper theological questions might be inserted, either overtly or covertly, into the phenomenological enterprise. But the motives underlying this rehabilitation of the concept of revelation within twentieth-century phenomenology should not be immediately dismissed on those grounds. To do so would be to ignore the crucial role that revelation plays within the wider critique of previous philosophical attitudes, a critique that is arguably internal to philosophy and phenomenology themselves.

3. TWO FACES OF PHENOMENOLOGY

Just as phenomenology's critical dimension has taken various forms over the course of the twentieth century, so has its appropriation of the concept of revelation. In fact, this appropriation has been just as complex and varied as the ways phenomenologists have sought to question the epistemological status of modern subjectivity, undermine the priority of theoretical knowledge, and challenge an exclusively technologico-scientific conception of reality. While this diversity is certainly reflected in the works of Heidegger, Marion, and Ricoeur, their formulations of revelation can nonetheless be roughly schematized in terms of the two contrasting attitudes toward language alluded to in the preface. For the sake of exposition, I will refer to these opposing positions as the "radical" and the "hermeneutical" attitudes. A brief discussion of the differences between them will help to account for the differences between the competing conceptions of revelation with which they are associated.

From the perspective of the radical attitude, the various philosophical positions that phenomenology seeks to overcome can be consolidated under the single, all-encompassing banner of "metaphysics," and its critique of metaphysics is almost always accomplished by means of a "step back"—a step back from *being* to *Beings* (as in Heidegger), from the *said* to the *saying* (as in Levinas), or from the *conditioned phenomenon*, which is subject to the horizons of being and objectivity, to an *unconditional givenness* (as in Marion).[18] This radical attitude begins to take shape in the works of early Heidegger, whose *Destruktion* of the metaphysical tradition involved a return to "the beginning, the primal, the originary,"[19] and thus moves in the direction of what might be called the pre-linguistic. It is important to note that the suspicion that this radical attitude harbors towards the "language of Metaphysics" often extends towards language in general—at least insofar as "certain conceptual formulations, derived from the original language of metaphysics, have impressed themselves into the living languages of present-day speech communities."[20] Only by returning to the very origin of speech, to its beginning or its "primordial sources," can we be certain to have attained a standpoint that is free of any such metaphysical contaminations. This partly explains why Heidegger's destructive (*destruktiv*) project was leveled against ordinary language—everyday chatter or idle talk (*Gerede*)—as much as it was against the distinctively philosophical language of modernity.[21] As Hubert Dreyfus notes, in *Being and Time* the very structure of language is said to lead Dasein "away from a primordial relation to being and to its own being," and thus it entails a falling away "from primordiality to groundlessness" under the tutelage of the one (*das Man*).[22] For early Heidegger, then, the quest for the meaning of Being necessitates a return to a primordial experience which precedes (or cuts beneath) certain forms of linguistic articulation and sedimentation.

Marion's attempt to pass beyond metaphysical thinking by means of a phenomenology of givenness displays a similarly "radical" attitude toward language. Here, again, linguistic mediation is regarded with a great deal of circumspection, as an instrument through which the given is constituted, thematized, and thus brought back into the fold of metaphysical thought. Put simply, Marion's central idea of the saturated phenomena is based on a recognition that the given often outstrips the conceptual and linguistic categories used to understand or interpret it. Phenomena, such as revelation, which are said to be doubly saturated, are practically defined in terms of their conceptual indeterminateness, by their resistance to linguistic determination, predication, or nomination. The call of revelation is therefore an anonymous call, one that defies all names. It must be noted that Marion has recently tried to accommodate a more hospitable attitude toward language and signification within his phenomenology of givenness by carving out a place for hermeneutics. However, that place not only remains secondary with respect to givenness—and is thus marked by its "essential lateness"—but he continues to portray hermeneutics as a kind of substitute for, or analogue of, constitution itself. Hermeneutics involves an imposition of the subject's finitude upon the given, a finitude that is constantly "brought out, by contrast, against the infinity of the obscure givenness [. . .]."[23] This purported correlation between language, finitude, and belatedness helps explain why Marion's phenomenology ultimately seeks the support of mystical theology, which he characterizes as a radicalization of an *apophatic* approach, which constantly un-says what is said, relentlessly deconstructing the divine names in order to preserve the unspeakable, nameless Name that lies on the far side of language.[24]

In contrast to this radical tradition, hermeneutical phenomenology actually draws upon the emancipatory dimension of language itself in order to overcome enlightenment paradigms. This can be seen in the work of Hans-Georg Gadamer, whose *Truth and Method* is often regarded as the single most significant contribution to twentieth-century hermeneutical thought. In that work, his critique of modern objectivism and its Cartesian ground was tied to a project of "thinking out the consequences of language as a medium."[25] Language is not the prison house of consciousness, according to Gadamer; rather, it is that by which we are able to possess what he calls a "world"—a network of meanings which extends beyond our merely physical "environment" (*Umgebung*). On this view, it is only through language itself that we escape the narrow confines of objectivistic modes of thinking.

Heidegger was foundational for this hermeneutical strand of phenomenology as well. Given what I have just said above—that Heidegger played an essential role in establishing a radical attitude—this might seem rather counterintuitive. But Heidegger contained multitudes. The hermeneutical strand of phenomenology picks up on his views regarding the manner in which language remains the necessary "medium" of thought or, as he would later come to call it, "the house of being." In fact, it is a remarkably thin line that separates the conception of language as idle talk, as the site of unproductive sedimented meanings that conceal our view of being, from the conception of language as a necessary condition of our belonging to being. Whereas the early Heidegger regarded language as a site of metaphysical sedimentation, Gadamer (and those most influenced by him) generally regard it as the creative source of new meaning and belonging (*Gehörigkeit*), and thus as a site of genuine understanding. As Gadamer famously put it: "*Being that can be understood is language.*"[26] The notion that, in the name of the critique of metaphysics, one might discard the linguistic heritage of the western tradition wholesale is not only incredibly naïve; it would amount to throwing the baby out with the bathwater. For understanding always involves an appropriation or exploitation of certain concrete potentialities embedded within a heritage or linguistic tradition, even when the conceptual frameworks handed down by that tradition may appear prejudicial or unproductive. In fact, the belief that critical thought might be capable of overcoming or suspending all such prejudices is an expression of the influence of the Cartesian tradition itself—in other words, it is part of our enlightenment inheritance. Such considerations ultimately serve to justify Gadamer's "rehabilitation of prejudice," his claim that the contents handed down by tradition, while in some sense prejudicial, are nonetheless productive for understanding.[27] These so-called prejudices actually represent "the background network of meaning-relations lying at the basis of all speech." Therefore, "From the perspective of hermeneutic philosophy, Heidegger's doctrine of the overcoming of metaphysics, with its culmination in the total forgetfulness of Being in our technological era, skips over the continued resistance and persistence of certain flexible unities in the life we all share [. . .]."[28] What needs to be rejected is not language or our linguisticality (*Sprachlichkeit*) as such, but merely the limiting of language to its technological or propositional forms.[29] The fact that language, at its core, is not merely a tool that can be controlled or manipulated, that language

constitutes us more than we control it, that we ourselves are carried along and sustained by the being of language—these insights provide the foundation for the hermeneutical critique of the autonomy of the modern enlightenment subject.

Nevertheless, this hermeneutical critique of modern subjectivity marks only the negative side of a predominantly positive discovery concerning the capacity of language to disclose new worlds, beyond the enlightenment's naturalistic, empiricist, and scientific visions of reality. This positive dimension of the hermeneutical problematic became one of the central themes of Paul Ricoeur's work on poetic and religious discourse during the nineteen sixties, seventies, and eighties.[30] But the basic principle was already present in Gadamer, whose analysis of the speculative structure of language in *Truth and Method* culminates with the poetic: "The poetic statement is speculative inasmuch as it does not reflect an existent reality, does not reproduce the appearance of the *species* (Lat.) in the order of essence, but represents the new appearance of a new world in the imaginary medium of poetic invention."[31]

Therefore, whereas radical phenomenology seeks to overcome metaphysics by sidestepping language in its ceaseless quest for the primordial givenness, hermeneutical phenomenology challenges enlightenment paradigms through language itself, or by insisting upon a richer conception of linguisticality and the inexorable connection between language and being. Bearing this fundamental difference in mind, it becomes less difficult to understand why the radical phenomenologists and the hermeneutical phenomenologists situate revelation on opposite sides of the linguistic divide: the former identifying revelation with a primal, originary moment that is claimed to be epistemologically prior to all language and linguistic mediation; the latter identifying it with the surplus of meaning that stems from the referential power of language itself.

So, I will insist that there is no such thing as *the* phenomenology of revelation. There are, rather, two quite distinct manners in which phenomenology approaches the phenomenon of revelation, and these manners reflect two fundamentally opposed attitudes toward historical, linguistic, and textual mediation within post-Husserlian continental philosophy indicated above—namely, one concerned with fundamental or primordial structures, and the other concerned with the productive imagination and the effective nature of texts. While radical phenomenologists tend to characterize revelation as an "originary" encounter with alterity that fractures, disrupts and in a crucial sense precedes the domains of history and language, hermeneutical phenomenologists regard revelation as an eruptive event which unfolds within these very domains. Thus, on the one side, one finds a variety of strategies for radicalizing the phenomenological reduction to the point where it would finally be capable of disclosing a purely heterological thinking of the other (namely, "revelation"), one that is anterior not only to theoretical reflection, but also to linguistic and textual mediation. On the other side, one sees a strategy of grafting a hermeneutical problematic onto a phenomenological method, a strategy that results in a conception of revelation as a surplus of meaning which unfolds itself in front of concrete texts that are always already located within the historic-linguistic milieu. In the chapters that follow, I will seek to trace the development of these two essentially dichotomous phenomenological views of revelation as they emerge in the works of Heidegger, Marion, and Ricoeur.

4. THE CONTENT OF CHRISTIAN REVELATION

But I must confess at the outset that my objective in this book is not *merely* to present an account of these opposed approaches from the disinterested standpoint of a spectator or intellectual historian. My ultimate aim is show that, unless supplemented by a genuine hermeneutic, the radical approach to revelation runs the risk of divesting revelation of its meaning and content, leaving us with a merely formal concept of revelation—a revelation *without* Revelation.[32] My exposition is thus admittedly quite polemical. It is intended to demonstrate the indispensability of the kind of hermeneutical phenomenology exemplified in the works of Ricoeur—works that have been relatively, though I think quite unjustifiably, neglected by the majority of phenomenologists operating within the purview of the theological turn. But before I can offer even a rough sketch of my argument, it is first necessary to say a few words about the idea of revelation as it developed within the context of its native soil, namely biblical theology. For that theological context forms an essential backdrop to the phenomenological elaboration of the concept of revelation.

The history of the idea of revelation within Christian thought is so long and complex that it is hard to say anything about it without running the risk of oversimplification. That said, scholars who have taken this risk often note that the concept of revelation engenders an essential ambiguity: it can either refer to the *means* (i.e., the process) through which God makes certain truths known to human beings, or it can refer to the *contents* (i.e., the body of truths) which are thereby made known.[33] While theological discussions of revelation often emphasize one sense over the other, neither of these two senses (marked in Latin by the distinction between *revelation* and *revelata*) can be fully collapsed into the other.

This basic double-sided formula is a rather late development in this history of theology, but it nonetheless provides a useful framework for examining the meaning of revelation within the Judeo-Christian tradition, beginning with its earliest deployment in the Hebrew Old Testament, where the vocabulary of revelation is used in a variety of ways: "to disclose or unveil" (*glh*) God's intention[34]; "to proclaim or make known" (*yd'*) through speech or actions;[35] "to communicate" (*nggd*) God's name or God's plan,[36] etc.[37] By and large, the Hebrew scriptures give the impression that humans cannot come to know God on their own, but must depend upon God's own initiative to reveal Himself to them[38]—and that idea has had a lasting impact on the Christian understanding of revelation up to the present.[39] This divine act of revelation takes place through nature, visions, dreams, etc. But, above all, God is said to be revealed in history, that is, the course of events experienced by His people. If history is the primary *means* (or process) through which God is thought to be revealed to the people of Israel, then—at the risk of oversimplifying matters—it could be said that the primary *content* of this revelation is the will of God, or, more specifically, God's promise to or covenant with His people.[40]

In the New Testament, of course, the notion of revelation is strongly associated with the person of Jesus Christ, who is regarded either as the content of revelation (i.e., as the fulfillment of God's promise in the Old Testament) and as the means through which revelation takes place. As Norbert Schiffer observes: "In St. Paul, God remains the revealer, as in the OT. The mystery of his will had been hidden in him, till executed in time through the death and resurrection of Jesus. [. . .] According to St. Paul, Christ is the content of the mystery of God (Rom 3:21–24; Gal 1:16; Eph 3:3, 5; 1 Tim 3:16) and he is not so much the revealer as the revealed."[41] For John, on the other hand, the situation is reversed. For Christ is regarded by John as the revealer himself, that is, as the one who, through his words and deeds, serves to reveal God the Father (*Jn* 1:14). The Father, according to John, is known only through Christ: "No one has ever seen God. It is God the only Son, who is close to the Father's heart, who has made him known" (*Jn* 1:18). In either case, the New Testament portrays Christ as the fullness of revelation—as both the *means* and the *content* of revelation, an idea which played an especially crucial role in early twentieth-century theology.

Given the centrality of revelation within contemporary Christian theology, it is a bit surprising that the topic remained of only subsidiary interest to the Church Fathers.[42] Indeed, the vocabulary of revelation (Latin *revelatio, manifestation*, etc.; Greek *apokalupsis, epiphaneia, dèlôsis*, etc.) was employed for centuries in a rather loose sense before becoming a central topic of theological discussion during the Scholastic period. By the thirteenth century, however, the term had taken on a slightly more coherent (though hardly uncontested) conceptual determination, one which received its classic elaboration in the work of Thomas Aquinas,[43] where it is often associated with a distinction (though not necessarily an opposition) between the "truths of reason" and the "truths of revelation."[44] The distinction was essentially one between natural and supernatural knowledge—that is, between truths learned by means of one's own natural faculty of reason or the observation of nature, on the one hand, and truths that are directly revealed to us by God, usually through "Holy Scripture," on the other.[45] According to renowned Thomistic scholar Etienne Gilson, Aquinas did not regard the two as being totally opposed, but as partially overlapping. Perhaps the most well-known example of this overlapping of reason and revelation in Aquinas concerns the unity of essence and existence in God's pure "act-of-being," a truth which Aquinas claims to have reached through complex metaphysical reasoning. "However, this pure act-of-being which St. Thomas the philosopher met at the end of metaphysics, St. Thomas the theologian had met too in Holy Scripture [i.e., in *Ex.* 3:14]. It was no longer the conclusion of rational dialectic but a revelation from God Himself to all men that they might accept it by faith."[46] Reason and revelation were like "two beams of light so conversing that they fused into each other."[47]

Nevertheless, this "fusion" did not necessarily rule out the existence of certain revealed truths that exceed the power and scope of human reason. As Gilson reminds us, Aquinas maintained yet another crucial distinction regarding the nature of revelation—namely, the distinction between the "revealable" (*revelabilia*) and the "revealed" (*revelatum*). On the one hand, the category of the so-called revealable included all that God has revealed or may reveal through reason, through nature, through Holy Scripture, or by any other means. The latter category, on the other hand, included only those truths that could be obtained through revelation in the strict sense—that is, through truths that are beyond the scope of natural reason. While certain truths, such as the unity of essence and existence in God, could be known through two separate channels (i.e., through either reason or Scripture), other truths, such as the doctrine of the Holy Trinity, could only be made known to us directly through God, which is to say, only through revelation properly speaking, in contrast to reason and natural knowledge.[48] Therefore, the *content* of the so-called revealed (understood in this strict sense of the term) was comprised of a set of propositional statements, i.e., doctrines that could not be obtained through human reason, but depended upon God's active revelation.

Nevertheless, Aquinas left plenty of room for the idea of natural revelation, that is, for the idea that God reveals himself to human beings *through* his creation, which consists of both the physical world and the human intellect. And this conception of revelation remained an incredibly influential one, especially within the Roman Catholic tradition, where it was reinforced by the First Vatican Council in 1870.[49] By then, however, the notion of natural revelation had already been subjected to harsh criticism, especially by the first generation of Reformation thinkers. For instance, in his *Heidelberg Disputation* (1518), Luther opposed this so-called theology of glory to a "theology of the cross" according to which God is said to be revealed in the suffering of Christ on the cross rather than in the power and glory of his creation. The locus of God's revelation is neither nature nor reason, but sacred scripture, i.e., the word which speaks of the scandal of the cross.[50] In opposition to the Reformation principle of the 'sufficiency of scripture,' the Catholic tradition has maintained a more optimistic attitude toward the use of reason but, more importantly still, toward tradition, which it views as a separate means through which God reveals himself to the church.

Returning now to the twofold nature of revelation as understood within Christian theology, one cannot help but notice that most of the differences so far discussed have primarily revolved around revelation's first meaning—that is to say, they have concerned the *means* or *process* by which God is revealed to human beings. But, in fact, there has also been much disagreement concerning the second meaning, i.e., the nature of the *content* that is revealed. I have mentioned in passing that the content of revelation was traditionally associated with a set of doctrines that were often expressed in proposition statements (the so-called *revelata*). Twentieth-century theology, however, witnessed a transition away from conceiving of this content in terms of a set of "communicated" propositional truths. In the Roman Catholic tradition, this shift can be measured in terms of the differences between the first and second Vatican Councils. As Lacoste observes, the first council "placed any personal dimension [of revelation] in the background; revelation was understood as a 'that,' as a body of *revelata*, rather than as a divine action."[51] In the second council, the "*revelata* almost disappear in favor of the revelation, itself thought of from the outset on the basis of Christ."[52] The content of revelation was by no means eliminated, but rather it was simply consolidated or absorbed within Christ, who is regarded as "both the mediator and the fullness of all revelation."[53] This changing attitude toward the content of revelation occasionally led to an increasing emphasis on the subjective rather than the objective dimension of revelation. This is particularly true of so-called existentialist theologies. Thus, for example, Rudolf Bultmann, Heidegger's Marburg colleague, insisted that revelation does not involve the communication of a doctrine of God, but a call to conversion in the face of the coming of the kingdom of God (a view which I hope to show in the following chapter is not all that far from Heidegger's own).[54]

But some theologians, most notably Karl Barth, were wary of the growing emphasis on the subjective experience of revelation, arguing that it leads to an anthropologizing of theology that places the human being rather than God at its center. In fact, this anthropologizing tendency could already be detected a century earlier in the work of Schleiermacher. While Barth himself had been fascinated with Schleiermacher as a young man, he eventually came to see him as instigating a trend among modern neo-protestant theologians that ultimately reduced Christian faith to a mere "'feeling,' in which all objectivity, and all *contents* characteristic of it, were supposed to be sublated [*aufgehoben*]."[55] If indeed revelation were to be principally defined by this subjective feeling or a distinctive capacity for such a feeling rather than by the material content or substance of a tradition, then theology would begin and end with an analysis of human subjectivity.[56] But Barth, who half-jokingly referred to himself as a "supernaturalist" and a "revelational positivist,"[57] insisted that any conception of revelation that focuses attention upon the human being rather than God is fundamentally misguided. Revelation, in his view, does not entail merely a modification of a natural human capacity, but rather it marks a complete break with what is human and with what is natural. And furthermore, Barth maintained that such an anthropocentric conception of revelation would be completely severed from the concrete contents of Christian tradition:

> I can see no way from Schleiermacher, or from his contemporary epigones [such as Bultmann], to the chroniclers, prophets, and wise ones of Israel, to those who narrate the story of the life, death, and resurrection of Jesus Christ, to the word of the apostles—no way to the God of Abraham, Isaac, and Jacob and the Father of Jesus Christ, no way to the great tradition of the Christian church.[58]

This is not to suggest that Barth advocated a return to the notion of revelation as a body of propositional truths concerning God or reality. Instead, his polemical engagement with Schleiermacher and his progenies gives voice to an important strand within twentieth-century theology, one that was rooted in the conviction that revelation cannot be produced or achieved through human initiative but must be received as a gift from God. It was, at least as far as Barth was concerned, an obvious consequence of this conviction that the theological treatment of revelation could not begin with an investigation of the human being or the conditions of human subjectivity.

More—indeed, considerably more—could be added to this discussion of the concept of revelation within Christian thought. After all, as Stephen Sykes has observed, "a history of the modern understanding of revelation would amount to a history of modern theology"—and that history would obviously exceed the scope and purpose of the present work.[59]

5. REVELATION WITHOUT REVELATION

In fact, this brief theological survey has led to a position from which one can better appreciate the true stakes of my project. Again, I contend that the phenomenological appropriation of revelation has all too often been accomplished at the price of a radical formalization and even an attenuation of its meaning. What the phenomenological discourse on revelation has generally lost sight of, in my view, is the material content of revelation itself. The phenomenological treatment of revelation (with the exception of its hermeneutical representatives, such as Ricoeur) is vulnerable to a criticism quite similar to the one Barth had launched against the anthropocentric, existentialist theologies of the nineteen twenties and thirties. Could one not say, at the risk of gross oversimplification, that phenomenology, too, begins with the human subject, with the analysis of consciousness, with the patient description of things as they appear within the flux of human experience? And if that is the case, will any phenomenological description of revelation be doomed from the start?

To be sure, phenomenology always entails a certain process of formalization. It moves, that is, from the concrete phenomenon as it is given within consciousness to the formal structure, essence (*eidos*), or its transcendental conditions of possibility. This intuition of essences is, as it were, achieved through a process of abstraction based upon a series of imaginative variations on concrete experience. It is precisely this ascension to a formal-transcendental register that distinguishes phenomenology from merely empirical sciences, such as psychology. But this formal analysis of consciousness is for phenomenology only a preliminary, methodological procedure or starting point, in much the same way that radical doubt serves as a momentary heuristic device in the initial stage of Descartes's *Meditations*.[60] The natural attitude's manner of positing a reality is, to be sure, momentarily put on hold; the world of manipulable objects is placed in suspense, and we are asked to attend to it in such a way that everything which is not immanent within consciousness be excluded. But lest we slip back into the same psychologistic skepticism to which Husserl's phenomenological breakthrough was believed to be the antidote, this methodological act of suspension should never be thought of as undermining or placing in doubt our belief in the existence of our world or the tangible content of our immediate experience. The material richness of lived experience is not lost with the *epochē*; rather, it is won, it is gained anew.[61]

Nevertheless, I will argue that in the texts of Heidegger and Marion (though, again, less so in those of Ricoeur) the formalization that revelation undergoes is not thought to result from the *descriptive* attitude of the phenomenologist; it is not thought to be purely or strictly methodological. Rather, this formalization is believed to be *constitutive* of the phenomenon itself. Put differently, I argue that revelation is not only described by these philosophers in terms of its most general or formal features; it is actually thought to be characterized by formalism itself, by a certain lack of determinate content. This claim is bound to be controversial, and I realize that it can only be justified on the basis of a meticulous reading of the texts in which this attenuation-formalization actually occurs. Generally speaking, however, my argument hinges upon the different ways in which Heidegger, Marion, and Ricoeur envision the relationship between their own phenomenological concepts of revelation, on the one hand, and the concrete expressions of revelation as found within religious discourse, on the other. This relationship between phenomenological discourse and religious discourse is governed by a series of distinctions—such as the distinction between the *ontic* and the *ontological*, *regional* hermeneutics and *general* hermeneutics, *revelation* and *revealability*, etc.—all of which effectively function to preserve the distance between philosophy and theology. What is at stake in each of these distinctions is nothing less than the ability of phenomenologists to take up the religious phenomenon of revelation without surreptitiously adopting theological presuppositions, or without abandoning their claim to neutrality or philosophical rigor.

A number of genuine questions present themselves: Can the phenomenologist (*as* philosopher) arrive at the phenomenological meaning, essence, or structure of revelation without having to draw from the well of theological discourse? If not, then does this mean phenomenology is inevitably dependent upon its engagement with religious language? Would this mean that the phenomenological analysis of revelation is inescapably (and indeed irreparably) "contaminated" by a certain theological orientation or bias? Moreover, can the phenomenologist avoid such theological orientations by adopting the perspective of a fundamental ontology (as Heidegger does) or by employing an increasingly rigorous form of the phenomenological reduction (as Marion does)? If such biases are indeed neutralized or held in check, or if the affiliation with concrete religious discourse is entirely eliminated, then what is left for the phenomenologist to investigate? What would the phenomenological meaning of revelation *mean* in the absence of any reference to concrete religious discourse? Would it represent an empty figure, a mere shadow? Or would it mark the ultimate essence of revelation *as such*, beyond any of its particular historical, linguistic, or textual instantiations?

Each of the figures investigated below has, in one way or another, had to confront this line of questioning. And although each offers a distinct response, one cannot fail to recognize the remarkable consistency of the specific set of problems and issues associated with the phenomenology of revelation. My objective in the following three chapters is to reconstruct, as best I can, these problems and issues through a series of interconnected readings that serve to draw the works of Heidegger, Marion, and Ricoeur into a dialogue which, though occasionally antagonistic, is ultimately productive.

NOTES

1. Edmund Husserl, "Phenomenology and Theology," in *The Religious*, ed. John Caputo (Oxford, UK: Blackwell Publishers, 2002) / "Phänomenologie und Theologie" *Wegmarken, Gesamtausgabe* vol. 9, Frankfurt: Vittorio Klostermann, 1996. Hereafter indicated by PT, followed by two sets of page numbers: the first refers to the English translation, the second to the German text.

2. Kisiel, *The Genesis of Heidegger's 'Being and Time'* (Los Angeles: University of California Press, 1995), especially Chapters 1–3.

3. For a nuanced treatment of these parallels, see Hent de Vries, *Philosophy and the Turn to Religion* (Baltimore: Johns Hopkins University Press, 1999), 104–5.

4. As we shall see in the following chapter, Heidegger goes to considerable lengths during the mid-1920s in order to conceal the religious provenance of many of the core categories of his phenomenological ontology—and I will argue that this attempt to cover his theological tracks will prove to have an enduring significance for all subsequent attempts to understand revelation in terms of phenomenology.

5. Jean Héring, *Phénoménologie et philosophie religieuse* (Paris, F. Alcan, 1926). For a brief discussion of these works, see Samuel Moyn, *Origins of the Other: Emmanuel Levinas Between Revelation and Ethics* (London: Cornell University Press, 2005), 38–45, 127.

6. This group was established in 1905, just six years after the publication of Husserl's *The Logical Investigations*. For more about the Göttingen Circle and its influence upon later interpretations of Husserl's phenomenology, see Ethan Kleinberg's *Generation Existential: Heidegger's Philosophy in France 1927–1961* (New York: Cornell University Press, 2005), 27–29.

7. Heidegger, on the other hand, was less enthusiastic about Otto's approach, seeing it as a mere extension of the neo-Kantian problematic rather than a true phenomenology. As Theodore Kisiel observes: "Admirable as he finds Otto's quasi-phenomenological attempt to single out the 'thing itself' proper to religious experience, Heidegger [. . .] begins to express reservations about the neo-Kantian distinction which makes the irrational parasitic upon the rational [. . .]." Kisiel, *The Genesis of Being and Time*, 96. For a discussion of Husserl's assessment of Otto's work, see Moyn, *Origins of the Other*, 38–45 and 127.

8. For a provocative, if highly problematic, study of the relationship between the phenomenology of religion and philosophical phenomenology, see George James's essay "Phenomenology and the Study of Religion: An Archeology of an Approach." James essentially argues that while the two disciplines are not entirely isolated from one another, they nevertheless arise from two independent pre-twentieth-century uses of the word 'phenomenology.' Thus, philosophical hermeneutics employs the term as it arose within German idealism, whereas the phenomenology of religion draws from its use within British empiricism. One obvious difficulty with this thesis is that Husserl's project draws its inspiration from the empiricism of Locke and Hume as much as (if not even more than) it does from German idealism. While James's thesis has a certain heuristic value, it loses all validity if it is pushed too far—as is, perhaps, the case with most arguments that are based solely on the history of the use of words.

9. See, for example, Husserl's *Ideas I*, §24, 44–45.

10. PT 57/54.

11. There are no lack of examples here. One could point to Kierkegaard, whose *Philosophical Fragments* directly respond to Lessing by advancing the thesis that a historical moment (revelation) can in fact provide the basis for an eternal truth. Within twentieth-century theology, one cannot fail to mention the neo-orthodox conception of revelation articulated by Karl Barth, which responds to the liberal protestant theology of his day, as yet another noteworthy example of this desire to restore revelation to its "proper" place of dignity—to the non- or supra-rational, to a place beyond the domain of human rationality. See Trevor Hart's essay on "Revelation" in *The Cambridge Companion to Karl Barth*, ed. John Webster (Cambridge: Cambridge University Press, 2000), 37–56.

12. When it comes time to say precisely what revelation means, we shall see that some phenomenologists (especially those who belong to what I refer to as the radical strand) find themselves reverting back to this merely negative and formal definition: revelation as that which lies outside of reason, as that which gives itself without being subject to and limited by the condition of sufficient reason, etc.

13. Jean-Francois Courtine, "Introduction: Phenomenology and Hermeneutics of Religion," in *Phenomenology and the "Theological Turn,"* trans. Bernard Prusak (New York: Fordham University Press, 2000), 123.

14. Ibid., 122.

15. Jean-Luc Marion, *Givenness and Revelation*, trans. Stephen Lewis (Oxford: Oxford University Press, 2018), 7.

16. Ibid. 7.

17. Kosky, "Translator's Preface," 113.

18. My use of Levinas's philosophy as an example of "radical" phenomenology is, admittedly, complicated by the fact that the term "metaphysics" is given a wholly positive signification in his work, since it is associated with Kantian ethics and is opposed to the ontological tradition he seeks to overcome. Nevertheless, for my purposes here his attitude toward metaphysics per se is less significant than the radical nature of his thought, which requires a step back from the said (which operates at the level of the proposition) to the saying (which constitutes the raw exposure of one face to another). In Levinas, the return from the said to the saying involves a correlative shift from ontology to ethics. But it also entails a shift away from actual determinate language toward that ethical relation (the so-called relation-without-relation) which *precedes* linguistic communication as its condition of possibility. It is the connection between this radical style of interrogation and this depreciation of language or linguistic mediation that interests me here, and to which Levinas's work singularly attests. See, for example, Emmanuel Levinas, "Language and Proximity," in *Collected Philosophical Papers*, ed. by Alphonso Lingis (Dordrecht: Martinus Nijhoff Publishers, 1987), 109–26.

19. See Hans-Georg Gadamer's insightful discussion of the Heideggerian critique of metaphysics in *"Destruktion* and Deconstruction," in *Dialogue and Deconstruction: The Gadamer-Derrida Encounter*, eds. Diane P. Mchelfelder and Richard E. Palmer (Albany, NY: SUNY Press, 1989), 104.

20. Ibid., 106.

21. BT, 169/212.

22. Hubert Drefus, *Being-in-the-World: A Commentary on Heidegger's* Being and Time*, Division I* (Cambridge, MA: The MIT Press, 1995), 229–30.

23. Jean-Luc Marion, "The Hermeneutics of Givenness," in *The Enigman of Divine Revelation: Between Phenomenology and Comparative Theology*, eds. Marion and Jacobs-Vandegeer (Cham, Switzerland: Springer, 2020), 39 and 42.

24. One cannot overstate the influence that Marion's confrontation with Derrida had upon his characterization of "mystical theology" as a "third way" that escapes or transcends the dialectic of affirmation and negation, of kataphatic and apophatic discourses. Roughly speaking, Derrida claims that apophatic discourse involves a negative but nevertheless ontotheological determination of the divine—a kind of hypostatization of the negative. Marion responds by claiming that mystical theology involves neither affirmation nor negation, but rather an unsaying or "un-naming" which could no longer be accused of being metaphysical because it no longer says "anything determinative about God." In this way, mystical theology represents a radicalization or realization of the negative way, especially insofar as language and predication are concerned. For a brief discussion of these themes in relation to prayer, see Christina M. Gschwandtner's *Degrees of Givenness: On Saturation in Jean-Luc Marion* (Bloomington: Indiana University Press, 2014), 150–53.

25. Hans-Georg Gadamer, *Truth and Method*: *Second, Revised Edition*, trans. Joel Weinsheimer and Donald G. Marshall (New York: Continuum, 1998), 461.

26. Gadamer, *Truth and Method*, 474. The italics are Gadamer's.

27. Paul Ricoeur states his objection to Heidegger's radical project even more forcefully: "This enclosure of the previous history of Western thought within the unity of 'the' Metaphysical seems to me to express a sort of vengefulness [. . .]. The unity of 'the' metaphysical is an after-the-fact construction of Heideggerian thought, intended to vindicate his own labor of thinking and to justify the renunciation of any kind of thinking that is not a genuine overcoming of metaphysics. But why should this philosophy claim for itself alone, to the exclusion of all its predecessors, that it breaks through and innovates? It seems to me time to deny oneself the convenience, which has become a laziness in thinking, of lumping the whole of Western thought under a single word, metaphysics" (RM, 311).

28. Gadamer, "Destruktion and Deconstruction," 109.

29. See, for instance, Gadamer, *Truth and Method*, 444.

30. For a good example of Ricoeur's approach, see Paul Ricoeur, "Word, Polysemy, Metaphor: Creativity in Language," in *A Ricoeur Reader: Reflection and Imagination*, ed. M. Valdes (New York: Harvester-Wheatsheaf, 1991), 86–98.

31. Gadamer, *Truth and Method*, 470.

32. I more or less borrow this expression from Jacques Derrida, who speaks of "a *thinking* that 'repeats' the possibility of religion without religion," in Jacques Derrida, *The Gift of Death*, trans. David Wills (Chicago: The University of Chicago Press, 1995), 49.

33. To cite just three examples: "What is the meaning of revelation?—The word stands either (a) for the process by which God makes known to man the truth which

he requires, or (b) for the body of truth which God has made known" (taken from H. L. Goudge's entry on "Revelation" in *Encyclopaedia of Religion and Ethics*, ed. James Hastings [New York: C. Scribner's Sons, 1928]); "In Christian theology the word is used both of the corpus of truth about Himself which God discloses to us and of the process by which His communication of it takes place" (taken from the entry on "Revelation" in *The Oxford Dictionary of the Christian Church, Third Edition*, ed. E. A. Livingstone [Oxford: Oxford University Press, 1997]); and, finally, "The term 'revelation' may refer either to the act of revealing (*revelatio*) or the things that have been revealed (*revelata*)" (taken from Stephen W. Sykes entry on "Revelation" in Lacoste, ed., *The Encyclopedia of Christian Theology* [New York: Routledge, 2005], 677).

34. As in *1 Sm* 9:15–16: "Now the day before Saul came, the Lord had revealed to Samuel: 'Tomorrow about this time I will send to you a man from Benjamin, and you shall anoint him to be ruler over my people Israel.' (Note: Unless otherwise stated, all translations of biblical passages are from *The New Oxford Annotated Bible: New Revised Standard Version with the Apocrypha* (third edition), ed. Michael Coogan (New York: Oxford University Press, 2001). NB: all subsequent biblical passages will refer to this translation and edition.

35. As in *Ez*. 20:9: "But I acted for the sake of my name, that it should not be profaned in the sight of nations among whom they lived, in whose sight I made myself known to them in bringing them out of the land of Egypt."

36. *Gn*. 41:25: "Then Joseph said to Pharaoh, 'Pharaoh's dreams are one and the same; God has revealed to Pharaoh what he is about to do.'"

37. For a more comprehensive list, see Johannes Deninger, "Revelation," in *The Encyclopedia of Religion*, ed. by Mircea Eliade (New York: Macmillan, 1987).

38. See, for example, *Deut*. 4:32–34.

39. This idea played an especially crucial role during the Reformation and, more recently, in the thought of Karl Barth.

40. As Norbert Schiffers writes, "God's revelation takes place in history and the history of God with man is both the *object* and the *means* of his revelation" (italics mine). *Encyclopedia of Theology*, ed. Karl Rahner (London: Burns & Oats, 1975), 1454.

41. Ibid., 1456.

42. Although the term *revelare* was already employed by Tertullian, it remained little more than a "subsidiary interest" within Patristic theology. See Jean-Yves Lacoste, *Encyclopedia of Christian Theology* (New York: Routledge, 2005), 1383–84.

43. John Baillie, *The Idea of Revelation* (New York: Columbia University Press, 1965). See Baillie's "Historical Reminder," 3–18.

44. F. L. Cross and E. A. Livingstone, *The Oxford Dictionary of the Christian Church* (London: Oxford University Press, 2005), 1392.

45. Gilson, *The Christian Philosophy*, 93.

46. Ibid.

47. Ibid.

48. "According to St. Thomas, the *revelatum* embraces solely that whose very essence it is to be revealed, because we can only come to know it by way of

revelation. [. . .] What constitutes 'the revealed' as such is not the fact that it has been revealed but rather its character of not being accessible save by revelation. Thus conceived, 'the revealed' is all knowledge about God beyond the grasp of human reason. God may in addition reveal things accessible to reason, but since they are not inaccessible by the natural light of human understanding, such knowledge is not part of 'the revealed.'" Gilson, *The Christian Philosophy*, 11–12.

49. *Decrees of the Ecumenical Councils*, ed. by Norman Tanner (Washington, DC: Georgetown University Press, 1990). See Chapter 3 of the second session.

50. This principle of the absolute sufficiency of Scripture which permeates Reformation thinking was not entirely incompatible with a theory of "natural revelation," as Calvin's insistence on the dual knowledge of God (*duplex cognition*) confirms: God, according to Calvin, can be known through God's Word as well as through God's creation (both the natural world and the human intellect) (Lacoste, *Encyclopedia of Christian Theology*, 1386–87). See Calvin's *Institutes of the Christian Religion*, trans. Henry Beveridge (Grand Rapids, MI: Wm. B. Eerdmans Publishing Company, 1989), Chapter 2: Book II, §18, 238.

51. Lacoste, *Encyclopedia of Christian Theology*, 1389.

52. Ibid.

53. Ibid.

54. Rudolf Bultmann, *Theology of the New Testament*, trans. Kendrick Grobel (Waco, TX: Baylor University Press, 2007), 49–59.

55. Karl Barth, "Concluding Unscientific Postscript on Schleiermacher," in *Karl Barth: Theologian of Freedom*, ed. Clifford Green (Minneapolis: Fortress Press, 1991), 79 (italics mine).

56. As we shall see in Chapter 2, despite the obvious differences in their vocabularies, this is precisely the kind of theology that Heidegger advocates in his essay on "Phenomenology and Theology." This similarity is hardly a coincidence, since the position Barth criticizes here was first adopted by Bultmann from Heidegger.

57. Barth, "Concluding Unscientific Postscript," 80.

58. Ibid.

59. Sykes, "Revelation," 677.

60. See Chapter 1 of Husserl, *Cartesian Meditations: An Introduction to Phenomenology*, trans. Dorion Cairns (London: Kluwer Academic Publishers, 1997).

61. Thus, regarding the new field opened by way of the phenomenological reduction, Husserl remarks: "Though we have 'excluded' the whole world with all physical things, living beings, and humans, ourselves included [. . .] Strictly speaking, we have not lost anything but rather have gained the whole of absolute being which, rightly understood, contains within itself, 'constitutes' within itself, all worldly transcendencies." Husserl, *Ideas*, 113.

Chapter 2

Phenomenology, Theology, and Counter-Contamination in Early Heidegger

> *The Bible [. . .] has thus been excluded by Heidegger from the domain of thinking, all the while being constantly called upon by him.*
>
> Marlène Zarader, *The Unthought Debt*

1. AN ITINERARY

In the previous chapter, I argued that phenomenology's turn toward the theological did not begin in the nineteen eighties. It was already well underway by the time Heidegger delivered his lecture on "Phenomenology and Theology" in 1928. In this chapter, I will argue that the fundamental themes and problems pertaining specifically to the phenomenology of revelation were already present, albeit in an embryonic form, in that lecture itself (although it must be said that making sense of that lecture will require us to view it within the broader context of Heidegger's work during that period). The reading of early Heidegger which I present in this chapter will furnish the thematic structures and interpretive framework for each of the investigations that follow: the distinction between revelation (*Offenbarung*) and revealability (*Offenbarkeit*), the so-called logic of presupposition, the problem of contamination and counter-contamination, and the tendency toward formalization/attenuation. Since these issues will continue to haunt all subsequent phenomenologies of revelation—whether they be of the 'hermeneutical' or 'radical' type—we will need to pay careful attention to context in which they originally emerged.

My itinerary runs as follows: I begin with a discussion of Heidegger's characterization of the phenomenology's relationship to theology in terms of the distinction he proposes between ontic science and ontological science (Sections 2 and 3). As Heidegger himself admitted in a 1961 postscript to

"Phenomenology and Theology,"[1] this characterization cannot be understood apart from the discussion of ontology and ontic science found in the introductory sections of *Being and Time*.[2] There, one discovers that the relationship between these two sciences involves a hierarchical ordering (a "logic of presupposition") whereby ontic investigation is subordinated to phenomenological ontology (Sections 4 and 5). After analyzing both the substantive and methodological arguments for the primacy and autonomy of phenomenology vis-à-vis ontic science (Sections 6 and 7), I turn to a consideration of his claim that theology (as the science of faith or revelation) must itself be classified as an ontic science (Section 8). This claim, however, seems to contradict the central role assigned to primal Christian experience within Heidegger's earlier lecture courses on the phenomenology of religious life (Section 9). Since this Christian experience served as a sort of template for Heidegger's later fundamental existentials of *Being and Time*, it would appear that *at least one* ontic science (namely, the science of this Christian revelation) violates the hierarchical ordering referred to above—that is to say, it suggests an ontic *contamination* of ontology. I explore this so-called problem of contamination by way of several deconstructivist readings of Heidegger's phenomenology of religion (Derrida, de Vries, Zarader), where the issue gets worked out in terms of an aporetical affiliation between revelation (*Offenbarung*) and revealability (*Offenbarkeit*) (Section 10). In the course of this analysis, I argue that a correlative problem comes into view: namely, Heidegger's phenomenologico-ontological approach seems to entail—and even necessitate—a certain formalization of revelation (*Offenbarung*), a formalization that threatens to 'contaminate' the supposedly concrete character of revelation itself. Since this process of formalization appears to involve an inversion of ontic contamination, I refer to it as the problem of counter-contamination (Section 11). These two problems—namely, ontic contamination and counter-contamination—are then shown to be operative at certain crucial junctures within Heidegger's lecture on "Phenomenology and Theology." I argue that the process of counter-contamination ultimately functions as a sort of protective strategy[3] whereby Heidegger is able to maintain the primacy of phenomenology over theology (Section 12) while also inoculating himself against the charge of ontic contamination. This primacy is finally confirmed and solidified in the 1928 lecture by phenomenology's claim to correct (or, better, "co-direct") theological analysis of *Christlichkeit*. Through a detailed reading of that lecture, I argue that this correction is accomplished by way of an appeal to certain, supposedly deeper "pre-Christian" ontological structures (Section 13). This move, I claim, effectively involves illegitimately superimposing the formal character of revealability back upon revelation itself, so that the latter is purged (in advance, as it were) of any ontic content that might threaten to contaminate the ontological character of the analytic of Dasein that is built upon it. Such is the long and arduous path demanded by Heidegger's own complex thought about the interrelationship between phenomenology, theology, and revelation.

2. PHILOSOPHY AND THEOLOGY AS SCIENCE

Heidegger opens his lecture with a discussion of what he refers to as the "popular conception" of the relationship between theology and philosophy, namely, as involving a tension or struggle between two competing *worldviews*—faith versus knowledge, revelation versus reason. According to this conception, both theology and philosophy concern the same subject matter— the world, human life, etc.—though each of them *interprets* this subject matter according to its own unique principles or point of view. Whereas theology is regarded as the "expression of the credal understanding of the world and life," philosophy is thought to provide an "interpretation of the world and of life that is removed from revelation and free from faith" (PT 50/47). It is to be expected that Heidegger, who rejects any characterization of philosophy as worldview, rejects this popular characterization.

Nevertheless, Heidegger does not move directly to this crucial distinction between philosophy and worldview. Rather, in the immediate context of the lecture, he begins with the observation that the kind of oppositional thinking involved in the popular conception serves to prevent genuine reflection on the relationship between religion and philosophy. After all, if each represents merely its own interpretation of the world, then their relationship could only be decided "by the manner, the extent, and the strength of the conviction and the proclamation of the worldview" rather than by "scientific argument" that would appeal to some mutually agreed upon principles (PT 50/47). In that case, philosophy and theology would remain two isolated and mutually exclusive worldviews, and nothing would enable us to mediate or arbitrate between them. Instead of establishing a relationship between philosophy and theology, the popular conception actually precludes the possibility of making any determination regarding that relationship. As a result, any examination of their relationship which takes this popular conception as its starting point would be forced to vacillate between two irreconcilable perspectives: *either* reason *or* revelation.

The boldness of Heidegger's lecture lies in its attempt to re-conceive this relationship as a relation between two sciences rather than two competing worldviews: "We, however, see the problem of the relationship *differently* from the very start. It is for us rather a question about the *relationship of two sciences* [*Wissenschaften*]" (PT 50/47, author's italics). But if Heidegger rejects the popular conception as false, naïve, or overly antagonistic, this does not mean that his own approach aims to reconcile philosophy and theology, nor even to demonstrate some degree of compatibility between them. In good Pauline fashion, he will insist to the very end upon the mortal opposition between faith and philosophy.[4] Nonetheless, his goal is to establish a framework within which it finally becomes *meaningful* to discuss their *possible* relationship, even if, as we will shortly see, this relationship entails an *absolute* difference.

Heidegger's reconceptualization, however, raises its own set of questions. If, as he suggests, their relation is to be understood as a relation between two sciences, does this mean that we should compare and contrast the conclusions or 'findings' of these sciences? Are we to seek out the parallels, discrepancies, and potential points of agreement between their respective truth claims? Areas where their results are mutually corroborated? Areas where they have diverged? Heidegger's response to this kind of approach is clear:

> It is not a case of comparing the factical circumstances [*faktischen Zustandes*] of two historically given sciences. And even if it were, it would be difficult to describe a unified state of affairs regarding the two sciences today in the midst of their divergent directions. To proceed on a course of comparison with respect to their factical relationship would yield no *fundamental* [*grundsätzliche*] insight as to how Christian theology and philosophy are related to one another. (PT 50/47)

This passage suggests at least two reasons for rejecting a comparative approach sought at the factical level of two existing sciences. First, in order to pursue this comparison, one would need to assume (mistakenly, it seems) that the claims of philosophy and the claims of theology concern the same subject matter (i.e., the same region of beings) and that they therefore represent two different takes on one and the same thing. Heidegger appears to regard this assumption as blatantly false: first because it threatens to lapse back into an opposition between two irreconcilable worldviews, and secondly, because he takes it as obvious that philosophy and theology (at least today) are not directed toward the same objects, nor do they even involve the same style of questioning.[5] But more importantly, Heidegger suggests that this kind of comparative approach—directed at the current methods and contents of these sciences—would fail to see what is most essential or "fundamental" to them. Presumably, this is because the methods and claims of any "historically given" science are subject to change and revision. Any similarities or parallels between their present styles of investigation or their current findings would be merely contingent, accidental, and, thus, incapable of revealing an essential or fundamental (*grundsätzliche*) relationship between philosophy and theology.

Consequently, Heidegger suggests that their relationship is not to be established on the same plane as their factual content or collected results (BT 29/9), but on the more fundamental level of their "ideal construction" (*idealen Konstruktion*), that is, on the basis of the respective "possibilities" they hold as sciences: "One can decide their possible relationship to one another from the possibilities they both have as sciences" (PT 50/47). But what does Heidegger mean by the "possibilities" of a science? What is the significance of his differentiation between a science's possibility or ideal aim, on the one hand, and its "factual circumstance," on the other?

3. ONTIC AND ONTOLOGICAL SCIENCES

Heidegger realizes that posing the question of the relationship between philosophy and theology in terms of two different kinds (or possibilities) of science "presupposes that we have [already] established the idea of science in general, as well as how to characterize the modifications of this idea that are possible in principle" (PT 50/47–8). It would be impossible to determine, at least with any precision, what his view of that relationship is without first determining what he means by science. In fact, Heidegger later claimed that his lecture presupposed the "idea of science" that he had already worked out in §3 and §7 of *Being and Time*, where he first posited a distinction between two general types of science—*ontic* science and *ontological* science. There, one discovers that this distinction is itself grafted onto the ontological difference, or the difference between beings (entities) and Being (the Being of entities). Science, taken in its most general sense, is defined by Heidegger as "the founding disclosure, for the sake of disclosure, of a self-contained region of beings, *or* of [B]eing [as such]" (PT 50/48, my italics). The division between ontic and ontological sciences derives from these two radically different manners of disclosure—ontic sciences are founded upon a disclosure of a being or a region of beings, whereas ontology involves the disclosure of Being as such.

Sciences that are founded on a disclosure of a specific "region of beings" are typically associated throughout Heidegger's texts of this period with two adjectives: they are said to be "ontic," as well as "positive." As the double predication suggests, this form of science exhibits not one but two essential features—features which are never systematically worked out by Heidegger himself. Still, one can infer that sciences that are referred to as ontic (rather than ontological) are so classified precisely because their mode of investigation never engages the question of Being as such, but is rather limited and in fact delimited by certain fields or regions of entities. They are always already preoccupied with a particular set of *present-at-hand* or *ready-to-hand* entities, to the exclusion of Being. Such sciences are also called "positive" sciences in order to highlight the fact that these specific regions of being are "in a certain manner always already disclosed prior to [the] scientific disclosure" as such (PT 50/48). As Heidegger writes:

> We call the sciences of beings as given—of a *positum*—positive sciences. Their characteristic feature lies in the fact that the objectification of whatever it is that they thematize is oriented directly toward beings, as a continuation of an already existing prescientific attitude toward such beings. (PT 50/48)

Ontic sciences serve to conceptualize, objectify, or thematize a set of (ontic) beings that have already been disclosed (posited) in a prescientific, pre-theoretical manner. The Being of the objects under investigation is regarded (naively, to be sure) as having already been disclosed, already laid out, already placed before us: hence his use of the word "*positum*." However, this pre-theoretical disclosure is never made explicit, never rendered transparent within the science itself (with the exception, that is, of rare moments of profound crisis, in which case their operations give way to genuinely ontological ones). Ontic-positive sciences are engaged in second-order operations—experiments, data collection, etc.—that are propped up upon and sustained by the "rough" and "naive" interpretations of their respective fields—interpretations which they inadvertently inherit from ordinary, pre-scientific experience without ever radically calling them into question.

This secondary operation of thematization is the central trait of such disparate disciplines as history, biology, and geometry, each of which has its own corresponding field of investigation: the past, life, space, etc. And each is said to be "positive" in part because the meaning of their respective fields is not originally established by the sciences themselves, but are simply adopted or taken over from our ordinary ("rough and naïve") conceptions of them. This by no means indicates a deficiency of these sciences *as* science. It is not as if they could proceed otherwise. On the contrary, it represents a constitutive characteristic of this kind of scientific activity. It constitutes the condition under which this type of ontic research can accomplish its own proper "ideal aim." The historian, for example, inquires about the past without ever posing the question of what the past *is* as such. Instead of asking about the nature of the Being of the entities which he or she studies (i.e., the nature of their past-ness, so to speak), the historian simply proceeds on the basis of our average or ordinary understanding of 'the past.' And that's a good thing—for a philosophically inclined historian, obsessed with the question about the Being of past as such, is not likely to be very a productive one. So, far from indicating a shortcoming of his or her research, this manner of proceeding actually represents the appropriate aim of ontic-positive scientific inquiry.[6]

That said, this does suggest that ontic-positive science is, strictly speaking, incapable of either establishing or clarifying its own direction, its own limits, its own field. It can only get started once this direction and delimitation has already been established. The historian, to return to our example, will always operate on the basis of our ordinary understanding of the nature of the past, which she simply adopts from our pre-philosophical intuitions, or our average, everyday discourse. As Heidegger puts it in *Being in Time*:

> Scientific research accomplishes, roughly and naively [*naiv und roh*], the demarcation and initial fixing of the areas of subject-matter. The basic structures [*Grundstrukturen*] of any such area have already been worked out after a fashion in our pre-scientific ways of experiencing and interpreting [*die vorwissenschaftliche Erfahrung und Auslegung*] that domain of Being [*des Seinsbezirkes*] in which the area of subject-matter is itself confined. (BT 29/9)

Although the ontic-positive sciences begin with—and are in a certain sense bound by—the "pre-scientific" comportment towards their respective domains, they nevertheless purport to move beyond this original disclosure, to "discover" more about the objective character of the entities under investigation. However, since they generally do so by conducting empirical experiments and accumulating data rather than by returning to the meaning of the Being of these domains, this leaves the uncritically adopted ontological presuppositions of the science fully intact, unquestioned and unchanged. Barring a genuine scientific crisis, no amount of such ontic-positive research will ever lead to the establishment of a new paradigm or to a genuine reevaluation of the Being of the things themselves.[7]

4. HEIDEGGER'S "LOGIC OF PRESUPPOSITION"

Each ontic science, insofar as it is determined by its own particular positum, by the region of beings which it thematizes, is said to be "heterogeneous" from every other. The differences between these sciences are merely relative differences when compared to the radical heterogeneity that exists between philosophy (ontological science) and the ontic-positive sciences as a whole. In utter contrast to these ontic-positive sciences, philosophy—understood here as phenomenology, the *Urwissenschaft*—is said to be concerned with Being as such, with the Being of beings, with Being *wholly other than* beings. Consequently, Heidegger insists that philosophy is the one and only *ontological* science and, as such, it fulfills its highest and most proper ambition in the form of a *fundamental* ontology, a questioning and clarifying of the meaning of Being (BT 31/11). Needless to say, this science of Being does not occupy the same register as those other, ontic-positive sciences. The respective "aims" of these two types of science could not in fact be more different. The one thematizes an already disclosed set of beings; the other digs beneath this scientific thematization in order to disclose, in increasingly rigorous and explicit fashion, the Being that is presupposed therein.

In fact, the relationship between the two types of sciences entails what Jacques Derrida has aptly called a "logic of presupposition." In *Aporias*, Derrida elucidates this logic in light of Heidegger's existential analysis of death and how it is said to differ from the various "scientific" (i.e., ontic-positive) treatments of death—that is, anthropological, psychological, bio-genetic treatments. Although we are not interested here in death *per se*, Derrida's reading of the significance of death in *Being and Time* serves well to elucidate this Heideggerian logic in its generality.

Summing up Heidegger's position, Derrida writes that "no matter how necessary and enriching [the anthropological and bio-genetic interpretations of death] may be, these forms of knowledge must presuppose a concept of death properly speaking."[8] That is to say, they "must already [i.e., prior to the second order activities of these sciences] know what death means and how to recognize [it]."[9] And yet, Derrida observes, "only an existential analysis can provide such a concept of death to these forms of knowledge," i.e., to the "ontic-positive sciences."[10] This is because the concept of death that always already operates within any given scientific study of death is left unchecked and un-interrogated by these sciences—in other words, it never becomes the object of ontic-positive investigation as such (just as the work of the historian never elucidates or conceptualizes the meaning of 'past-ness'—i.e., the Being of history—even though this work constantly presupposes a basic understanding of the past as the condition of its own possibility). Heidegger's existential analysis, on the other hand, takes this yet-to-be-clarified concept as its theme. One could say that the aim of his fundamental ontology in general is to clarify or to make explicit the meaning of Being that operates subterraneously within other modes of inquiry. The task of Heidegger's existential analysis of death, then, is to render this presupposed meaning of death transparent to itself.[11]

If anthropology, demography, biogenetics, psychology, thanatology, and even theology are to avoid erecting themselves upon unexamined grounds, they will have to be preceded, guided, and corrected by ontological science. The question of the meaning of Being takes precedence over the accumulation of data, the conducting of empirical experiments, the analysis of statistics, etc. Thus, for example, the fundamental existential analysis of death ought to come *before* the ontic-positive science of death (thanatology). But what is the meaning of this "before"? What is the nature of the priority accorded to ontology vis-à-vis ontic science?

One can detect a fundamental ambiguity at the very heart of Heidegger's logic of presupposition. At first glance, it appears as though this priority simply stems from Heidegger's recognition of a basic hermeneutical fact—namely, that all interpretation must begin with some prejudice, with the interpreter's own pre-understanding about that which he or she interprets. A certain methodological precaution follows directly from this fact:

> our first, last, and constant task is never to allow our fore-having, fore-sight, and fore-conception to be presented to us by fancies and popular conceptions, but rather to make the scientific [i.e., ontological] theme secure by working out these fore-structures in terms of the things themselves [i.e., in terms of the Being of the beings in question]. (BT 195/153)

If ontology is merely understood as the task of working out these fore-structures "in terms of the things themselves," then its priority simply follows as a natural consequence of this procedural imperative. But the logic of presupposition seems to involve both an *epistemic* and an *ontological* order. In fact, Heidegger implies that the latter serves to justify or ground the former—in much the same way that some rationalists claim that the *ordo cognoscendi* is grounded in an *ordo essendi*—so that the merely methodological priority (or procedure) reveals a deeper, more fundamental ontological structure beneath it. In any case, the order implied within this logic of presupposition is, as Derrida rightly points out, an order in every sense of the word—it signifies both a sequencing, a method, a manner of proceeding *as well as* a demand, prescription, requirement.[12] It is demanded by the ontological constitution of the things themselves.

Nowhere is this demand more evident than in Heidegger's discussion of the relationship between the ontological structure of understanding and the (apparent) circularity to which it gives rise at the epistemological level. A more accurate understanding of the priority of ontology over ontic-positive science can be gained by considering that particular discussion. As is well known, Heidegger warned his readers not to misinterpret the hermeneutical structure of understanding in terms of a *circulus vitiosus* which could somehow be avoided or overcome simply by developing a more rigorous epistemological method or procedure (BT 194/152–53). His solution to the problem of the circularity of all understanding (if it really is a problem at all) is to move back from the epistemological level to an ontological level.

> The 'circle' in understanding belongs to the structure of meaning, and the latter phenomenon is rooted in the existential constitution of Dasein—that is, in the understanding which interprets. An entity [namely, Dasein] for which, as Being-in-the-world, its Being is itself an issue, has an ontological, circular structure. (BT 195/153)

The epistemological structure is driven back into the ontological constitution of Dasein itself. In other words, the methodological order is itself shown to be merely derivative; it derives from a fundamentally ontological structure—and, as we shall see, from an ontological stratification according to which certain experiences or modes of existence are more primordial than others. Since the (epistemological) circularity reflects an ontological structure, it should not be mistaken as an imperfection of the understanding. The goal is not to overcome the circle but to enter into it in the appropriate manner.[13] And this means, to begin with, that one must place ontological science before ontic-positive science: one must "make the scientific theme secure by working out these fore-structures in terms of the things themselves," i.e., in terms of the Being of the being in question (BT 195/153). So, in the end, the priority of ontology does have a methodological pertinence. However, if the priority (or anteriority) of ontology over ontic-positive science entails a "correct" manner of proceeding (that is, an appropriate methodological procedure), this is only in order to meet the demands of this underlying ontological order. In other words, the so-called logic of presupposition is ontological more than it is methodological.

Derrida is right to conclude that Heidegger's logic of presupposition involves a *radical* gesture—one that goes well beyond merely methodological concerns and hermeneutical precautions. Insofar as ontology claims to penetrate deeper the epistemological problematic, its priority is irreducible to the methodological priority implicated by the "pre-" in pre-understanding, pre-comprehension, or even pre-supposition. To be sure, ontology may proceed by way of a clarification of the naive concepts presupposed by ontic-positive sciences. But this clarification is not solely aimed at improving or contributing to our scientific knowledge about entities and their ontic properties, but rather at disclosing or retrieving more fundamental (i.e., founding) ontological structures of factical life experience—the so-called existentials worked out in *Being and Time*.

The priority of fundamental ontology, then, has to do with its claim to reveal deeper structures of experience, which are more primordial than the modes of experience unearthed by ontic-positive analysis. The existential analysis of death is telling in this regard. For here we see that the existential being-towards-death involves a more radical, authentic, and fundamental experience of death than can be found within the ontic-positive sciences. And yet, this existential structure is presupposed, albeit in a naïve fashion, by those sciences themselves. Thus, Heidegger's analysis entails a stratification or layering of these structure of existence—one is more primordial or foundational, while the other is derivative. As Derrida notes,

Heidegger describes this relation of dependence using the classical idea of order, an order of priority, precedence, and presupposition (*vorliegen, voraussetzen*), which is also an order of foundation: there is the *founding* basis of the foundation and the *founded* structure that presupposes it.[14]

The radicalism implied by the logic of presupposition, then, has to do with this return to "presupposed" foundations, to the fundamental structures of existence or factical life experience.

That these structures are thought to be more primordial than the theoretical mode of experience operative within ontic-positive science is hardly surprising. What is surprising, however, is that Heidegger appears to situate these structures beneath or beyond the domains of language, culture, and religion in general. Derrida catches sight of this double radicality when he writes:

> If one wants to translate this situation in terms of disciplinary or regional borders, of domains of knowledge, then one will say that the delimitation of the [ontic-positive] fields of anthropological, historical, biological, demographic, and even *theological* knowledge *presupposes* a nonregional onto-phenomenology that not only does not let itself be enclosed within the borders of these domains, *but furthermore does not let itself be enclosed within cultural, linguistic, national, or religious borders either* [. . .][15]

The fundamental experiences disclosed by ontological analysis are not enclosed within the domains of history, language, and culture since they actually serve to *found* these domains themselves.[16] I will eventually examine the ultimate consequences of Heidegger's claim that the fundamental structures uncovered by his existential analysis come *before* cultural, linguistic, and religious domains. However, in order to do so, the "hierarchical order" that supposedly separates ontology from ontic-positive science will need to be more clearly determined.

5. THE PRIORITY OF ONTOLOGY IN *BEING AND TIME*

How exactly does Heidegger conceive of the priority of ontological science over and above ontic-positive science? Again, Derrida's text provides us with some clues:

> A hierarchical order thus delimits the field; it rigorously superordinates or subordinates the questions, themes, and in fact, the ontological regions. According to Heidegger, these regions are legitimately separated by pure, rigorous, and indivisible borders. An order is thus structured by *uncrossable* edges.[17]

Derrida is correct to see in Heidegger a tendency towards such border-control, but his characterization slightly oversimplifies the situation. For, in truth, Heidegger does permit certain border crossings, but only those traveling in one direction. It would be more accurate to say that Heidegger envisions a sort of *one-way filiation* or *derivation* between the ontic and the ontological. On the one hand, ontic science must be preceded, founded, guided, "corrected," and, therefore, to a certain extent informed by the fruits of a fundamental ontology. Fundamental ontology, on the other hand, must maintain its absolute independence from those ontic sciences which it, in turn, serves to ground. Ontology, Heidegger claims, serves both to ground and correct ontic research, without ever borrowing from or being affected by the content of the positive sciences themselves. Therefore, the border between the two types of sciences can be crossed in the direction moving from ontological to the ontic. Ontology can inform ontic-positive science—and only when it does can a science be confident that its presuppositions and procedures are adequate to the Being of that which it thematizes.[18] But to travel in the opposite direction would be to violate Heidegger's hierarchical, methodological apparatus and to threaten the autonomy of ontology which this apparatus seeks to preserve.

This one-way filiation will prove essential for understanding the relationship between theology and phenomenology in Heidegger's 1928 lecture. And so we must try to formulate this relationship with as much precision as possible.

The autonomy of Heidegger's fundamental ontology is marked by a double indifference, a kind of independence which situates it at a level that is not once but *twice* removed from every possible ontic orientation—and, I might add, twice removed from the spheres of language, culture, and religion. This double indifference is tantamount to ontology's foundational function—that is, its role as a "preliminary research" that "must run ahead of [i.e., precede] the positive sciences" in order to lay their foundations (BT 30/10). This preliminary research aims to uncover the ontological conditions that make a given ontic science possible. In that respect, Heidegger's conception of ontology remains rather conventional, even classical.[19] For the foundational status vis-à-vis the empirical sciences had in fact already been claimed by that "venerable tradition" of ontology which Heidegger's work seeks to destroy and ultimately to overcome. Thus, for example, Heidegger readily acknowledges that the positive outcome of Kant's first *Critique* was to lay the foundations for the natural sciences—not, to be sure, by explicating a "theory of knowledge," but by establishing a natural ontology, "an *a priori* logic of the subject-matter of that area of Being [*Seinsgebietes*] called 'Nature'" (BT 30–31/11). In contrast to the positive sciences (and Newtonian physics in particular) whose work unfolds *within* that region of Being called Nature, Kant set down the ontological conditions of possibility governing this region as a whole. From this perspective, it could be said that Kant's project had been accomplished "without favoring any particular ontological directions [*Richtungen*] or tendencies [*Tendenzen*]" (BT 31/11). Consequently, it could be argued that traditional ontology, even in its pre-Heideggerian manifestations, *already* maintained a degree of independence with respect to the contents of the positive sciences—and, this, by Heidegger's very own admission.

Nevertheless, Heidegger moves beyond this conventional understanding of ontology and its manner of laying foundations. For, according to Heidegger, this sort of ontology "remains itself naïve and opaque [*undurchsichtig*] if in its researches into the Being of entities it fails to discuss the meaning of Being in general" (BT 31/11). Heidegger's *fundamental* ontology, by contrast, lays the foundation not only with respect to ontic sciences, but also with respect to those traditional (regional) ontologies that had in the past served to lay the foundation for particular ontic sciences:

> The question of Being aims therefore at ascertaining the *a priori* conditions not only for the possibility of the sciences which examine entities as entities of such and such a type, and, in so doing, already operates with an [naïve] understanding of Being, but also for the possibility of those ontologies themselves which are prior to the ontical sciences and which provide their foundations. (BT 31/11)

On the basis of this radicalization of ontology itself, Heidegger's fundamental ontology may be said to occupy a depth that is twice removed from the level of ontic-positive scientific research. In a manner that might first appear paradoxical, fundamental ontology comes to occupy its position of ultimate foundation only so long as it maintains its distance from both traditional (regional) ontologies and the ontic-positive sciences. While the ontic sciences, by definition, orient themselves toward some particular empirical content, fundamental ontology must be kept free—indeed, *absolutely* free— from any and every ontic orientation. It must remain 'directionless' and, as it were, 'contentless' if it is to "make the Being of entities stand out in full relief" (BT 49/27).

Heidegger supplies two different explanations for this absolute difference between ontic science and his fundamental ontology. The first, "substantive" explanation, found in the first chapter of the Introduction to *Being and Time* (§§1–4), concerns the peculiarity of ontology's object of study; the second, "methodological" explanation, found in the second chapter of the Introduction (§§5–7), concerns the particular method of his fundamental ontology. I will consider Heidegger's methodological explanation and the questions raised by it, before turning to his substantive explanation.

6. PHENOMENOLOGY AS A NON-ORIENTED SCIENCE

The methodological requirements of a 'directionless' investigation demand a particular sort of rigor, one that is only attainable by way of the phenomenological approach which, according to Heidegger's formulation, brings into view not a particular region of beings, but Being and its manner of manifestation. Or, as he occasionally puts it, phenomenology concerns not the "what" but the "how" of manifestation.[20]

> With the question of the meaning of Being, our investigation comes up against the fundamental question of philosophy. This is one that must be treated *phenomenologically*. Thus our treatise does not subscribe to a 'standpoint' or represent any special 'direction'; for phenomenology is nothing of either sort, nor can it become so as long as it understands itself. The expression "phenomenology" signifies primarily a *methodological conception*. This expression does not characterize the what of the object or of philosophical research as subject-matter, but rather the *how* of that research. [. . .] Thus, the term 'phenomenology' is quite different in its meaning from expressions such as 'theology' and the like. [Unlike the term "phenomenology"] those terms designate the objects of their respective sciences according to the subject-matter which they comprise [. . .]. (BT 50/27 and 58–59/34)

Phenomenology, then, is absolutely different from a standpoint or worldview. To have a worldview means to take up a certain standpoint, a certain position or angle from which to view life, the world, etc. Phenomenology, however, does not involve taking a position or approaching something from some particular angle. This is because it does not concern any "thing" at all—or, at least, it is not defined by the things which it investigates. That is to say that, unlike other "-ologies," phenomen*ology* is defined not by the thing but by the manner (the "how") of its investigation. (It is worth noting that this methodological point underscores Heidegger's earlier refusal to characterize the relationship between theology and philosophy in terms of two worldviews—for, as it turns out, philosophy is not properly speaking a worldview at all.)

The most crucial question raised by Heidegger's discussion of methodology concerns the fate of the "what" (i.e., the ontical content) within phenomenological analysis itself. What happens to the concrete, ontical content in the transition from the "what" to the "how"? Does this content disappear behind the curtain of Being? Must ontic beings be passed over, or overlooked, so that our gaze can be redirected toward the ontological such? Does ontology's quest for Being result in a kind of indifference or even blindness towards beings, towards the concrete objects of ontic investigation? I am not yet prepared to answer these questions, since doing so would first require us to consider ontology's relation to a *particular* ontic science and its specific content, rather than to ontic science *in general*. Later, I will have occasion to give this issue the attention it deserves by examining the fate of the content of revelation when it is approached within the phenomenological mode (see Section 11, below). For the moment, my aim is considerably more modest. I am interested here in the ways in which Heidegger understands and justifies his distinction between ontic and ontological sciences, and the logic of presupposition that this understanding implies. Thus far, I have only considered his methodological justification: unlike other scientific approaches—the other "*-ologies*"—phenomen*ology* is not defined by a pre-established set of entities, but by the "how," the way, the manner in which these entities are manifest.

But this formulation of phenomenology already seems to be at odds with Heidegger's own characterization of the nature of inquiry in general (BT, §2). The revival of the question of Being, according to the argument of *Being and Time*, can only be accomplished by rigorously adhering to a basic hermeneutical principle: namely, that every inquiry—and this would, above all, include ontological inquiry—"is guided beforehand by what is sought [*Jedes Suchen hat seine vorgängige Direktion aus dem Gesuchten her*]" (BT 24/5). Though we need not concern ourselves here with the details of his revival of the *Seinsfrage*, it is worth noting that this hermeneutical principle seems on its surface to contradict the expressed aim (or, shall we say, *non*-aim, *non*-directionality) of the phenomenological method as conceived by Heidegger.[21] According to this principle, it belongs to the structure of all inquiry to involve not one, but two elements—not only that which one seeks to discover, but also that which one interrogates in his or her effort to make this discovery. As Heidegger puts it, "in addition to what is asked about [in this case, Being as such], an inquiry has *that which is interrogated* [*ein Befragtes*]" (BT 25/5). A simple example may help clarify Heidegger's point here: If a botanist wants to discover the essential features of a certain type of shrub, then he or she will need go out and collect samples from shrubs that appear to belong to this type, rather than from trees, weeds, or shrubs which obviously belong to a different type. In order to discover the essential features, the botanist will have to examine particular entities, namely, certain shrubs and shrub specimens. The important point here is that all investigation will have to be oriented toward particular entities and this orientation is secured or guided by a pre-understanding of those entities. This, however, seems to rule out the possibility of "phenomenology" as defined by Heidegger (namely, as a non-oriented science), since the hermeneutical character of all inquiry would imply that ontology's quest for Being must also begin with some being, with some entity or entities, with some thing (i.e., the *that* which is to be interrogated).

Indeed, by the time of *Being and Time*'s composition, this hermeneutical insight had led Heidegger to recognize the impossibility of proceeding directly to Being. For even *as* phenomenology, ontology must first pass by way of beings.[22] Since Being is always the Being of some entity, it must always be read on the face of some entity (BT 29/9). But this insight would seem to undermine the distinctive (if not the defining) feature of the phenomenological method, namely, its supposed *non-directionality*. How could Heidegger continue to insist on phenomenology's exceptional character, its radical difference from the ontic-positive sciences, when it too must be directed toward a particular being?

7. THE SIGNIFICANCE OF DASEIN FOR PHENOMENOLOGY

An answer to this question is found in the first introductory chapter of *Being and Time* (§§1–4), where Heidegger seeks to justify the fundamentality of phenomenological ontology on the basis of that peculiar entity which it takes as the starting point of its investigation. As it turns out, there is a particular kind of being that can prepare the ground for a genuine science of Being by allowing us to pass through it—and this is the Being of the inquirer itself: namely, Dasein. In fact, the entire analysis of *Being and Time* is first made possible by Heidegger's strategic decision to take Dasein as the starting point of the inquiry. Dasein's precedence over and above other entities within *Being and Time* is notoriously complex, and often mistaken. To be sure, this being is for Heidegger no ordinary being. It would be mistaken, though, to interpret the priority accorded to it as signaling a move towards some form of philosophical anthropology or existential humanism, as did certain of his French interpreters—most notably, Jean-Paul Sartre. Such interpretations not only misconstrue the nature of Dasein as understood by Heidegger, but, more importantly still, they overlook the preparatory status of the analytic of Dasein within the overall project of a fundamental ontology.[23] Dasein is "selected" as the theme of his phenomenological analysis because it, unlike other ontic entities, does not deflect us away from the question of Being. On account of the peculiar character of Dasein, Heidegger suggests, his analysis can be delimited and directed toward a particular being (namely, Dasein) without fear of losing sight of the ontological question (namely, of the meaning of Being as such).

Why? Heidegger's answer is deceptively simple: because of Dasein's so-called ontico-ontological constitution—that is to say, on account of the fact that an "understanding of Being is itself a definite characteristic of Dasein's

Being" (BT 32/12). In contrast to every other ontic entity, it is distinguished—indeed, "ontically distinguished"—by the very fact that "Being is an issue for it" (BT 32/12). The essential character of Dasein lies "in the fact that in each case it has its Being to be, and has it as its own" (BT 32–33/12). It follows that Dasein cannot be defined "by citing a 'what' of the kind that pertains to a subject-matter" (BT 32/12).

This point was made famous and, for a time, even fashionable by Sartre, who formulated it by inverting the classical (i.e., metaphysical) relationship between essence (*essentia*) and existence (*existentia*). Ever since Plato, existence had been subordinated to essence. However, Sartre insisted that in the particular case of human beings, "existence precedes essence." Humans exist; but unlike other existing beings, their existence lacks the support of some underlining universal nature or a predefined, predetermined human essence.[24] This existentialist (even "humanistic") formulation was surely inspired by *Being and Time*. And though it provides a useful "shorthand" explanation of the philosophical meaning of Dasein, Heidegger remained extremely wary and indeed critical of it—insisting that it risked overemphasizing the question of the human being to the detriment of the question of Being as such.[25] In contrast to Sartre, then, Heidegger's analytic of Dasein is meant to open a window onto Being, rather than onto the human being *per se*. To the extent that Sartre's formulation reveals a unique humanism, it actually conceals the more fundamental question of Being.[26]

This contrast between Sartre and Heidegger is telling, in that it helps to clarify the real significance of Dasein within *Being and Time*: Whereas every other science covers over the meaning of Being by losing itself in the beings that it investigates, the science of Dasein, so to speak, leaves the question of Being in play—if for no other reason than that Dasein itself leaves this question in play. The importance of Dasein, therefore, needs to be understood in terms of Heidegger's concern to secure a science of Being in contrast to a science of ontic beings.[27] Like every inquiry (including ontic-positive inquiries), Heidegger's phenomenology begins with the analysis of one particular kind of entity (i.e., Dasein). However, in this case the existence of the entity in question (i.e., Dasein) is never given, never laid out in advance, never given as a kind of "positum," as is the case with the present-at-hand and ready-to-hand entities examined by the ontic-positive sciences.[28]

Herein lies the distinctiveness of Heidegger's phenomenological analytic of Dasein: though it, too, is subject to the general structure of inquiry, this analytic is not properly speaking a *positive* science—at least not in the same manner as other ontic-positive sciences. Unlike ontic-positive sciences, the analysis of Dasein does not naively presuppose a meaning of the Being of its object (Dasein), but rather it keeps the meaning of its Being in question, in view, and indeed at the center of its analysis. Any inquiry into this particular entity always entails inquiry into the Being of this entity. Dasein, then, does not represent one region of beings among others, one field of investigation among others. It represents a unique, though preliminary, point of departure for a science of Being as such. Thus, Heidegger's decision to begin with Dasein is determined by his quest for a fundamental science of Being (phenomenological ontology) that would ground all other sciences, or that would be presupposed by all forms of ontic-positive investigation.

When taken together, the methodological and substantive discussions of the existential analytic of Dasein exhibit what I, following Derrida, have called a logic of presupposition—a logic which entails a hierarchical relation between ontic and ontological sciences. In short, "Ontological inquiry is indeed more primordial, as over against the ontical inquiry of the positive sciences" (BT 31/11).

8. THEOLOGY AS AN ONTIC-POSITIVE SCIENCE

I will have more to say about the nature of this singular style of inquiry in a moment. For now, it is enough to note that this fundamental "shift in view" from beings to Being sets philosophy absolutely apart from every other science. Each science, of course, has its own unique founding disclosure which distinguishes it from ever other science. But ontological science is set apart from all ontic sciences in ways that are vastly more profound.

> Within the circle of actual or possible sciences of being—the positive sciences—there is between any two only a relative difference, based on the different relations that in each case orient a science to a specific region of beings. On the other hand, every positive science is absolutely, not relatively, different from philosophy. (PT 50/48)

We have seen that the two types of sciences stand in an imbalanced and indeed hierarchical relationship to one another: ontic science is subordinated to an ontological science that serves as its condition of possibility. Now we come to see that, in addition to this *imbalance*, Heidegger's typology also exhibits a certain *lopsidedness*. That is to say, while the class of ontological sciences includes but a single member—namely, *the* fundamental, phenomenological ontology—the class of ontic-positive sciences casts an incredibly large net, including nearly every actual science (in fact, all but one: viz., ontological science), as well as any number of possible sciences yet to be realized.

This brings us to yet another momentous move in Heidegger's 1928 lecture. The first move, we recall, was to have characterized the relation between philosophy and theology in terms of two different kinds of science, rather than, say, two worldviews. Now we discover—and by now it comes as no surprise—that theology is to be grouped together with the ontic-positive sciences, such as chemistry and mathematics. "Theology," he writes, "is a positive science and as such is absolutely different from philosophy," that is, from fundamental ontology (PT 51). Given the lopsidedness of his typology, this conclusion seems all but inevitable. His strict definition of ontology leaves no room for theology, or any other "-ology" for that matter. However, from the perspective of the "popular conception" with which Heidegger's lecture began, the suggestion that theology (as an ontic science) is "in principle closer to chemistry and mathematics than it is to philosophy" could only appear paradoxical, if not preposterous.

In truth, the classification of theology as ontic science might even seem problematic from the perspective of the development of Heidegger's own thinking. As we have seen, ontology must keep itself absolutely free of any and every ontic-positive determination. In determining existential structures, ontology can neither borrow from nor be guided by the content of an ontic-positive science without violating the logic of presupposition and the hierarchical apparatus deployed by Heidegger throughout the nineteen twenties in order to maintain the fundamental character of his ontology. If, as Heidegger insists, it turns out that theology is such a science, then it, too, must be held at an absolute distance from his fundamental ontology. However, with the growing body of research devoted to Heidegger's early lecture courses on religious life, it is becoming increasingly evident that the development of his ontological project was inextricably tied to his theological interests, his deep appreciation for certain dimensions of religious experience, and, particularly, the eschatological experience of the early Christian community.[29] One of the most crucial problems raised by the publication of these early lecture courses—as Theodore Kisiel, Hent de Vries, Marlène Zarader, and others have noted—concerns the ways in which the existential structures articulated by Heidegger's fundamental ontology seem to be rooted within his early phenomenological-theological reflections on primal Christian experience. The question, therefore, is whether or not Christian theology (and here it is a matter of "revealed" rather than "speculative" theology) can be legitimately held at such an "absolute" distance from his fundamental ontology—and, if it is held at such a distance, at what price?

9. HEIDEGGER'S EARLY PHENOMENOLOGY OF RELIGIOUS LIFE

This question obliges us to turn momentarily from the 1928 lecture on "Phenomenology and Theology," back to the pair of lecture courses on religion which he delivered almost a decade earlier, in the years immediately following the First World War: "Introduction to the Phenomenology of Religion" and "Augustine and Neoplatonism." Kisiel and de Vries have shown that during this period Heidegger employed the terms "Christianity" and "phenomenology" (or "metaphysics," as Heidegger still called it then) almost interchangeably, "trading off each other in their progressive unfolding."[30] While Heidegger maintains that the two must be kept at an absolute distance in his 1928 lecture, this is not so obviously the case a decade before, when his theological provenance still exerted a tremendous—and for the most part explicit—influence on his teaching and his philosophical interests. Kisiel goes so far as to claim that "Heidegger's breakthrough to his lifelong philosophical topic is inherently tied to a personally felt religious topic, in ways we have yet to 'divine.'"[31] In his early years, this so-called lifelong topic went by a variety of names: "the primal something, life in and for itself, factical life, the historical I, the situated I, factical life experience, facticity, Dasein, being."[32] We are only now beginning to recognize the full extent to which his formulations of these critical themes appear to have been shaped by his then-recent turn toward Protestantism in January of 1919, and his subsequent preoccupation with Luther's theology of the cross and Pauline eschatology. In hindsight, it is difficult to imagine how the particular conception of fundamental ontology expressed in *Being and Time* could have ever taken shape in the absence of these three interrelated features of Heidegger's intellectual development. This is not the place, however, for a discussion of the biographical details of this development. In what follows, I will limit myself to sketching only the most salient features of the two early lecture courses on religion.

The course on the "Introduction to the Phenomenology of Religion" was initially intended to focus on a highly abstract, methodological problematic.[33] Heidegger realized that before proceeding directly to the experience of religious life, he would first need to secure a method capable of grasping this experience without subjecting it to a conceptual determination that would compromise its elusive, concrete, situational, and singular quality.[34] At stake, it seems, is the possibility of articulating the general features or universal structures of an experience which is inherently and absolutely singular, that is, which can only be "understood" by being taken up by the individual Dasein. Consequently, he begins the course with a highly technical treatment of the classical problem of universals, in which he tries to demonstrate the difference between traditional theoretical concepts and what he calls "formal indications" (*formale Anzeige*)—a kind of non-theoretical, pre-conceptual "grasping" that "points" to the concrete without taking it up into a universal.[35] Formal indication serves as *both* a means for articulating general structures of concrete experience *as well as* a sort of guide or stepping-stone that places us before certain concrete possibilities of existing, certain *ways* of being.

This notoriously enigmatic idea has been a stumbling block for even Heidegger's most formidable commentators.[36] For my purposes here, it is enough to note the continuities between the formal indication and his later formulation of phenomenological method in *Being and Time* (§7), which I have already discussed at length above (Section 6). The central point is that the formal indication does not involve a conceptual comprehension or thematization, for that kind of comprehension would be wholly antithetical to the "thing" in question—which is not an (present-at-hand or ready-to-hand) entity, but a concrete, factical experience. Its function, rather, is to grant us access to this pre-theoretical experience, to factical life, to Being. But how this access is accomplished remains somewhat of a mystery. The difficulties are compounded by the fact that Heidegger's only detailed discussion of formal indication was cut short. Less than ten hours into the course, Heidegger caught word that the "less methodologically minded students" had complained to the dean about the lack of "religious content" in his seminar. As a result, Heidegger "abruptly—and angrily—cuts short his abstruse methodological discussion with the announcement that, beginning with the next class, the course will henceforth be concerned solely with concrete religious phenomena."[37] Although the formal indication represents what Kisiel calls "the secret password of his early work," Heidegger never returns to the topic in any systematic way.

In the second half of the lecture, Heidegger offers an interpretation of the Epistles of Paul (specifically, the letter to the Galatians, the second letter to the Corinthians, and the two letters to the Thessalonians) in order to get at the unique temporal modality implicit within the primal Christian eschatological experience. He is especially interested in Paul's conception of hope in the second coming (the *parousia*) on which Christian life is said to be based. It is of utmost significance, according to Heidegger, that Paul refuses to ascribe a date to this coming. Heidegger claims that instead of speaking of the event in *chronological* terms—as if it were a future, objective event that could be awaited, anticipated, foreseen, or calculated—Paul speaks of it in *kairological* terms. That is to say, the *parousia* is discussed in terms of a practical and imminent decision (or conversion) that must be taken up and reenacted in the moment (*Augenblick*) by each individual Dasein.

> The *chairos* (a time reckoned according to significant events rather than by some scientific standard of measurement [. . .]) places it on the razor's edge in the decision. Chairological characteristics do not reckon with and master time; rather they place one into the threat of the future. They belong in life's history of *performance* which cannot be objectified. [. . .] If man tries by means of

chronological computations or content-oriented characterizations to define the inaccessible event which suddenly bursts upon the scene, the event upon which his life is based, he then eliminates that which should determine his life as the always inaccessible and replaces it with the secured, the accessible.[38]

Again, the important point is that Paul stresses not the time of the coming of the *parousia*, but the *mode* of this coming—namely, its suddenness. It comes, according to the well-known passage from 1 Thessalonians, "like a thief in the night."[39] The original Christian community lived in a state of constant insecurity, "in a resolute and open *wachsam sein*, being-wakeful for the incalculable Coming within the eye-opening moment."[40] Simply put, the primal Christian experience displays (or at least appears to display) what Heidegger will come to call in *Being and Time* an "openness" to Being and an "authentic resoluteness."

In the second course, "Augustine and Neoplatonism," Heidegger argues that this authentic experience of "temporal urgency" (i.e., *kairos*) which is constitutive of Christian faith (and which is given paradigmatic expression within Paul's Epistle to the Thessalonians) was diminished, if not completely eradicated, by subsequent theological interpretations which sought to capture the essence of the *parousia* with the help of Neoplatonic concepts. Augustine, for example, in spite of his own attentiveness to the authentic Christian experience, occasionally adopts a Neoplatonic conception of God as "repose" which suggests a sense of security and quietude that, according to Heidegger, flatly contradicts the urgency and wakefulness of *kairological* experience itself. Unlike many of his German predecessors and colleagues (viz., Harnack, Troeltsch, and occasionally even Dilthey), Heidegger was nothing but suspicious of Augustine's periodic attempts to accommodate Christian thought to Greek concepts.[41] Such attempts only served to conceal what was most essential.

> The eschatological [*das Eschatologische*] in Christianity was already obscured by the end of the first century. Later, all the original Christian concepts are misconstrued. In contemporary philosophy, too, the Christian conceptualizations are still hidden behind the Greek attitude [*Einstellung*].[42]

Heidegger argues that the intrusion of speculative concepts into Christian thought led to a forgetfulness of the original experience of Christian faith—an argument clearly influenced by his recent turn to Luther and his reading of Kierkegaard. He therefore calls for a destruction of traditional theological concepts in order to retrieve the concealed nature of Christian faith: its inherent uneasiness, its *cor inquietum*, its lack of security, its emphasis on the moment of decision—in short, its *facticity*.

Our discussion of Heidegger's lecture courses on religion has by no means been exhaustive, but it has served its purpose nonetheless, for it has already become evident that key features of his later existential analysis in *Being and Time*—historicity, facticity, care, fundamental temporality, anxiety, etc.— were anticipated in and prefigured by his lecture courses on religion.[43] To state some of the most obvious examples: the distinction between chronological time and *kairological* time corresponds to the later distinction between history (*Historie*) and historicity (*Geschichtlichkeit*); the being-wakefulness of faith anticipates the authentic resoluteness of Dasein; the anxiety regarding the *parousia* bears structural resemblances to the existential anxiety involved in being-towards-death; and, more generally speaking, his characterization of the process by which primal Christian experience becomes concealed by Greek conceptuality prefigures his later description of the history of the forgetfulness of Being (*Seinsvergessenheit*).

These and other parallels invite speculation about the status of this primal Christian experience and the ontic-positive science which takes this experience as its *positum* (namely theology) within Heidegger's overall project. Is Heidegger's interpretation of primal Christianity (*Urchristentum*) meant merely to serve as one concrete, historical *example* that helps illuminate the fundamental existential structures—that is, as one example among other possible examples? If so, he would have to explain why Christian experience *appears* to supply the example *par excellence* for his fundamental existentials (an explanation which he never provides). Or, on the contrary, does this primal Christian experience constitute a *privileged event* (a particular "revelation," as it were), one that would prove *indispensable* for Heidegger's later fundamental ontology—that is, an event in the absence of which the fundamental existentials of *Being and Time* could not have been thought. If, as I strongly suspect, this is the case, then it seems that Heidegger would be forced to grant theology (and here, again, it is a matter of revealed rather than speculative theology) the upper hand in its relationship with ontology. Or, at the very at least, the relationship between theology and ontology would have to be rethought on the basis of what Heidegger actually does rather than what he says he does. If revealed theology has as its basic task the interpretation of this event, of the revelation constitutive of primal Christian experience, then this supposedly "ontic-positive science" would seem to serve as a guide (or even a foundation) for Heidegger's ontological science. (Though, as we will see shortly, Heidegger says quite the opposite in his 1928 lecture on "Phenomenology and Theology.")

10. *OFFENBARUNG* UND *OFFENBARKEIT*: DECONSTRUCTING HEIDEGGER

This general line of interrogation has been pursued within a number of deconstructivist readings of the religious dimension of Heidegger's thought. Hent de Vries, in his work on *Philosophy and the Turn to Religion*, poses the question in the following terms: "why exactly is it that the shortest route to the explication of the phenomenon of the historical [that is, to Heidegger's lifelong topic: facticity, Dasein, etc.] is found in the phenomenology of religion?"[44] According to de Vries, we are faced with two possible interpretations of the relationship between Christian life and the existential analytic. *Either* Christianity serves as an external proof, an actual historical confirmation, of Heidegger's ontological existentials; *or* it serves (in ways yet to be "divined") as the foundation for these existentials themselves. Now, according to Heidegger's stated intentions, the existential analytic aims to articulate the general structures of existence, of factical life experience, of Dasein's most basic possibilities. These general structures (or, as it were, *sub*structures) are claimed to serve as the condition of possibility for every concrete way of existing—*including* the particular, Christian way of existing. Accordingly, the Christian experience articulated in Heidegger's early lecture courses would be, at most, an example or material fulfillment of these formal substructures. De Vries, however, in clear opposition to Heidegger's own interpretation of his work, argues the following (and does so precisely on the basis of a reading of Heidegger's texts):

> But then again, should one not rather maintain that originary Christian experience of factical life provides at least just as much a key to the understanding of factical life as the other way around? Is originary Christian life experience for Heidegger merely an "example" (*Exampel*), albeit the most revealing instantiation of a general structure, called facticity? Or does the reverse of these hold true as well?[45]

A similar suggestion is raised within Marlène Zarader's *The Unthought Debt: Heidegger and the Hebraic Tradition* (a text to which I shall return in greater detail below). While acknowledging Heidegger's insistence that the existential structures of Dasein constitute the condition of possibility for the *kairological* experience of time, she argues that it seems just as likely (again, on the basis of Heidegger's texts themselves) that the Christian (and, she would add Judeo-Christian) experience constitutes the event which first renders possible Heidegger's existential reinterpretation of time as fundamental, ecstatic temporality.[46]

This problem—which, I might add, is not merely a problem of interpretation, as it concerns not only Heidegger's texts but also the fate of the relation between phenomenology and revelation more generally—finds its clearest expression in Jacques Derrida's 1995 address on "Faith and Knowledge." Here, Derrida characterizes the dilemma in terms of a relation between revelation (*Offenbarung*) and revealability (*Offenbarkeit*), a relation that is said to be aporetical rather than dialectical. Simply put, *Offenbarkeit* denotes for Heidegger the general structure of experience that shapes, conditions, and makes possible any and every actual (i.e., positive, historical) *Offenbarung*. This relation can be articulated in terms of the logic of presupposition described above: any science which takes as its object, as its positum, an actual (in this case Christian) revelation must already presuppose a rough and naïve conception of revealability. Accordingly, the aim of a phenomenology of revelation (or, in this case, an existential analytic of religious life) would be to explicate or render explicit this general structure of revealability, without affirming or denying the existence of revelation as an actual, given event. The aporia comes to light, however, as soon as one considers how revealability is itself manifested or phenomenolized, that is to say, how it comes into view in the first place. Does not the phenomenality of revealability presuppose or depend upon the manifestation of a particular event of revelation, of an event which would both attest to and engender it? How else could revealability as such first become visible? How else could it become the rightful object of phenomenological analysis?

It is worth citing Derrida's formulation of the aporia in its entirety, as it provides the basic interpretive framework for both de Vries and Zarader.

> In its most abstract form, then, the aporia within which we are struggling would perhaps be the following: is revealability (*Offenbarkeit*) more originary than revelation (*Offenbarung*), and hence independent of all religion? Independent in the structures of its experience and in the analytics relating to them? [. . .] Or rather, inversely, would the event of revelation have consisted in revealing revealability itself [. . .].[47]

The question, then, is whether Heidegger's analyses winds up privileging revelation over revealability rather than revealability over revelation. Derrida, de Vries, and Zarader insist that Heidegger's texts remain open to either interpretations, or, more interesting still, to *both* interpretations *at once*—and that they do so in spite of Heidegger's best intentions. As we shall see below, Zarader favors a reading that places revelation over and above revealability, whereas Derrida and de Vries favor a deconstructivist interpretation which keeps the tension between these two possibilities forever in play, in a state of constant oscillation and undecidability (though again, it is worth stressing that they attribute this undecidability not to Heidegger himself, but to certain possibilities opened up by Heideggerian texts).[48]

Nevertheless, there can be no question regarding Heidegger's *explicit* intentions. Despite the ambiguities, gaps, and inconsistencies in his texts—and despite the intriguing interpretations which they have provoked—Heidegger rather unambiguously insists on the priority of revealability over and above revelation. This position is expressed in a little-known text that records Heidegger's response to the question, "Is it proper to posit Being and God as identical?"[49] Heidegger begins by saying that "Being and God are not identical and I would never attempt to think the essence of God by means of Being." But he then shifts the discussion from the question of God to the question of God's revelation, suggesting that while the former is not conditioned by Being, the latter most certainly is. "I believe that Being can never be thought as the ground and essence of God, but that nevertheless the experience of God and of his manifestedness [*Offenbarkeit*], to the extent that the latter can indeed meet man, flashes in the dimension of Being [. . .]"[50] We must be extremely cautious when formulating Heidegger's position regarding revelation. Above all, we must be careful not to confuse the relation between revelation and revealability with the relationship between God and Being and all the associated problems concerning ontotheology—problems which our analysis has intentionally left aside. What is at stake in the problem of revelation is not the status of God as such, but only God's manifestation, the manner in which God opens onto Dasein. Though Heidegger is careful to keep God as such free from ontology, he nevertheless claims that God's revelation is contained or conditioned by "the dimension of Being," by the existential structures of Dasein, by "revealability"—and not the other way around. God may be above and beyond all matters of Being and ontology, but if God is to be revealed to Dasein, this revelation (*Offenbarung*) must conform to the ontological conditions of experience, that is, to revealability (*Offenbarkeit*).

This decision to hand revelation over to the "dimension of Being," and thereby subordinate revelation to revealability, is entirely consistent with the Heideggerian logic of presupposition. After all, if God's revelation (that is, a particular, ontic, positive, or historical event) were to exceed or occur independently of the ontological conditions of revealability, this event would threaten to destroy or at least destabilize the hierarchical structure, the disciplinary boundaries, and the one-way filiation between ontology and ontic-positive sciences which, as we have already seen, served to organize and legitimate Heidegger's entire ontological project of the nineteen twenties. "Even the most undisputed conceptual and disciplinary boundaries," de Vries writes, would "thus threaten to break down, or are at least robbed of their ultimate justification."[51] Therefore, "[i]t would accordingly be necessary [in order to preserve these boundaries] that a revealability (*Offenbarkeit*) be allowed to reveal itself, with a light that would manifest (itself) more originarily than all revelation (*Offenbarung*)."[52] The general structure of revealability would need to reveal itself prior to and independent of any and every revelation. And, in keeping with the logic of presupposition, this structure would not only be deeper and more radical than any (Christian) revelation but the former would also be presupposed ("roughly and naively") by the latter as its condition of possibility.

As one might expect, the deconstructivist interpreters with whom we are presently engaged tend to exploit those points in Heidegger's texts where this logic is violated—where revelation (*Offenbarung*) appears to precede revealability (*Offenbarkeit*), or, at least appears to be co-originary with it. De Vries's own constructive project is to demonstrate that the logic of presupposition must be subverted, displaced, and overcome by a "logic of substitution" best exemplified in Derrida's late writings on religion. According to this other logic, the general structure of revealability and the revelation of particular positive religions continually trade places, continually "substitute" for one another, to the point where they become mutually conditioning and mutually conditioned. In a clever, if convoluted, play on Heidegger's logic of presupposition, de Vries argues that the conditioned (revelation) conditions the conditioning (revealability) just as much as the other way around.[53] "I [. . .] simply wish to stress, once more, that the so-called ontic and empirical determinations and overdeterminations are conditions of the possibility of the question of Being—of Being as such—*at least as much* and *for the same reason*—as they are in turn made possible by this question—by the notion of Being."[54]

My aim, however, is not to assess the legitimacy of this quasi-Derridian move. Rather, I embarked on this detour through recent deconstructivist interpretations of Heidegger—most notably de Vries's—in order to bring to the fore two problems that seem to plague Heidegger's project from within. These problems have serious consequences for the fate of his logic of presupposition and the conception of revelation which follows from it. And, as we will see in the next chapter, they will continue to haunt and perhaps even threaten phenomenological conceptions of revelation up to the present.

11. CONTAMINATION AND COUNTER-CONTAMINATION

We will need to formulate these questions as explicitly as possible. The first and most obvious problem concerns the seemingly incontestable existence of certain ontic contaminations or illicit borrowings from ontic-positive domains by existential ontology. We have just seen that de Vries, Zarader, and

Derrida have each sought to detect the traces of "contaminating contraband" and to spell out their full implications for the phenomenology of religion. Nothing more needs to be added to our previous discussion of that problem.

But there is a second, albeit less obvious, question that I have yet to raise. In seeking to avoid, manage, or reduce such contaminations, has Heidegger not committed an equally problematic offense—that is to say, has he not hollowed out or slimmed down revelation itself? This line of questioning suggests the following possibility, which at this point remains nothing more than a hypothesis: In order to maintain the pure, originary, formal character of revealability—and, which amounts to the same thing, in order to preserve the strictly philosophical character of his phenomenological analyses—Heidegger seems to employ (implicitly, perhaps not even deliberately) a rather ingenious stratagem: he simply folds the "purity" or "formality" constitutive of revealability over into the ontic-positive domain of revelation. In other words, he purges "revelation" (in this case, Christian revelation) of its ontical "content" so that any potential "theological contamination" on the side of revealability would be immediately mitigated, indeed, mitigated *in advance*. Heidegger appears to have eliminated the ontic content of determinate revelation before that content could ever pose a risk to his formal existential analysis, that is, before his existentials could become contaminated by revelation, and in this case, by that particular mode of existence exhibited in certain Christian texts. Revelation is then divested and deprived of anything—that is, any determinate content, any ontic orientation—that might have otherwise threatened the integrity and fundamentality of Heidegger's ontological existentials (which, as we have seen, are in fact rooted in a particular, Christian revelation, the example *par excellence*). Revelation itself gets recast as a pure, formal structure; and revealability, in turn, becomes what might be described as the structure of a structure.

This "divestment," "attenuation," or "hollowing out" of Christian revelation must not to be confused with the phenomenological gesture itself, which rightly moves from the concrete ontic experience of revelation (*Offenbarung*) to the ontological structure of revealability (*Offenbarkeit*). That an ontological analysis should involve some kind of "formalization" of religious motifs is entirely justifiable—and Heidegger made this point explicitly in his discussion of the method of *formale Anzeige*. The problem of counter-contamination lies elsewhere, and should not be confused with the legitimate methodological process of formalization as such.[55] On the contrary, I am suggesting that the process of formalization which is constitutive of ontological analysis (and which is entirely appropriate in that register) gets deflected back onto the ontic-positive register itself, so that the so-called religious experience with which Heidegger is supposedly concerned never really appears in itself or on its own terms—what appears, rather, is merely an empty shell, a mere abstraction of the concrete phenomenon from which the investigation ought to have proceeded. There is, in other words, a *counter-contamination*, whereby revealability (*Offenbarkeit*) intrudes upon and violates revelation (*Offenbarung*). (Strictly speaking, counter-contamination is the exact inversion of ontic contamination—though, of course, one does not provide a satisfactory solution or antidote to the other.)

While the first problem (i.e., the problem of ontic contamination) has received a great deal of attention in the deconstructivist literature surveyed above, the second problem (the problem of formalization, or counter-contamination) has largely remained below the radar—it surfaces here and there, but it is seldom ever treated as a problem in its own right. The one exception to this rule is found in the work of Merlène Zarader, where this process of counter-contamination is diagnosed as a symptom of Heidegger's refusal to acknowledge his indebtedness to the Hebraic tradition.[56] Although Zarader never explicitly formulates the problem, she catches sight of it while analyzing how the determinate, ontic, religious contents that threaten to contaminate (or "pass into") Heidegger's fundamental "concepts" are forced to undergo a formalization or purification which effectively uproots them from their material "source." As Zarader writes: "The kairological essence of time, which thus 'passes,' in [Heidegger's] oeuvre, right into the heart of the Heideggerian [ontological] concepts, *only enters it after having been cut off from its source.*"[57] The "source" to which Zarader refers is the Hebrew Old Testament: i.e., the cultural and linguistic background of the New Testament, and hence of the primal Christian experience of the *kairos*. What Zarader contests is Heidegger's "curious reduction of all theology to a single, New Testament theology,"[58] a reduction which would totally disassociate the New Testament from the Old.[59] Thus, although Christian eschatology illicitly passes into Heidegger's ontology (as a potential contamination), it does so "only *after* having been cut off artificially from the Old Testament" and—which is to say the same thing—only after having been divested of its initial cultural and linguistic contents.[60]

Moreover, this process of divestment is not arbitrary, but rather involves a counter-contamination in which certain "philosophical" (or "ontological") biases are visibly present—most notably, Heidegger's preference for the Greek language. Heidegger's interpretation of the concrete, Christian revelation is tainted (or counter-contaminated) from the very outset by certain ontological motives which lead him to focus exclusively on Greek texts, to the exclusion of Hebraic ones. This exclusion is hardly accidental. For, as Zarader notes, "if Scripture is condensed into the New Testament, then Greek is the language of Revelation."[61] Heidegger's exegesis, then, quite literally makes revelation speak the language of philosophy. And this counter-contamination (that is to say, this philosophical contamination of revelation) is precisely what renders

Christian revelation suitable for ontological formalization in the first place. Christian revelation is first made palatable to philosophical thinking through a suppression of its Hebraic content.[62]

Zararder's aim in all of this is to highlight the importance of the Old Testament for adequately understanding the New Testament, and thereby to demonstrate the failures of Heidegger's biblical exegesis. Drawing on the work of several notable biblical scholars (such as Paul Beauchamp and James Barr), she argues that the Hebraic language of the Old Testament "is *constitutive* of the Neo-testamentary language itself."[63] This, she continues, explains why James Barr insists that the "essential lexical" task of New Testament exegesis is to investigate "the way in which Greek words are *vessels* for a *content* of Semitic thought."[64]

I, however, am less concerned with the shortcomings of Heidegger's biblical exegesis than with the ways in which this exegesis betrays—and indeed initiates—a broader process of formalization (or counter-contamination) of Judeo-Christian revelation, which, in turn, renders Heidegger's indebtedness to this revelation unproblematic from the point of view of a "strictly" ontological mode of thought. If, as Barr suggests, "Greek words are *vessels* for a content of Semitic thought," then we could say that Heidegger's Greco-centric interpretation of Scripture, which supplies the hidden basis for his analytic of Dasein, had already reduced revelation to a mere vessel, to its Greek figure, to the mere form "revelation" devoid of any determinate (ontic) content.[65]

But this "formalization" of revelation (*Offenbarung*) should not be confused with the ontological gesture itself, in which the formalization of Christian content is accompanied by an explicit move from the ontic (*Offenbarung*) to the ontological (*Offenbarkeit*) in an effort to exhibit the essential structure of the singular, concrete experience of *Offenbarung*. In fact, the ontologizing gesture that seeks to develop a kind of generalization (or universalization) starting from, or on the basis of, the concrete religious motifs would be entirely justifiable, since that move (from the ontic to the ontological) is essential to the phenomenological method itself, taken in its broadest sense. And this method could be interpreted as involving some kind of hollowing out of those religious motifs. Derrida made reference to this ontological formalization when he posed the following rhetorical question in 1995: "[D]oes not Heidegger proceed, from *Sein und Zeit* on, with an ontologico-existential repetition and rehearsal of Christian motifs that are *at the same time hollowed out* and reduced to their originary possibility?"[66] Christian motifs are redeployed, rehearsed, repeated in Heideggerian ontology in the precise measure that they are *simultaneously* hollowed out, formalized, emptied. They are hollowed out *in the process of* being repeated within existential analytic; the repetition *effects* a certain hollowing out of what is repeated in this repetition.[67]

But that is not the process I refer to as counter-contamination. On the contrary, I am arguing—along with Zarader—that another kind of "hollowing out" takes place in Heidegger's texts, one that is neither constitutive of, nor *simultaneous* to, the ontological gesture, but rather one that *precedes* it. This hollowing out of Christian revelation occurs even before it is taken up into the existential analytic. In this case, Christian factical life experience is shown to be abstract and formal in and of itself (i.e., independently and in advance of its ontological repetition). De Vries catches sight of this fact in the following passage:

> Of course, to argue that any general structure [revealability] remains parasitic upon that which it makes possible [revelation] is not to imply that the latter takes the function of a *concrete*, that is to say, ontic or empirico-positive, condition of the possibility of the former. For, as we have seen, the concreteness of the unrest and the flux of Christian factical life experience is much less that of a mediatizable whole (as would be the implication of the Latin *concrescere*) as that of an absolute yet repeatable *singularity*. As a matter of fact, this singularity would therefore be at least as elusive—indeed, as abstract or as formal—as the most abstract and most formal of all structures (categories, transcendentals, existentials, universals).[68]

De Vries suggests, with characteristic ambiguity, that Christian factical life experience is itself *already* rendered "abstract" and "formal" before it is taken up by or within an ontological formalization. In spite of, and perhaps even on account of, its radical singularity, concrete Christian factical life experience is already thought to be marked by a certain structural formality, or formalism. Primal Christian experience has already undergone a certain formalization within Heidegger's lecture courses—a formalization which in some sense *makes possible* and *paves the way for* the second, properly ontological formalization which, in turn, culminates in the fundamental existential structures of *Being and Time*. Christian experience is, as it were, emptied-out or slimmed-down to its most basic, "abstract," and "formal" elements, to the point that it is thought to defy or exclude any content-orientation. And yet, de Vries himself does not seem to view this abstraction or formulization of Christian factical life experience as problematic and, consequently, he never explicitly poses the question of counter-contamination.

There are seemingly good reasons for this omission, as well as for the general lack of attention paid to counter-contamination. To begin with, nothing in Heidegger's ontological project—neither the logic of presupposition, nor the hierarchical ordering of ontology and ontic-positive science—seems to prohibit counter-contamination. It would appear from our previous discussion of the *one-way filiation* or *derivation* between the ontic and the ontological (Section 5) that Heidegger's project even necessitates certain ontological contaminations, so long as these involve border crossings *from* the ontological *to* the ontic-positive. Ontological analysis claims to place the ontic-positive sciences on firmer ground by reexamining their fundamental concepts, and this means redirecting or returning them to the meaning of the Being of the entities in question. This redirection naturally requires the ontic-positive sciences to adopt a certain ontological inflection. We have already examined this process in great length above and will not repeat our analysis here. But it is worth recalling that in the course of that analysis, I encountered a question that I was then unable to answer, a question regarding the fate of the ontic content within this process of redirection. This question imposes itself upon us once again: does the thought of Being as such lead to a sort of blindness towards the ontical content of the regional sciences? This is indeed the primary question or issue raised by what I am here calling counter-contamination.

I am now in a position to venture a more or less precise answer: From the perspective of a fundamental ontology (such as Heidegger's), which is primarily concerned with the disclosure of Being as such, this blindness remains something of a virtue. It is permitted and even encouraged by the phenomenological method as defined in §7 of *Being and Time*, namely, as a science of the "how" rather than the "what" of appearances. This, perhaps, explains why the problem of counter-contamination has been given less attention than the problem of ontic contamination. Nonetheless, from the perspective of the ontic-positive sciences themselves, the preoccupation with the radical question of Being remains a virtue only so long as it provides science with a more genuine, more fundamental conceptual understanding of the nature of the ontic entity (or region of entities) in question. If, on the contrary, this preoccupation with ontology prevents one from traveling the return route (that is from Being back to beings, from questions of ontology back to questions of epistemology), or, if, in the process of this return to epistemological questions, the ontological preoccupation obscures or clouds one's view of the material (ontical) richness of the entities rather than contributing to our understanding of them, then serious problems do arise (problems which I have assembled under the banner of counter-contamination).[69] But these problems are not problems for ontology as such.

Nevertheless, if the problem of formalization or "counter-contamination" may not pose a direct threat to Heidegger—whose primary interest lies in the question of Being as such—it still remains a fundamental problem for all subsequent phenomenologies of revelation (such as those found in the work of Emmanuel Levinas and Jean-Luc Marion) that seek to overcome the ontological biases of Heideggerian phenomenology as well as to preserve the full weight, density, and substantive meaning of "revelation" within its phenomenological descriptions. We will see more clearly in our discussion of Levinas and Marion in the following chapter that this process of formalization presents serious problems for a phenomenology that takes revelation as its subject matter, and strives to remain "faithful" to it.

For now, it is enough to recognize that we are dealing with two unique problems: *contamination* (which, properly speaking, consists of an "ontic contamination" of the ontological) and *counter-contamination* (which technically consists of an "ontological contamination," a premature formalization of the ontical). While the former poses a threat to the philosophical status of phenomenology in general, the latter poses a problem (perhaps even *the* problem) for the phenomenology of revelation *qua* revelation. And, yet, we must never cease to see these two problems in relation to each other. For it is my general thesis that counter-contamination results from (or even functions as) a sort of reflex mechanism for managing, reducing, and limiting ontic contamination and, as such, is most likely to occur when the philosophical rigor of phenomenology is threatened by incursions from the ontic domain. In the following chapter, this thesis will be given its fullest and most concrete demonstration by way of an analysis of Jean-Luc Marion's distinction between Revelation (as event) and revelation (as its phenomenological figure). But in Heidegger the situation remains extremely complex. We might hypothesize—without claiming to demonstrate conclusively—that the "formalization" of revelation is motivated by his efforts to mitigate or alleviate the effects of any potential ontic contamination of his existential analysis. With the help of Marlène Zarader, we were already able to perceive how this process of formalization gets worked out in terms of Heidegger's New Testament exegesis. The time has now come to test this hypothesis against Heidegger's 1928 lecture.

12. *CHRISTLICHKEIT* IN "PHENOMENOLOGY AND THEOLOGY"

With these two problems in mind (contamination and counter-contamination), we now resume our reading of Heidegger's 1928 lecture on "Phenomenology and Theology." Our aim will be to test our working hypothesis, which is essentially twofold: namely, (1) that Heidegger seeks to preempt any potential accusation that his ontology might be "contaminated" by an ontic orientation and/or content derived from a particular revelation (*Offenbarkeit*), in this case Christian revelation; (2) and, paradoxically, that he accomplishes this goal of preserving the autonomy and priority of his fundamental ontology only by carrying out a kind of formalization or hollowing out of Christian theology *and* its *positum* (i.e., *Christlichkeit*), to the point where theology begins to resemble phenomenology and to the point where the positum of theology begins to resemble factical life experience itself.

The *first part* of our hypothesis is relatively uncontroversial. Heidegger's desire to preserve the autonomy, independence, and superiority of ontology vis-à-vis theology (i.e., the science of a revelation) is made clear from the start, from the very moment he announces that "*theology is a positive science, and as such, therefore, is absolutely different from philosophy*" (PT 50/49). Since theology is characterized as an ontic-positive science, we may already anticipate that it, too, will become vulnerable to the logic of presupposition and to the hierarchical order implied by that logic. Like every other ontic-positive science, theology will be subject to and dependent upon the "correction" or "co-direction" of a phenomenological ontology, which, in turn, remains independent and wholly autonomous. This imposition of the ontic/ontological relationship onto the theology/phenomenology relationship represents Heidegger's most obvious (and, for the most part, explicit) attempt to preserve the autonomy of phenomenological ontology. But the complex relation between theology and phenomenology is in no way exhausted by the ontic/ontological dynamics that we have already considered above (Sections 2–4). Over the course of Heidegger's lecture, it becomes increasingly evident that theology remains subordinate to and dependent upon the resources of ontological science (and the analytic of Dasein) in ways that other, ontic sciences are not. In other words, theology's relation to and dependence on phenomenology is utterly unique. We will soon discover that this dependency is actually exacerbated by the exceptional character of theology's *positum* and, specifically, by the unique manner in which this *positum* is disclosed, or "revealed." What is most astonishing, though, is that this dependency appears not to result from theology's ontic character, but rather from a certain affinity between theology and phenomenology: namely, the object of theology (like Being itself, or the "object" of phenomenological ontology) exceeds the thematization and objectification constitutive of most, if not all, other ontic-positive scientific activity.

And here is where the *second part* of our hypothesis concerning counter-contamination comes into play: paradoxically, it is the formalization or purification of the ontical content of revelation—to the point where revelation begins to resemble Being as such and where theology begins to resemble phenomenology—that enables Heidegger to preserve the priority of phenomenological ontology (the science of Being) over theological science (the science of revelation). This observation is as complex as it is counterintuitive. Simply put, theology remains dependent upon phenomenological ontology precisely because its *positum*, like Being as such, is said to be characterized by a certain resistance to any ontic determinations and, thus, to the modes of thematization and objectification found within other ontic-positive sciences. Because of this resistance, theology must enlist the support of phenomenology—and, particularly, its method of formal indication—in order to come to grips with its own subject matter. Therefore, it is only on account of the strange affinity between Being, on the one hand, and revelation, on the other, that Heidegger is finally able to insist that ontology alone can provide the guidelines for thematizing theology's positum. In other words, Heidegger avoids the problem of contamination by deflecting the formalism of phenomenology back onto the ontic-positive science of theology and reducing revelation itself to its most abstract and formal structures. In short, he seeks to avoid, manage, limit, and suppress contamination by means of counter-contamination.

Our first task, then, will be to determine the nature of theology, and this means coming to grips with its peculiar *positum*. A science, we recall, is said to be positive if the object of its investigation is already disclosed in some rough and naïve fashion before the investigation begins (Section 3). Its positivity, then, concerns its object and the manner in which this object is laid out (i.e., posited) in advance—that is, in advance of the conceptual articulation or thematization characteristic of all scientific activity. So, we must ask, what constitutes the proper object of this theological science? Heidegger does not fail to pose the question himself, devoting an entire "division" of his lecture to an analysis of "The Positive Character of Theology."[70] Heidegger, it seems, refuses to define this *positum* in terms of any determinate content. Rather than offering his readers a substantive account of its nature or contents, he simply supplies us with a name: *Christlichkeit*.[71] It is by no means obvious just what is meant by this ostensibly vague and indeterminate term, which was most likely adopted from Franz Overbeck, whose work *Über die Christlichkeit* helped shape the young Heidegger's interests in early Christian eschatology.[72] But the designation seems to act as a sort of 'protective strategy' within his lecture, telling us less about what theology *is* than about what it *is not*.[73] Thus, instead of describing the content or substance of *Christlichkeit*, Heidegger proceeds by ruling out a number of traditional ways of conceiving of theology's positum. He offers something of a critique of the self-understanding of certain dominant forms of Christian theology, spanning from Aristotelian Scholasticism all the way up to the historical-critical and liberal theologies of his German colleagues. And, in each instance, he insists that to the degree that theologians have misidentified the proper positum of theology, they have also erroneously adopted criteria of validity drawn from other ontic-positve sciences rather than from revelation itself. Let us examine two examples.

(1) The first concerns the possibility of treating theology as the study of the historical (*historisch*) events of Christianity—in which case, theology's

positum would be nothing other than the history of Christianity. Heidegger immediately rejects this possibility:

> That would evidently be an erroneous characterization of theology, for theology itself belongs to Christianity. Theology is something that everywhere in world history gives testimony to its intimate connection with Christianity as a whole. Evidently, then, theology cannot be the science of Christianity as something that has come about in world history, because it is a science that itself belongs to the history of Christianity, is carried along by that history, and in turn influences that history. (PT 52/51)

On the face of it, Heidegger's argument (if it is one) appears rather flimsy, as it would seem to call into question the legitimacy of all sorts of historiographical works. But the true significance of Heidegger's claim lies elsewhere. It concerns the manner in which the theological object is disclosed, or revealed, to the theologian: namely, through faith and faith alone. The theologian, therefore, does not *belong* to Christianity in the same way that, for instance, an American belongs to America. This particular Christian mode of belonging or "part-taking" is what Heidegger calls "faith." Thus, he states, "The occurrence of revelation, which is passed down to faith and which accordingly occurs in faithfulness itself, discloses itself only to faith" (PT 53/53). This is what (according to Heidegger) certain liberal Protestant schools of theology seem to forget when appealing to the critical methods of historiographical research. In treating the object of theology as a historical datum, as a subsistent, present-to-hand entity or "state of affairs," they wind up adopting secular criteria of truth which are foreign, if not even opposed to, faith and to its particular mode of *belonging*.

Jeffrey Barash has articulated the position which Heidegger took, during the nineteen twenties, towards those who sought to treat theological matters from this historical-critical point of view:

> In theological matters historical scholarship tended to impose the same kinds of secular criteria on theological phenomena as on other aspects of the cultural world. It subjected the personification of God in Christ to the same historical rules as other historical events. It applied the same categories of historical understanding to the primitive Church as to secular institutions. Theologians like [Adolph von] Harnack and [Ernst] Troeltsch simply failed to consider the possibility that religious belief might be irreducible to the same forms of analysis as other phenomena, that belief might potentially infuse existence with a meaning that could not readily be analyzed by the methods of investigation of secular disciplines.[74]

It is no surprise then that in order to designate the true object of theology Heidegger adopts a term—*Christlichkeit*—from someone who was himself an outspoken opponent of historical-critical trends within the theology of his day: namely, Franz Overbeck. For Overbeck—and following him, Heidegger—*Christlickeit* signified something that was irreducible to all verifiable, objective manifestations of culture or to any actual historical event or series of events. It was, therefore, impossible to capture the essence of *Christlichkeit* by means of critical procedures and methods. Heidegger recognized that such methods are designed to secure an "objective" perspective from which to assess historical data, and this perspective was allegedly achieved through an act of distanciation whereby the scientific observer becomes disengaged from what Hans-Georg Gadamer would come to call effective-history or *Wirkungsgeschichte*. However, according to Heidegger, this disengagement was antithetical to theological inquiry. Engagement, belonging, "par-*taking*," or "faith" is precisely what is required of the theologian if he or she is to gain access to theology's genuine 'object,' *Christlichkeit*.

Therefore, we are told that "faith [is] the essential constitutive element of Christianness [*Christlichkeit*]," which is in turn the *positum* of theology (PT 58/61). But does this formulation give us any clearer sense as to the meaning and content of theology? In truth, Heidegger tells us very little about that to which the Christian believer belongs through faith. He does, no doubt, tell us that this belonging or part-taking consists of a "'having part in' the event of the crucifixion," the event of the cross (PT 53/53). But, again, Heidegger's emphasis is placed on the fact that this event is not to be confused with some historical happening which could become susceptible to objective historical research. He emphasizes the mode of faith rather than its content, stressing that the burden of faith is something that one takes upon oneself, in one's own factical existence. (In this regard, one might observe that Heidegger's earlier interests in Luther's theology of the cross had lasting and widespread effects, contributing not only to his early rejection of medieval Aristotelian scholasticism but also to his critique of the liberal theology of his day—and, particularly, to the use of historical-critical methods in theology.)

(2) We have seen that Heidegger refuses to define theology as the science of the history of Christianity. He also considers a second alternative, one suggested by the word "theology" itself. Etymologically, of course, theology refers to the "science of God," in the same way, for instance, that zoology refers to the study of animals (PT 56/59). Not surprisingly, Heidegger rejects this interpretation of theology—though not for the reasons one might have expected. In this context, Heidegger's goal is not to rule out the possibility of speculative or metaphysical knowledge of God. It is not here a matter of refuting or overcoming ontotheology. Rather, he simply insists that speculative or metaphysical inquiry is no way theological, since it abides by criteria

of reason rather than criteria of faith. "Theology," he writes, "is not speculative knowledge of God" (PT 56).

> In that case theology would be the philosophy [. . .] of religion, in short, *Religionswissenschaft*. [. . .] [T]heology is not a form of the philosophy of religion applied to the Christian religion [. . .] In all such interpretations of theology the idea of this science [i.e., its positum] is abandoned from the very beginning. That is, it is not conceived with regard to the specific positive character of theology, but rather is arrived at by way of a deduction and specialization of nontheological sciences—philosophy, history, psychology—sciences that, indeed, are quite heterogeneous to one another. (PT 56/59–60)

Two observations must be made regarding Heidegger's thesis. First, theology is categorically distinguished from other, theoretical or empirically oriented modes of scientific inquiry, since its object—*Christlichkeit*—is accessible in and through faith alone. Its object is "revealed" only to those who believe (PT 52/51).

> The imparting of this revelation is *not a conveyance of information* about present, past, or imminent happenings; rather, this imparting lets one "part-take" of the event that is revelation (= what is revealed therein) itself. But the part-*taking* of faith, which is realized only in existing, is *given* as such always only through faith. (PT 53/52–53, my italics)

The founding disclosure of theological science is different from the founding disclosures operative within other ontic-positive sciences, in that it consists in a revelation whose meaning cannot be comprehended as an objective fact, a theoretic proposition, or *as an ontical content of any kind* for that matter, but can only be taken up as a particular way of being—i.e., as a particular *existentiell* modification of Dasein.

Secondly, just because theology is not the speculative science of God or the science of the *being* proper to God, this does not mean that theology is wholly independent from philosophy or even ontology. As a matter of fact, the reverse is true: by abandoning the philosophical-ontological questions concerning God's existence or the nature of that existence, theology becomes, in effect, absolutely dependent upon phenomenological ontology. For now it is no longer a question of God, but of God's revelation (i.e., the manner in which God is disclosed to Dasein through faith). We already encountered the reasons for this dependency (though without knowing it) when we considered Heidegger's 1951 response to the question about the possibility of identifying God and Being (above, Section 10). God as such, we were told, is not subject to ontology, to "the dimension of Being." *But* God's revelation most certainly is. Therefore, when Heidegger defines theology's positum as the founding disclosure of faith (i.e., revelation or *Christlichkeit*) rather than God as such, he is not freeing theology from ontology, but rather placing it squarely within ontology's jurisdiction.

It is not surprising, therefore, that Heidegger gives the term *Christlichkeit* a particularly philosophical, even *ontological*, inflection. And here we encounter the most illuminating clue regarding the nature of theology's *positum*. In Heidegger's lecture, the term *Christlichkeit* indicates the condition of possibility of Christianity itself—functioning, it seems, in much the same way that *Offenbarkeit* does with respect to *Offenbarung*. As the science of *Christlichkeit*, theology is said to consist of "a knowledge of that which initially *makes possible* something like Christianity as an event in world history. Theology is a conceptual knowing of that which first of all allows Christianity to become an originarily historical event, a knowing of that which we call Christianness [*Christlichkeit*] pure and simple" (PT 52/51, my italics). When defined in this way—as the science of *Christlichkeit*—theology gets (re)directed away from the actual, concrete contents of Christian revelation towards the conditions that would first render such an event possible (i.e., revealability)—redirected, that is, from the "what" of revelation to the "how." But, then, how will Heidegger be able to mark the difference between the theme of theological analysis and the theme of phenomenological analysis? After all, was phenomenology not defined in *Being in Time* as the study of the "how" rather than the "what" of appearances?[75] As a return to fundamental ontological conditions of possibilities? Was it not the case that the "ideal aim" of phenomenological ontology had been characterized by an ability to penetrate behind the second-order activities of scientific thematization? And was it not this "ideal aim" that was supposed to set it apart from theology as an ontic-positive science? Now, given the non-susceptibility of *Christlichkeit* to such second-order thematizations, and given theology's own, intrinsic demand for a return to the fundamental conditions of possibility, we ourselves (as careful readers of Heidegger's text) must wonder what finally authorizes Heidegger to lump theology together with the ontic-positive sciences.

This question imposes itself with even greater urgency as soon as we recognize that theology (in clear opposition to Heidegger's own definition of ontic science) is apparently not directed toward some "region of beings"— such as would be the case if its object were the Highest Being or a set of historical (*historisch*) events—but rather toward factical "existence" itself. This situation inevitably follows from Heidegger's decision to characterize revelation as a mode or way of being rather than as the disclosure of some ontic content or as the "conveyance of information" about a set of subsistent, present-at-hand entities (PT 53/52–53). But it leads to a rather peculiar picture of theology: not only is the object of theology *disclosed* (or revealed) only when it is taken up as a factical life experience, but the *modality* (rather than the content or the matter) of this disclosure, of this revelation, turns out to be the theme of theological science itself.

> As conceptual interpretation of itself on the part of faithful existence, that is, as historical knowledge, theology aims solely at that transparency of the Christian occurrence that is revealed in, and delimited by, faithfulness itself. Thus the goal of this historical science is concrete Christian existence itself. Its goal is *never* a valid system of theological propositions about general states of affairs within *one region of being* that is present at hand among others. The transparency of faithful existence is *an understanding of existence* and as such can relate only to *existing* itself. (PT 54/56)

There is therefore an unmistakable parallel between theology and fundamental ontology to the extent that each is held to be marked by a certain distance from all other sciences. At the outset of the lecture, Heidegger had argued that the difference between ontology and ontic-positive science is absolute, whereas the difference between the various ontic-positive sciences is merely relative—relative, that is, to their respective "regions of beings." But, in the case of theology—an *allegedly* ontic science—this relative distance turns out to be not so relative after all, since, much like phenomenological ontology, theology is also directed back to factical life experience, existence, Being, etc. In Heidegger's own lecture, the emphasis is, we have seen, placed on the degree to which theology differs from other ontic sciences: it is neither the philosophy of religion, nor the psychology of religion, nor the history of religion—a series of distinctions which cannot help but to remind us of the explanation in *Being and Time* for drawing a sharp line between phenomenological ontology on the one hand and all ontic sciences on the other (BT §3 and §10). Thus, contrary to his explicit claims, theology occupies a slippery, ambiguous, even liminal space within Heidegger's otherwise rigorous and watertight typology—a position that he constantly struggles to control, conceal, and keep in check through a persistent and vehement, though nevertheless thoroughly inconsistent, insistence on its ontic-positive character.

Nevertheless, the point that I want to stress here is that theology begins to resemble phenomenology only because the object of theology (faith, revelation, *Christlichkeit*) has already taken on a kind of abstract, formal character within Heidegger's analysis. In other words, *it has already been subject to a counter-contamination*. For if theology must remain open and free from the objective, thematizing tendencies operative within other ontic sciences (history, speculative theology, sociology, psychology, etc.), this is due solely to the fact that the particular way of being exemplified by Christian faith has been defined in terms of its own sort of "openness"—one that, as we recall from Heidegger's early lecture courses, was conceived of in terms of an authentic openness towards the "event" or the "moment of decision," the *kairos*. Moreover, insofar as this openness lacks and even resists all content and every "content-orientation"—as Pöggeler has aptly put it[76]—it remains by its very nature indeterminate and can therefore be said to consist of a pure form (or formalization) of experience itself. It is, as de Vries has put it, "at least as elusive—indeed, as abstract or as formal—as the most abstract and most formal of all structures."[77]

13. FROM *CHRISTLICHKEIT* TO THE PRE-CHRISTIAN

According to Heidegger, it is precisely the elusive, non-thematizable, and, we might add, purely formal character of *Christlichkeit* that requires theology to enlist the support and co-direction of phenomenological ontology. Why? The final, culminating division of "Phenomenology and Theology" is devoted to this very question ("C. The Relation of Theology, as a Positive Science, to Philosophy"). But Heidegger's answer is complex and, therefore, must be patiently laid out if we are not to miss the ultimate aim of the entire lecture.

Theology is not faith pure and simple; it is, rather, *faith seeking understanding*. Insofar as it is science, theology strives for a *conceptual* understanding *of* faith *through* faith: "this [conceptual] interpretation of faithful existence is the task of theology" (PT 58/62–63). Therefore, "[a]s science, theology places itself under the claim that its concepts show and are appropriate to the being that it has undertaken to interpret" (PT 57/62). But we have already seen that this "being" is not an ontic entity—it is not some subsistent or manipulable thing—but is actually a mode of factical life experience. Among the two scientific options or "possibilities" available to Heidegger—namely, ontic-positive science and ontological science (or phenomenology)—only the latter possesses a "method" capable of penetrating this kind of being. So it would appear that theology must borrow from or appeal to phenomenology if it is to accomplish its own fundamental aim as science. Hence, "the positive science of faith needs philosophy only in regard to its scientific character" (PT 57/61).

This recourse to phenomenology is, in fact, more puzzling than it would at first appear, for the situation is further complicated by the fact that access to the fundamental themes of theology requires the adoption of an attitude or way of being, namely, faithful existence, that is clearly opposed to the phenomenological attitude itself. If the theme of theology only comes into view in and through faith, then how can phenomenology become capable of accessing this theme without having first adopted a standpoint of faith—a perspective which is (like every other perspective, standpoint, or "worldview," for that matter) wholly antithetical to phenomenology as a non-oriented science? This problem is not lost on Heidegger, who himself poses the following series of questions: "But is it not the case that that which is to be interpreted in theological concepts is precisely that which is disclosed only through, for, and in faith?" (PT 57/62)

> But can [the themes of theology], which manifestly belong to the ontological context of Christianness, be understood specifically as to what they are and how they are, except through faith? How does one ontologically disclose the what (the essence) and the how (the mode of being) underlying these fundamental concepts that are constitutive of Christianness? Is faith to become the criterion of knowledge for an ontological philosophical explication? Are not the basic theological concepts completely withdrawn from philosophical-ontological reflection? (PT 58/62)

Heidegger's solution to this predicament is truly remarkable—and, as usual, it involves his characteristic (re)turning towards the primordial, the ever-deeper ontological structures.

Heidegger has already established that *Christlichkeit*, insofar as it marks the condition of possibility of the event of Christianity (i.e., of faith, revelation, or *Offenbarung*), occupies a certain ontological depth. But now Heidegger goes on to claim that *Christlichkeit* is itself derivative—it is founded upon a still deeper, more primordial pre-Christian structure. *Christlichkeit* has its ontological roots, as it were, in the pre-faithful, pre-Christian existence of Dasein. As a result of this intricate ontological stratification of *Offenbarung*, *Christlichkeit*, and finally the pre-faithful existence—a layering of the former (as derivative) upon the latter (as fundamental)—phenomenology's task vis-à-vis theology needs to be reconsidered. If, at first, it appeared as though phenomenology would have to adopt Christian faith in order to come to theology's rescue, this is certainly no longer the case. Now, phenomenology no longer needs to explicate *Christlichkeit per se* in order for it to be of assistance to theology, since it can now provide that assistance simply by formally indicating the neutral (i.e., pre-faithful) ground upon which *Christlichkeit* itself stands. Insofar as that ground is deeper than or prior to the attitude or way of being of faith, phenomenology can provide this elucidation—or, better, this *excavation—without* having to adopt the standpoint of faith. Phenomenology, in other words, can support theology without being contaminated by the specific attitude of faith itself.

To be sure, all of this would amount to a flagrant violation of theology's own self-understanding were Heidegger not able to demonstrate that some relation or reference to pre-faithful existence is intrinsic to Christian faith.[78] He will therefore go on to claim that pre-faith existence is in some sense constitutive of faithful existence, and that faith simply entails a modification of pre-faithful (pre-Christian) existence. According to Heidegger, this claim finds its confirmation in the fact that one is said to be born into faith. Faith, then, is a rebirth that involves taking on a *new* way of being. "Accordingly, the proper existentiell meaning of faith is: *faith=rebirth*. And rebirth does not mean a momentary outfitting with some quality or other, but a way in which a factical, believing Dasein historically exists in *that* history which begins with the occurrence of revelation [. . .]" (PT 53/53). On these grounds, Heidegger seeks to provide a theologically palatable explanation for the necessity and indispensability of phenomenology for the science of faith:

> [. . .] though what is revealed in faith can never be founded by way of a rational knowing as exercised by autonomously functioning reason, nevertheless the sense of the Christian occurrence as rebirth is that Dasein's prefaithful, i.e., unbelieving, existence is sublated [*aufgehoben*] therein. Sublated does not mean done away with, but raised up, kept, and preserved in the new creation. One's pre-Christian existence [*vorchristlichen Existenz*] is indeed existentielly, ontically, overcome in faith. But this existentiell overcoming of one's pre-Christian existence (which belongs to faith as rebirth) means precisely that one's overcome pre-Christian Dasein is existentially, ontologically included within faithful existence. (PT 58/63)

Therefore, "[a]ll theological concepts necessarily contain that understanding of being that is constitutive of human Dasein as such [*Dasein als solches*], insofar as it exists at all" (PT 58/63).

The aim of phenomenology (at least with respect to the foreign demands imposed on it by theology) is to *formally indicate* the general, universal region underlying properly theological concepts. But Heidegger's method of formal indication is, as we saw earlier, anything but clear,[79] and the lecture provides only one concrete example of this process. The paucity of examples alone justifies citing it in its entirety:

> Thus, for example, sin is manifest only in faith, and only the believer can factically exist as a sinner. But if sin, which is the counterphenomenon to faith as rebirth and hence a phenomenon of existence, is to be interpreted in theological concepts, then the *content* of the concept *itself*, and not just any philosophical preference of the theologian, calls for a return to the concept of guilt. But guilt is an original ontological determination of the existence of Dasein. The more originally and appropriately the basic constitution of Dasein is brought to light in a genuine ontological manner and the more originally, for example, the concept of guilt is grasped, the more clearly it can function as a guide for the theological explication of sin. (PT 58/64)

Thus, the actual conceptual content of sin can only be retrieved by way of a return to the more fundamental (or *radical*) ontological concept of guilt. The general lesson to be drawn from this example is clear: The phenomenological interpretation of faith (and even the theological interpretation of faith, to the extent that it involves conceptual understanding at all) is to be sought and worked out solely at the level of the "original ontological determination of the existence of Dasein." But, at that level, none of the determinate content of the way of being of faith remains—it has already been removed as part of the excavation process that served to expose its more radical foundations in the ontology of Dasein.

This *radical* process of ontological excavation, of returning to supposed foundations, has a convenient methodological consequence for a phenomenologist, such as Heidegger, who might be concerned to distance himself from the theological biases of the Christian faith, while simultaneously claiming to provide a philosophical foundation for it: for there is no longer any reason to worry that his phenomenological account of faith has been contaminated by certain religious biases or presuppositions, since the phenomena that it examines (guilt, the mode of being of Dasein, *Offenbarkeit*, etc.) has *already* been purged of its particular religious content (sin, the being of faith, *Offenbarung*, etc.). Nevertheless, while the problem of contamination has been thereby averted, I would argue that another closely related problem has arisen: namely, the problem of counter-contamination. After all, Heidegger's analysis of the religious phenomenon has now been co-opted, so to speak, by the analysis of Dasein itself, so that all that appears, and all that is conceptually worked out in it, is what was already there in his ontological account to begin with. Instead of returning to the thing itself (whether that be sin, faith, or revelation), instead of allowing the thing itself to appear *as itself*, Heidegger's analysis has rendered the religious phenomenon wholly transparent, so that our gaze passed right through it without catching sight of its distinctive content. Indeed, that religious content of sin (to take his own example) has been effectively eliminated and replaced by the purely ontological or philosophical concept of Guilt, which will now serve as our inevitable guide to sin's true meaning.

If Heidegger had once viewed genuine Christian life as offering an authentic attestation of the fundamental (i.e., ontological) possibilities of human existence, this is most certainly no longer the case in 1928. Although it is to be expected that Heidegger would maintain (in good Pauline fashion) a sharp division between faith and philosophy and their respective *existentiell* possibilities, Heidegger's decision to champion philosophy as the sole modality of being which is capable of attesting to the primordial ground of Dasein marks a serious departure from the position he held just a few years earlier, in the early nineteen twenties, when primal Christian experience was thought to provide the best possible model or the "shortest detour" to these ontological structures. This change in his attitude corresponds to a shift in focus with respect to Christianity itself—he went from emphasizing the *kairological* dimension of faith to emphasizing the notion of rebirth. And this notion of rebirth is itself placed in an entirely negative light—rebirth, for Heidegger, not only signifies redemption from sin, but above all it signifies the enslavement of Dasein. In taking up faith, Dasein is not only said to be "born again"; it is also said to have become a "slave" (PT 53/53). Thus, while Christian faith had been previously viewed as involving a genuine openness to the moment of decision, it is now characterized solely in terms of its state of dependency upon God. On the other hand, philosophy—and philosophy alone—is said to be capable of retrieving the fundamental structures of Dasein precisely because it involves a "free appropriation of one's whole Dasein" (PT 60/66).

It comes as no surprise, therefore, that Heidegger's 1928 lecture on "Phenomenology and Theology" represents his final serious engagement with theology and with revelation *qua* determinate (i.e., Christian) revelation.[80] Heidegger's obsession with ontological concerns and his constant quest for increasingly radical foundations or conditions of possibility eventually led him to view faith, *Christlichkeit*, and revelation (*Offenbarung*) as merely derivative phenomena. But this conclusion came only after a long period of philosophical labor in which the religious concepts underwent (or were subjected to) a series of progressive formalizations or radicalizations, which effectively purged them of their determinate contents. As we will see in the next chapter, the consequences of this fateful decision can be felt up to the very present.

NOTES

1. PT 49/45.
2. See, especially, BT §3 and §7.
3. Ever since the publication of Wayne Proudfoot's influential *Religious Experience*, "protective strategy" has been used as term of art among scholars of religious experience. While not entirely unrelated to those discussions, my use of the term here is quite idiosyncratic. In the context of Heidegger's work, something like a protective strategy functions, not to shield religious phenomena from reductive analyses, but, more precisely, to prevent the suspicion that his philosophical analyses (especially the ontological or existential structures involved in his analytic of Dasein) owe anything to the determinate content of religious phenomena. And this, I will argue, is achieved by first *purging* or *divesting* those phenomena of their determinate content. In other words, the protective strategy is designed to purify the fluid, so to speak, before it is ever ingested or taken up into the body of Heidegger's fundamental ontology.

Wayne Proudfoot, *Religious Experience* (Berkeley, CA: University of California Press, 1985).

4. "Faith is so absolutely the mortal enemy [*Todfeind*] that philosophy does not even begin to want in any way to do battle with it. This *existentiell opposition* [*existenzielle Gegensatz*] between faithfulness and the free appropriation of one's whole Dasein is not first brought about by the sciences of theology and philosophy but is prior to them" (PT 60/66, my italics).

5. In fact, we will see that, according to Heidegger, philosophy (as ontological science) is not directed at any particular region of beings. Nor can it strictly speaking be associated with any kind of perspective or view of things. Heidegger had already insisted on this important distinction (i.e., between worldview and philosophy as such) during his KNS course in 1919. For a further discussion, see, for instance, Theodore Kisiel, *The Genesis of Heidegger's Being and Time* (Los Angeles: University of California Press, 1995), 38–58.

6. In this regard, Heidegger's distinction between ontic-positive and ontological sciences can be illuminated by a comparison to a better-known (or at least better-understood) theory, for it bears a striking resemblance to Thomas Kuhn's later distinction between "normal" and "abnormal" (or "revolutionary") science in his *Structure of Scientific Revolutions*. Though it would be wrong to make too much of the comparison, it is not surprising to see someone like Richard Rorty make use of Kuhnian nomenclature when discussing Heidegger's views on science in *Philosophy and the Mirror of Nature*, especially in chapters VII and VIII. See, Richard Rorty, *Philosophy and the Mirror of Nature* (Princeton, NJ: Princeton University Press, 1979). Rorty writes that "'Normal' science is the practice of solving problems against the background of a consensus about what counts as a good explanation of the phenomena and about what it would take for a problem to be solved" (Rorty, *Philosophy and the Mirror of Nature*, 320). This is, in essence, ontic-positive science. "'Revolutionary' science is the introduction of a new 'paradigm' of explanation, and thus of a new set of problems" (ibid.). Kuhn's conception of revolutionary science approximates Heidegger's characterization of ontological science. But here we would need to add that, according to Heidegger at least, such revolutions usually occur when a science has momentarily lost touch with the Being that animates its field. For Heidegger, genuine scientific "revolutions" are possible only by way of a return to properly ontological questions. If, after all, the new "paradigm" is to have any merit, it must issue directly from the Being of the entities in question. It is important to note that according to Heidegger these properly ontological concerns (about which I shall say more in a moment) are largely antithetical to ontic-positive scientific research—they arise only at moments of extreme crisis. Normal scientific "research" could not proceed very far if it were constantly bogged down or preoccupied with fundamental, ontological questions. Thus, normal science (i.e., ontic-positive science) can be what it is, can live up to its own "ideal aim," only if it operates against the background of an as-of-yet unproblematic consensus about the nature of its regional (ontic) field. As soon as this consensus is broken or becomes problematic in some way, the scientific task (or aim) immediately changes registers—it is no longer normal but abnormal, no longer ontic-positive but ontological.

7. Heidegger writes in *Being and Time*: "The real 'movement of the sciences takes place when their basic concepts undergo a more or less radical revision which is transparent to itself. The level which a science has reached is determined by how far it is *capable* of a crisis in its basic concepts. In such immanent crises the very relationship between positively investigative inquiry and those things themselves that are under interrogations comes to a point where it begins to totter. Among the various disciplines everywhere today there are freshly awakened tendencies to put research on new foundations" (BT 29/9). It is made evident in the following paragraph of *Being and Time* that Heidegger includes theology among those sciences experiencing such crises. It would, therefore, be impossible to view his lecture on "Phenomenology and Theology" as anything but an attempt to put theological research "on new foundations."

8. Jacques Derrida, *Aporias*, trans. Thomas Dutoit (Stanford, CA: Stanford University Press, 1993), 44.

9. Ibid., 45.

10. Ibid., 44.

11. BT 195/153.

12. "There is a *methodological order* here in every sense of the term: (1) an order in the sense of the logic of a whole, an element, or a milieu (in the sense that one says: it is on the order of . . . ; in this case, on the order of method); (2) it is also an order as order of progression, sequence, forward motion, or irreversible procedure, a step, a way of proceeding or of progressing; (3) it is finally a given order, the double prescription to follow an order and to follow a give order of sequential linkage or of consequence: begin here and *end* there!" Derrida, *Aporias*, 45.

13. "What is decisive is not to get out of the circle but to come into it in the right way" (BT 195/153).

14. Derrida, *Aporias*, 44, my italics.

15. Ibid., 27, my italics.

16. Here we are anticipating the opposition between existential and existentiell.

17. Derrida, *Aporias*, 175. To be sure, Derrida is the first to admit that Heidegger violates these very same borders. In fact, the crux of his entire critical reading of *Being and Time* concerns the meaning of these violations, which according to Derrida, are at once intolerable and inevitable (even necessary). At this point, however, I am only concerned with Heidegger's own *conception* of this rigorous ordering. In other words, I am interested in what Heidegger *claims* to do, rather than what he actually does.

18. Heidegger describes the process whereby ontology informs science in *Being and Time*. This is said to occur most often during periods of crisis within a science, when competing theories force it to reconsider its most basic concepts and therefore to redirected itself (ideally, with the help of ontology) back to the Being proper to its particular field. As he writes: "The real 'movement' of the sciences takes place when their basic concepts undergo a more or less radical revision which is transparent to itself. The level which a science has reached is determined by how far it is *capable* of a crisis in its basic concepts" (BT 29/9).

19. This point is also emphasized by Derrida in *Aporias*, where he indicates the ways in which Heidegger's existential analysis of death "relies on a classical argument within the philosophical tradition." Derrida, *Aporias*, 28.

20. This lends further support for why Heidegger's fundamental ontology does not seek to resume the "venerable" tradition of ontology: "the methodology of ontology remains questionable in the highest degree as long as we merely consult those ontologies which have come down to us historically, or other essay of that character. Since the term 'ontology' is used in this investigation in a sense which is formally broad [i.e., in a sense that is not oriented towards or associated with regional ontologies—e.g., ontology of Nature], any attempt to clarify the method of ontology by tracing its history is automatically ruled out" (BT 49/27).

21. It is, nevertheless, worth noting the importance of the hermeneutical structure of understanding for this revival. Although Heidegger claims that philosophical discourse on "Being" had fallen into despair, he nevertheless maintained that the "vague average understanding of Being is still a Fact" which may supply the guidelines for ontological inquiry. In fact, *given the structure of inquiry itself*, this average understanding *can and must* serve as a guide. Therefore, we observe, it was only on the basis of the hermeneutical structure of understanding that Heidegger was able to hold together the two seemingly contradictory claims which legitimized his revival of the ontological question in the first place, namely: first, that the traditional philosophical conceptions of Being that we inherit are utterly inadequate and, secondly, that "the meaning of Being must already be available to us in some way" and must supply us with certain, albeit inexplicit, guidelines for fundamental ontological investigation (BT 24–25/4–5).

22. Theodore Kisiel suggests that this indicated a new development in Heidegger thought. The projective structure of understanding, the rooted-ness of all ontological knowledge in the ontic—all of this is new to *Being and Time*. Heidegger had never before discussed the matter in precisely those terms. See Theodore Kisiel, "Heidegger (1920–21) on Becoming a Christian: A Conceptual Picture Show," in *Reading Heidegger from the Start: Essays in His Earliest Thought*, eds. T. Kisiel and J. van Buren (New York: SUNY Press, 1994), 174–94.

23. That this analytic represents a preliminary stage within his overall fundamental ontology—and not an end in itself—was a point Heidegger emphasized in his celebrated "Letter on Humanism," in *Martin Heidegger: Basic Writings (Revised and Expanded Edition)*, ed. D. Krell and trans. F. Capuzzi (San Francisco: Harper San Francisco, 1993). But it was already stressed within the pages of *Being and Time* itself: "Yet the analytic of Dasein is not aimed at laying an ontological basis for anthropology; its purpose is one of fundamental ontology. This is the purpose that has tacitly determined the course of our considerations hitherto, our selection of phenomena, and the limits to which our analysis may proceed" (BT 244/200).

24. Jean-Paul Sartre, *Existentialism and Human Emotions* (New York: Citadel Press, 1997), 13–16.

25. This contrast needs to be stressed if we are to understand accurately the manner in which Heidegger comes to subordinate theology to phenomenological ontology. As we shall see, for Heidegger the subordinate (or secondary) status of theological

science vis-à-vis the analytic of Dasein has nothing to do with a celebration of a humanistic atheism over dogmatic theism, as may be the case with other forms of existential philosophy.

26. Therefore, Heidegger writes, "By way of contrast, Sartre expresses the basic tenet of existentialism in this way: Existence precedes essence. In this statement he is taking *existentia* and *essentia* according to their metaphysical meaning, which from Plato's time on has said that *essentia* precedes *existentia*. Sartre reverses this statement. But the reversal of a metaphysical statement remains a metaphysical statement. With it he stays with metaphysics in oblivion of the truth of Being." Heidegger, "Letter on Humanism," 232.

27. Perhaps Heidegger's clearest statement concerning the necessity of the preliminary analytic of Dasein for fundamental ontology is preserved in the published edition of his 1927 summer lecture course: "The method of ontology, that is, of philosophy in general, is distinguished by the fact that ontology has nothing in common with any method of any of the other sciences, all of which as positive sciences deal with beings. On the other hand, it is precisely the analysis of the truth-character of being which shows that being also is, as it were, based in a being, namely, in the Dasein. Being is given only if the understanding of being, hence Dasein, exists. This being accordingly lays claim to a distinctive priority in ontological inquiry. It makes itself manifest in all discussions of the basic problems of ontology and above all in the fundamental questions of the meaning of being in general. The elaboration of this question and its answer requires a general analytic of the Dasein. Ontology has for its fundamental discipline the analytic of Dasein. Ontology has for its fundamental discipline the analytic of the Dasein." Martin Heidegger, *The Basic Problems of Phenomenology*, trans. Albert Hofstadter (Bloomington: Indiana University Press, 1988), 19.

28. Were it not to carry us too far afield from our primary line of inquiry, more could be gained from further analysis of this crucial link between Dasein's ecstatic nature and its "peculiar neutrality" (BT, 171/136). We have merely touched upon what is most basic and essential for understanding Heidegger's prioritization of this being (i.e., Dasein) over all others.

29. Two courses ("Einleitung in die Phänomenologie der Religion" and "Augustinus und der Neuplatonismus") have recently been published as *Phänomenologie des Religiösen Lebens*, G.A. vol. 60. Both have been translated into English in a volume bearing the title *The Phenomenology of Religious Life*. Martin Heidegger, *The Phenomenology of Religious Life*, trans. M. Fritsch and J. Gosetti-Ferencei (Bloomington: Indiana University Press, 2004).

30. Kisiel, *The Genesis of Heidegger's "Being and Time,"* 19. See also Hent de Vries's *Philosophy and the Turn to Religion* (Baltimore: Johns Hopkins University Press, 1999), 177.

31. Kisiel, *The Genesis of Heidegger's "Being and Time,"* 19.

32. Ibid., 17.

33. Heidegger, *The Phenomenology of Religious Life*, §11–§13.

34. This challenge recalls the one faced by Schleiermacher (especially in his debate with Hegel over the nature of religious experience). It perhaps not surprising that

Schleiermacher's theological writings played a significant role in Heidegger's own confessional turn to Protestantism.

35. "[. . .] the formal indication is a defense [*Abwehr*], a preliminary securing, so that the enactment-character still remains free. The necessity of this precautionary measure arises from the falling tendency of factical life experience, which constantly threatens to slip into the objective, and out of which we must still retrieve the phenomena." Heidegger, *The Phenomenology of Religious Life*, 44/64.

36. De Vries uses the metaphor of a stepping-stone, or a ladder, that must be tossed aside once it has been ascended. The general idea is that the formal indication grants access to concrete factical life, or to Being, without thematizing it, without making it accessible in the ordinary sense of manipulabe and subsistent entities. John Caputo, on the other hand, uses the image of a finger pointing at the moon—the moon should never be confused with the finger. John Caputo, *The Prayers and Tears of Jacques Derrida* (Bloomington: Indiana University Press, 1997), 139. Kisiel's interpretation, which follows Heidegger's lectures more closely, is bit more perplexing. He likens the function of the formal indication to the function of the demonstrative "it," which serves to indicate any number of objects without further determination or specification. Kisiel, "Heidegger (1920–21) on Becoming a Christian."

37. Kisiel notes that the WS course of 1920–1921 turned out to be a *cursus interruptus*: "The interruption is most unfortunate for us who follow, since Heidegger [. . .] will never again return to this vital but esoteric subject in the deliberate and systematic way that he had begun here, usually preferring instead to mention it in passing, with little or no explanation, as he applies this method of philosophical conceptualization in one context or another in the years to and through *Being and Time*." Kisiel, "Heidegger (1920–21) on Becoming a Christian," 177–78.

38. "The structure of Christian hope, which in truth is the relational sense of Parousia, is radically different from all expectation. [. . .] The 'When' is already not originally grasped, insofar as it is grasped in the sense of an attitudinal 'objective,' time. The time of 'factical life' in its falling, unemphasized, non-Christian sense is also not meant. Paul does not say 'When' because this expression is inadequate to what is to be expressed, because it does not suffice." Heidegger, *The Phenomenology of Religious Life*, 71–2/102. See also Otto Pöggeler, *Martin Heidegger's Path of Thinking*, trans. D. Magurshak and S. Barber (Atlantic Highlands, NJ: Humanities Press International, Inc., 1987), 24–25.

39. 1 Thessalonians 5:2.

40. John van Buren, "Martin Heidegger, Martin Luther," in *Reading Heidegger from the Start: Essays in His Earliest Thought*, ed. T. Kisiel and J. van Buren, 159–74 (New York: SUNY Press, 1994), 163.

41. See, for example, Heidegger, *The Phenomenology of Religious Life* (especially "Augustine and Neoplatonism," §1–§3). For a detailed discussion of Heidegger's understanding of history and historicity, and how this understanding led him to break with several of his immediate theological predecessors, see Jeffrey Barash, *Martin Heidegger and the Problem of Historical Meaning* (New York: Fordham University Press, 2003), 143.

42. Heidegger, *The Phenomenology of Religious Life* (especially his "Introduction to the Phenomenology of Religion," 104–105/147–148).
43. See, for example, Hent de Vries's *Philosophy and the Turn to Religion*, 104–5.
44. Ibid., 178.
45. Ibid., 241.
46. Zarader insists that the most innovated traits of Heidegger approach to Being are the result of an often inexplicit confrontation of Greek and non-Greek (and specifically biblical) sources within his work: "if Heidegger so radically renewed the Greek comprehension of Being, he did so on the basis of thought forms drawn form another source, a source initially related, like the entire biblical universe, to God. That means that we find ourselves before the reappearance in Heidegger's work of categories closely tied to a certain [biblical] heritage, aiming to reflect on a question [i.e., of Being] come straight from an other [Greek] heritage as well" (137). Although Heidegger remains incontestably focused on a question (the question of Being) that was initially opened by a uniquely Greek mode of thinking, his manner of approaching this question is nevertheless determined by a series of categories that lack any Greek equivalents, such as "donation, welcome and passivity, memory and gratitude, promise and salvation, etc." (145). It is hardly a coincidence, Zarader argues, that these non-Greek categories "find something like an echo of anticipation in the universe of Hebraic thought"—and specifically in the categories developed within the biblical commentaries for articulating the "approach to God" (136). Marlène Zarader, *The Unthought Debt: Heidegger and The Hebraic Heritage*, trans. Bettina Bergo (Stanford, CA: Stanford University Press, 2006).
47. Jacques Derrida, "Faith and Knowledge: The Two Sources of 'Religion' at the Limits of Reason Alone," in *Religion*, ed. J. Derrida and G. Vattimo (Stanford, CA: Stanford University Press, 1998), 16.
48. "Now and then religion and the historical [i.e., facticity] seem merely to co-exist, albeit not altogether peacefully, as co-originary possibilities caught in a perpetual flight both away from and, oddly enough, also toward each other" (de Vreis, *Phenomenology and the Turn to Religion*, 177). Numerous examples of this sort of oscillation could be cited in Derrida, usually in the context of his distinction between messianism and messianicity, which more or less corresponds to the problem of revelation and revealability.
49. Martin Heidegger, *Seminare, Gesamtausgabe*, vol. 15 (Frankfurt: Vittorio Klostermann, 1996), 436–37.
50. "*Ich glaube, dass das Sein niemals als Grund und Wesen von Gott gedacht warden kann, dass aber gleichwohl de Erfahrung Gottes und seiner Offenbarkeit (sofern sie dem Menschen begegnet) in der Dimension des Seins sich ereignet* [. . .]" Heidegger, *Seminare*, 436–37.
51. De Vries, *Phenomenology and the Turn to Religion*, 177.
52. Derrida, "Faith and Knowledge," 15.
53. De Vries writes, "Yet while Heidegger thus claims that the revelation of positive religions is somehow made possible by the revealability or 'dimension' of Being, it can be argued on internal grounds that the reverse thesis holds true as well." *Phenomenology and the Turn to Religion*, 238, 242–43.

54. Ibid., 240.

55. For a relevant discussion of this proper method, see Lehmann's early analysis of the young Heidegger's religious thought. Karl Lehmann, "*Christliche Geschichtserfahrung und ontologische Frage beim jungen Heidegger*," *Philosophisches Jahrbuch* 74, 1966, 126–53. See also Zarader, *The Unthought Debt*, 155.

56. She is keenly aware of the problematical nature of Heidegger's formalization of the content of Hebraic tradition. Zarader, *The Unthought Debt*, 158.

57. Ibid., 159, my italics.

58. Ibid.

59. It is no mere coincidence that Zarader's comments are themselves inspired by a line of questioning first opened up by Paul Ricoeur, who had raised a similar objection to Heidegger directly during the Cerisy Colloquium in 1955. He rearticulated the problem twenty years later in his introductory note to *Heidegger et la question de Dieu*, which Zarader cites almost in its entirety: "What has often astonished me about Heidegger is that he would have systematically eluded, it seems, the confrontation with the whole [*bloc*] of Hebraic thought. He sometimes reflected on the basis of the Gospels and of Christian theology, but always avoided the Hebraic cluster [*massif*], which is the absolute stranger to the Greek discourse. . . . This misprision [*méconnaissance*] seems to me to run parallel to Heidegger's incapacity to take a 'step back' in such a way that might permit us to think adequately all the dimensions of the Western tradition. Does the task of rethinking the Christian tradition by way of a 'step backward' not require that one recognize the radically Hebraic dimension of Christianity, which is first rooted in Judaism and only afterward in the Greek tradition? Why reflect only on Hölderlin and not on the Psalms, on Jeremiah? There lies my question." Zarader, *The Unthought Debt*, 7, translation modified.

60. Zarader, *The Unthought Debt*, 159, my italics.

61. Ibid.

62. Moreover, given Heidegger's penchant for origins, for the originary, for Ur-phenomena, it is indeed surprising that he fails to take that final step back into the Old Testament Hebraic backdrop of the New Testament. Zarader writes, "It is utterly remarkable that Heidegger treats the Neo-testamentary test as a univocal point of departure, which would have no background at all. This leads him to comment on Paul's Greek without ever inquiring about what it was carrying, and what would come to it from a possible background language [*arrière-langue*]. Now, the existence of this background language is here much more than a possibility, much more even than a simple historical source. It is constitutive of the Neo-testamentary language itself, which is a language that precisely finds its meaning only as a sort of cauldron in which the difficult synthesis of Hebrew and Greek is brought about." Zarader, *The Unthought Debt*, 161.

63. Ibid., 161.

64. Ibid., 161, my italics.

65. Ibid., 161, my italics.

66. Derrida, "Faith and Knowledge," 15, my italics.

67. It is not surprising that Derrida comes to emphasize the role of repetition within Heideggerian ontology since, on Derrida's view, all abstractions or "idealities" are produced through processes of repetition, iteration, and reiteration. So the existential analysis is, for Derrida, just one example of this process.

68. De Vries, *Phenomenology and the Turn to Religion*, 241.

69. Paul Ricoeur has raised a similar question regarding the relation between ontological and epistemological issues within Heidegger's work: "With Heidegger's philosophy, we are engaged with going back to the foundations, but we are left incapable of beginning the movement of return which would lead from the fundamental ontology to the properly epistemological questions of the human sciences. Now a philosophy which breaks the dialogue with the sciences is no longer addressed to anything but itself." See Paul Ricoeur, *Hermeneutics and the Human Sciences* (hereafter: HH), 59.

70. "A positive science is the founding disclosure of a being that is given and in some way already disclosed. The question arises: What is already given for theology?" (PT 52). Heidegger articulates his response in division "A" of his lecture. See PT 52–54/51–55.

71. "Theology is a conceptual knowing of that which first of all allows Christianity to become an originarily historical event, a knowing of that which we call Christianness pure and simple. Thus we maintain that *what is given for theology (its positum) is Christianness*" (PT 52/52).

72. See Barash, *Martin Heidegger*, Chapter 4.

73. We employ the phrase "protective strategy" in its most general and nontechnical sense, and with only loose reference to its more technical meaning—as found in the work of Wayne Proudfoot, for instance, where such strategies are specifically shown protect the *sui generis* character of religious phenomena and are thought to combat the reductionist tendencies of certain scientific approaches to religious phenomena. At any rate, in Heidegger this protective strategy is put to rather curious ends: To be sure, it does serve to guard against the reduction of theology to any other scientific discipline (such as the history or psychology of religion). But, in doing so, it also serves to protect the fundamental status of that discipline which it most resembles—namely, phenomenological ontology. This would be an alternative way of expressing the thesis under consideration here. See Proudfoot, *Religious Experience*.

74. See Barash, *Martin Heidegger*, 144.

75. BT, §7, section C.

76. To cite once again some key passages from Pöggeler's important work, *Martin Heidegger's Path of Thinking*: "the thinking which computes time and turns toward accessible 'objective' contents, thereby distinguishing for itself its relation to the inaccessible future will not escape ruin" (25). Or, again: "The chairos (a time reckoned according to significant events rather than by some scientific standard of measurement [. . .]) places it on the razor's edge in the decision. Chairological characteristics do not reckon with and master time; rather they place one into the threat of the future. They belong in life's history of performance which cannot be objectified. [. . .] If man tries by means of chronological computations or content-oriented characterizations to define the inaccessible event which suddenly bursts upon the scene, the event

upon which his life is base, he then eliminates that which should determine his life as the always inaccessible and replaces it with the secured, the accessible" (24–25). Pöggeler, *Martin Heidegger's Path*.

77. De Vries, *Phenomenology and the Turn to Religion*, 241.

78. Interestingly, Paul Ricoeur claims that Saint Paul was the first to catch sight of this connection between "a nonspecifically religious phenomenon (or, at least, a nonspecifically Christian phenomenon), which he called *suneidesis*—knowledge shared with oneself—and the *kerygma* about Christ that he interpreted in terms of 'justification by faith.'" Conscience, for Paul, acts as a sort of anthropological presupposition without which justification by faith would be impossible. Paul Ricoeur, *Figuring the Sacred: Religion, Narrative, and Imagination*, ed. M. Wallace and trans. D. Pellauer (Minneapolis: Fortress Press, 1995), 271. (Henceforth, FS.)

79. See above, Section 9.

80. For Heidegger's later relationship theology, see John Caputo, "Heidegger and Theology," in *The Cambridge Companion to Heidegger: Second Edition*, ed. Charles Guignon (New York: Cambridge University Press, 2006).

Chapter 3

Marion's Radical Revelation
Givenness and the Anonymous Call

Thus one is most disclosed when one is most anonymous.
                                  Wallace Stevens, "Nudity in the Colonies"

He is a good man who can receive a gift well.
                                            Ralph Waldo Emerson, "Gifts"

1. RESISTANCE AND REPETITION

In the last chapter, I argued that Heidegger's effort to prevent theological "contaminants" from intruding upon his strictly philosophical articulation of fundamental existential structures led him to adopt a strategy of counter-contamination, whereby revelation (*Offenbarung*) was eventually purged, little by little, of its material contents and extricated from the "merely regional" textual-linguistic milieu of the Judeo-Christian heritage in which it was first encountered. I now turn to the work of Jean-Luc Marion, who is not only one of the central figures in the so-called theological turn, but also one of the most sophisticated critics of Heidegger's ontological characterization of revelation. Indeed, as we shall see, Marion's trailblazing theological work, *God Without Being*, specifically targets the picture of revelation presented in Heidegger's 1928 lecture on "Phenomenology and Theology." And his assault upon the Heideggerian conception of revelation continues right up through his most recent theological works, such as *Givenness and Revelation*, the published version of the Gifford Lectures.[1] But Marion's critique of Heideggerian ontology is not limited to theological considerations alone. In fact, he also tries to mount an objection on "strictly philosophical grounds," that is, on the basis of considerations that are entirely consistent with the original insights, motives, and concerns of Husserlian phenomenology. He does so by proposing a threefold historical framework or "scheme" for understanding the evolution of the phenomenological reduction. This threefold scheme functions as the theoretical armature of his entire philosophical enterprise, and it will therefore serve as a helpful organizing principle for my own analysis in this chapter.

According to Marion, the importance of Husserl's work cannot be understood in isolation, but only in relation to that which it follows (Descartes, Kant, Nietzsche) and that which it anticipates (Heidegger). Thus, in order to determine the rigor specific to Marion's version of phenomenology, one must turn not only to Husserl's texts, but to an entire complex of issues concerning the history of metaphysics which helped to set the stage for the initial phenomenological "breakthrough" and its subsequent developments. Marion conceives of this development as an "inevitable" succession of three increasingly radical forms of the phenomenological reduction, each of which draws us progressively closer to a "pure givenness," or the gift as such.[2] Husserl is said to have paved the way with his transcendental reduction, which, along with his "principle of principles," served to strip away (or reduce) the subjective conditions previously imposed upon appearances throughout the history of metaphysics. However, that reduction only partially cleared a path for that which "gives itself as itself," since it remained committed to "the constitutively metaphysical definition of presence—objectivity."[3] Heidegger's existential reduction offered the "second surge," leading us back from beings (i.e., objects constituted by a subject) to the Being of beings. Although Heidegger introduced an import radicalization of Husserl's founding insights, his preoccupation with ontology ultimately confined phenomena to the horizon of Being, and as a result he, too, failed to accomplish the return to the things as they give themselves. Therefore, it is finally up to Marion (or so he argues) to formulate his own radical version of the reduction, the so-called pure reduction—one that is finally capable of leading phenomenology beyond metaphysics, to a phenomenology of givenness as such.

Despite Marion's efforts to provide a strictly philosophical justification for this increasing radicalization, I claim that the transition from Heidegger's existential reduction to Marion's third and final reduction to pure givenness cannot be understood apart from a specific set of theological concerns initially developed in his groundbreaking book, *God Without Being*. What is perhaps most striking is that Marion's attempt to overcome Heideggerian ontology is both aimed at and sustained by a certain rehabilitation of the category of revelation. Nevertheless, through a patient reading of Marion's two major philosophical texts (*Reduction and Givenness* and *Being Given*), it will become clear that his attempt to conceal the theological motivations for his new brand of radical phenomenology ultimately led him to recapitulate the Heideggerian strategy, that is, the protective strategy which I sought to explain in the previous chapter in terms of a kind of counter-contamination. Marion's rehabilitation of revelation—his endeavor to make revelation a legitimate subject of phenomenological investigation—is justified on the basis of a distinction between revelation *as possibility* and Revelation *as actuality*.[4] Phenomenology, Marion insists, concerns the former, while theology concerns the latter. We shall see, however, that through a series of extremely complex and subtle philosophical maneuvers, Marion's phenomenological figure of revelation (as possibility) winds up imposing its own indeterminate status upon Revelation itself (i.e., upon Revelation as an actually given event, or Call). This indeterminacy (or "purity"), therefore, entails a hollowing out of "Revelation" that essentially extricates it from any determinate historical/religious context. Revelation, in the end, is described as a purely formal givenness, a givenness which, by definition, is given *before* any act of determination or nomination, before any Name can be "imposed" upon it. The concern that I will raise regarding this conception of Revelation as a pure form of givenness is whether or not it will be able to maintain any reference to the historical, linguistic, or textual richness of revelation in its religious/theological acceptation—be it Jewish, Christian, or otherwise. But before this question can be properly posed, we must first traverse the path of Marion's threefold schematism of the reduction, beginning with his reading of Husserl.

2. PHENOMENOLOGY AND METAPHYSICS

From the perspective of Marion's quasi-teleological interpretive framework, according to which the development of phenomenology consists of a series of radicalizations culminating in his theory of givenness, everything seems to hinge upon Husserl's original break with metaphysics—a break which, though incomplete, nevertheless succeeds in setting the entire process in motion. It is no surprise, then, that Marion insists that the true significance of Husserl's work (and, thus, the genuine destiny of phenomenology as a whole) can only be "measured" by "an interpretation that is itself awake to the essence [and, we might add, shortcomings] of metaphysics."[5] In order to demonstrate the (supposedly) "post-metaphysical" character of phenomenology, Marion harkens back to the golden age of metaphysics, to a kind of philosophical thinking which defined the metaphysical tradition before its culmination (Hegel?) or its decline (Nietzsche?): namely, to the critical philosophy of Emmanuel Kant.[6] Marion's primary interest in Kant concerns "the formal conditions of experience" elaborated in the first critique.[7] The Kantian conditions of possible experience are not given by phenomena themselves but are rather imposed upon phenomena by the subjective faculties of sensibility and understanding. "This means that intuition [which must always conform to the formal conditions of sensibility, i.e., time and space] and the concept[s of the understanding, i.e., the categories] determine *in advance* the possibility of appearing for any phenomenon."[8] According to Marion, Kant's decision to make all phenomena conform to the subjective powers of knowing reflects a broader trend within Western metaphysics that traces at least as far back as Leibniz's principle of sufficient reason, according to which "nothing happens without it being possible for the one who sufficiently knows things to give a Reason that suffices to determine why it is so and not otherwise."[9] This constitutes *the* characteristic feature of metaphysics, as defined by Marion: "In a metaphysical system, the possibility of appearing never belongs to what appears, nor phenomenality to the phenomenon."[10]

Here is where Husserlian phenomenology makes its great advance according to Marion:

> It is this aporia that phenomenology escapes all at once in opposing to the principle of sufficient reason the "principle of all principles," and thus in surpassing conditional phenomenality through a phenomenality without condition. The "principle of all principles" posits that "every originarily *donating* intuition [*Anschauung*] is a source of right [*Reschtsquelle*] for cognition, that everything that offers itself to us originarily in 'intuition' ['*Intuition*'] is to be taken quite simply as it gives itself out to be, but also only within the limits in which it is given there."[11]

According to Husserl's principle of all principles, intuition is seen as valid in and of itself—it gains its stripes, so to speak, of its own accord, without having to receive in advance the knowing subject's stamp of approval. Since each and every intuition is said to constitute its own "source of right" (*Reschtsquelle)*, the phenomenologist need not demand that intuition satisfy any pre-given (or shall we say non-given) set of requirements, such as the Kantian categories or the pure forms of sensibility. Marion writes that "the 'principle of all principles,' setting intuition to work as the ultimate instance of donation, gives rise to the extension of intuition beyond the Kantian prohibition."[12] In order to appreciate Marion's own constructive phenomenological project, we need to determine the nature and scope of the Husserlian extension of intuition.

A passage from *Ideas I* appearing just before Husserl introduces his principle of all principles will provide the key to understanding this extension: "the individual object can 'appear' [and] can be apprehended by consciousness but without a spontaneous 'activity' performed 'upon' it."[13] On its own, this passage illustrates with remarkable clarity the degree to which Husserl emphasizes the passivity of the subject in the face of giving intuition. When viewed in light of its context, however, this passage also reveals what for Marion marks a crucial development in Husserl's thought—namely the widening of the notion of intuition so as to include the intuition of essences in addition to sensuous intuition. Now, the passage in question has been extricated from a rather complex line of argument in which Husserl tries to show that the essence of that which is imagined (in this case, a "flute-playing centaur") must not be conflated with the act of imagination itself.[14] Though it is customary to conceive of imaginary essences as the products of the understanding (in particular, of the faculty of imagination) and therefore as being located within the subject alone, Husserl claims that essences (imaginary or otherwise) are in fact *given to*, rather than *created by*, consciousness. In order to appreciate the innovation of Husserl's thesis, we need only to recall Kant's definition of the imagination as "the faculty for representing an object even without its presence in intuition."[15] The faculty of the imagination, it would appear, would be capable of re-producing or re-presenting the essence of a thing without the aid of intuition—without having to receive something from outside itself. Husserl's analysis, however, aims to demonstrate that even this apparently spontaneous (and thus autonomous) act of imaginative representation requires the support of intuition—the support, that is, of a certain givenness. Far from being a product of a merely subjective activity involving no givens (i.e., no intuition), imaginative essences are, according to Husserl, received in and through intuition. Thus, Husserl writes, "*seeing essences is an originary presentive* [i.e. giving] *act* and, as a presentive act, is the *analogue of sensuous perceiving* and *not of imagining.*"[16]

In fact, Husserl's argument for the intuition of essences is really only an elaboration of a theory already found in the *Logical Investigations*—namely, the theory of categorial intuition.[17] There, too, Husserl had extended the scope of intuition beyond the Kantian conception of sensibility, so as to include the intuition of not only sensible objects but of ideal objects as well (such as aggregates, numbers, states of affairs, totalities, etc.).[18] Husserl writes, "Sensuous or real objects can in fact be characterized as objects of the lowest level of possible intuition, categorial or ideal objects as objects of higher levels."[19] Rather than acting as the subjective doorways through which intuition must pass, Husserl had claimed that categories (higher level intuitions) are themselves founded upon and given through (lower level) intuition.[20] Thus, Marion suggests that Husserlian phenomenology marks an important break with the metaphysical tradition. Intuition is no longer governed by the rules or restrictions of the knowing subject (such as the Kantian categories) but, rather, the categories themselves are now shown to be given to the subject by higher-level "donating" intuitions.

Marion's suggestion that Husserl's discovery of 'categorial intuition' constitutes an important break with traditional metaphysics is by no means new—after all, Heidegger's early fascination with the *Logical Investigations* was driven by this same insight. In his summer course of 1925, Heidegger had already claimed that the first "decisive character of the discovery of categorial intuition" was that "there are acts in which ideal constituents show themselves in themselves, which are not constructs of these acts, functions of thinking or of the subject."[21] And with this he believed "phenomenological research . . . arrives at the form of research sought by ancient ontology. There is no ontology *alongside* phenomenology. Rather, *scientific ontology is nothing but phenomenology*."[22] Thus, according to the standard interpretation of the development of twentieth-century phenomenological philosophy, Husserl's discovery of categorial intuition cleared the path for Heidegger's fundamental ontology.

3. FIRST SURGE: FROM INTUITION TO GIVENNESS (. . . AND BACK)

Nevertheless, in spite of Heidegger's own admission that categorial intuition provided a foundation for *Being and Time*, Marion rejects the standard interpretation which portrays an almost seamless continuity between the discovery of categorial intuition and the question of Being, in favor of a far more nuanced understanding of the relationship between metaphysics and phenomenology, and between Husserl and Heidegger—more nuanced, perhaps, than even Heidegger himself would have supposed.[23] As Marion writes,

> It thus seems to be self-evident, as much for Heidegger as for his interpreters, that categorial *intuition*, by fixing Being itself at work in the expression, defines the hyphen—tenuous but obstinate—between the last metaphysician and the first "thinker." [. . .] But the sanctioned interpretation (or indeed self-interpretation) of Heidegger, as right as it seems literally, perhaps masks what is essential. (RD 35)

But then what, for Marion, is the essential? What essential insight of Husserl's provided the break with metaphysics and the ground for genuine thought? Marion's use of italics in the above quotation offers us the first clue, by hinting at what is essentially non-essential, namely, *intuition*. Marion's suggestion seems to be that the standard interpretation misses what is most essential by focusing exclusively on this extension of intuition.

In order to make sense of the non-essentiality of intuition, one must take a closer look at the first chapter of *Reduction and Givenness*, in which the Heideggerian interpretation of Husserl is supplemented by another interpretation—the one offered by Derrida's *Speech and Phenomena*.[24] To be sure,

Marion's intention is not to conceal but rather to highlight the apparent conflict between the standard (i.e., Heideggerian) interpretation and the Derridian interpretation: according to the former, the elevation of intuition marks a promising break with metaphysics and supplies a new ground for the question of Being; according to the latter (to which we will return in a moment), the promotion of intuition marks the fatal step which led Husserl back into a metaphysics of presence. In spite of this difference, Marion suggests that these two perspectives can be reconciled within a single interpretation, which would be all the more profound since it is informed and supported by both.[25]

The true novelty of Marion's analysis of Husserl's relation to metaphysics surfaces in Marion's juxtaposition of these two influential readings. Marion presents the Derridian argument as follows: Even though Husserl's analysis of signification in the First Investigation would appear to prove that "the absence of intuition [. . .] is not only *tolerated* by speech, it is *required* by the general structure of signification," Husserl's metaphysical presuppositions ultimately overshadow this discovery, so that Husserl finally concludes that intuitive fulfillment is needed in order to secure signification in "evident presence."[26] In other words, Husserl reaffirms the authority of presence by subordinating the absence (or non-presence) of signification to fulfilling intuition (presence). Therefore, Derrida concludes that, in spite of his potential advance, Husserl's thought is ultimately re-inscribed within a metaphysics of presence.[27] Now, it must be observed that only a modified version of Derrida's interpretation is actually accepted by Marion. On the one hand, Marion argues that Husserl eventually succumbs to the Derridian critique. But, on the other hand, Marion claims that Husserl does not reach (at least not in the First Investigation) the conclusion that Derrida attributes to him: namely, that signification requires the support of intuition and thus of presence. Marion insists to the contrary that Husserl never retracts his initial position—he never claims that signification requires intuitive fulfillment. Rather, "Husserl's thesis [in the First Investigation] will consist, conversely, in refusing to refuse a signification its 'truth' under the pretense that it lacks a fulfilling intuition" (RD 25).

I do not need to retrace the laborious textual exegesis which led Marion to revise Derrida's position in order to point out the primary implication of Marion's alternative interpretation. On Marion's reading, Husserl felt a need to broaden the field of signification beyond the already extended field of intuition; "but how can a field that is already broadened and *already* total be transgressed? [. . .] To where would this realm extend itself if intuition already covers and discovers everything, including the categorial, in evidence alone?" (RD 30). Marion argues that Husserl's desire to extend signification beyond intuition is driven by a vague—and, as we shall see, ultimately suppressed—recognition of a givenness which precedes both intuition and signification (RD 32). Marion writes: "For both [intuition and signification] must allow themselves to be reinterpreted as two modes of the one givenness which alone is originary" (RD 33). So, in the end, Marion sees the real breakthrough of the *Logical Investigations* not as the broadening of the field of intuition or signification, but as the implicit, and indeed never fully appreciated, uncovering of the "unconditional primacy" of givenness itself.

Still, Marion admits, it is no wonder that neither Derrida nor Heidegger were able to bring into focus the implicit centrality of givenness within Husserl's text—for the deficiency belongs to Husserl, not his interpreters.

> What constitutes the weakness? No doubt this: that [Husserl] contents himself, too easily, with naming that givenness without truly thinking it. How does he name it? Through the finally very rough analogy of a categorial intuition. . . . The breakthrough goes as far as the givenness of Being, but recoils in the face of its abyss, by closing it again through the unquestioned because problematic, but structurally traditional, concept of categorial intuition. (RD 36)

Husserl was unable to register the true significance of his own discovery. Fluent in the language of metaphysics alone, he was incapable of understanding the voice of givenness, and could make sense of it only by translating it back into familiar, wholly metaphysical terms, such as "intuition," "evidence," "objectivity," etc. "Husserl, indeed, completely dazzled by unlimited givenness, seems not to realize the strangeness of such an excessiveness and simply manages its excess without questioning it" (RD 38). In order to manage givenness, he conceals it within and limits it to an expanded, but still traditional (i.e., still metaphysical) theory of intuition (ibid.).

If Marion regards Husserl's breakthrough as the discovery of the unconditional primacy of givenness, he nevertheless admits that this discovery was only partial—the instant givenness is unearthed by Husserl, it is immediately covered over by a classical (i.e., "metaphysical") theory of intuition. At this point it would have been perfectly plausible for Marion to have resumed Derrida's line of attack, targeting Husserl's inability to appreciate the absence of intuition as a structural feature of signification itself. But, as will soon become clear, Marion takes his cue from Heidegger instead. "Heidegger, as opposed to Husserl, will seek to think givenness, and therefore he will destroy categorial intuition—indeed, he will no longer evoke it either in *Sein and Zeit* or later." Marion even wonders: "Could one risk saying, without declaring it, that Heidegger opposes categorial intuition to givenness?" (RG 36). In the end, Marion credits Heidegger rather than Derrida for advancing phenomenology past its Husserlian limit, beyond intuition and, finally, beyond metaphysics.

4. SECOND SURGE: FROM HUSSERL TO HEIDEGGER

In order to understand this advance, it is important to clarify a bit further why Marion had argued that intuition blocks the way to givenness as such. Marion characterizes the pitfalls of Husserl's conception of givenness *as* intuition in several ways. In his article on "The Saturated Phenomenon," for instance, he locates the problem within the final lines of the principle of principles: "intuition justifies phenomena, 'but also only [*aber auch nure*] within the boundaries in which' it gives itself."[28] The problem, according to Marion, stems from the fact that givenness *as* intuition would always remain inscribed within and therefore bounded by the horizon of objectivity intended by consciousness. Hence, phenomenality would forever be determined by consciousness, "which reigns unquestioned" (RG 50–54).

Marion illustrates Husserl's position by means of a familiar, if deceptively simplistic, example:

> The function of the horizon cannot be underestimated. In effect, when it is a question of seeing an object, transcendental by definition, I cannot apprehend it all at one fell swoop. The sides of the cube are six in number, but no one has ever perceived in lived experience more than three sides together [i.e., at once]. We therefore must, by moving the observer or the object, add new experiences for each of the missing sides; however, this movement carries with it the disappearance of the previous sides. . . . It is therefore necessary that the irrepressible novelty of the flux of lived experiences, therefore of *intuition, remain*, de jure, *always included within an already defined horizon* where lived experiences not yet given could simply be united with the lived experiences already given . . . in one and the same objective *intention*. (BG 185–6, my italics)

Furthermore, Marion not only insists that Husserl winds up limiting intuition to a subjective condition—namely, the predefined horizon intended by consciousness—but that this has the additional consequence that any given phenomenon inevitably "suffers from a deficit of intuition, and thus from a shortage of *donation* [i.e., givenness]."[29] That there is, according to Husserl, always a shortage of intuition can be seen by returning to Marion's example of a cube: For even though the cube as a whole (i.e., as a six-sided object) is intended by consciousness, only three sides of a cube can be intuited at any given moment. It follows, according to Husserl, that the aim of an intentional subject always exceeds that which is given in intuition (viz., up to three of its intended sides). Or, to put the matter another way, one might say that what is given is never quite enough, it never quite lives up to the concept of the intended object. The given always needs to be supplemented by an intentional gaze that would, so to speak, fill in the gaps leftover by intuition.[30] As Marion puts the matter in *Being Given*, "Intentionality renders what appears immanent to consciousness, based on the simple fact that appearance (genuinely immanent to be sure) never appears except as always already ordered to its object by intentionality" (BG 24). Givenness is always accompanied by the non-given, by what consciousness alone can supply—imminence, permanence, in short, presence. It never appears as pure givenness, but is once again submitted to the activity of a constituting transcendental subject.

Returning to *Reduction and Givenness*, we discover that this interpretation of Husserl's principle of principles has already been sanctioned by a comment Heidegger made in *Zur Sache des Denkens*, which Marion does not fail to cite: "If one wanted to ask: Where does the 'principle of all principles' get its unshakable right, the answer would have to be: from the transcendental subjectivity that has already been presupposed as the matter of philosophy."[31] The shortcoming of the *Logical Investigations*—the fact that the phenomenological breakthrough was hampered by an adherence to the traditional theory of intuition—is still present in *Ideas I*. For however radical the principle of principles is, it is still expressed in terms of intuition (and, thus, in terms that will become unacceptable for Heidegger, and, later, for Marion).

Nevertheless, it is of even greater importance for Marion that Husserl's conception of the reduction itself continues to operate along these same lines. It, too, privileges the kind of certitude which objectivity alone can afford. According to Marion, this reduction can be reduced to the following four points:

> (1) It is deployed for the intentional and constituting *I*. (2) It gives to the *I* constituted objects (3) taken within regional ontologies which, through formal ontology, are in full conformi[t]y with the horizon of objectivity. (4) It thus excludes from givenness everything that does not let itself be led back to objectity, namely, the principal differences of ways of Being (of consciousness, of equipmentality, of the world). (RG 204)

Husserl thereby reduces all givenness to that which can be given "objectively," or according to the horizon of the object. Marion asks: "is it self-evident that objectivity offers the only face of being?" "Is it self-evident, finally, that the phenomenon must reduce its phenomenality to objectivity, itself understood as an assured permanence?"[32] His answer, of course, will be negative. By excluding all that could not be reduced to immanent presence, Husserl leads us to a one-dimensional conception of phenomena.

To this *flat* phenomenon, Marion will oppose the *depth* of the Heideggerian phenomenon. But what is this depth? First, we must note that for Husserl, a phenomenon "becomes immanent only to the extent that consciousness becomes intentionally immanent in what itself appears" (BG 25). In other words, the phenomenon does not appear of its own accord—it does not present itself by itself—rather, it needs to be represented by consciousness, that is, re-presented by consciousness to itself. Indeed, the primacy that Husserl accords to this type of theoretical reflection, in which consciousness gains mastery over the phenomenon by representing it within its own immanent stream, is precisely what Heidegger's analysis of being-in-the-world placed in question. For Heidegger, on the other hand, a phenomenon "is not *represented*, [rather] it *presents* itself. And precisely because it presents itself by itself, it can also be absent" (RD 57). In fact, the phenomenon "is first characterized by its unapparentness."[33] Or, as Heidegger himself put it during his summer course of 1925, "What can be a phenomenon is first and foremost covered up."[34] On these grounds, Marion claims that "instead of offering the certain evidence of an object for consciousness [as in Husserl], the [Heideggerian] phenomenon offers itself as the enigma of the forever unobjectifiable play of the apparent with the unapparent" (RD 59). As a result, the Heideggerian phenomenon is said to possess two levels—the *apparent* as well as the *unapparent*—rather than just one.

According to Marion, this deepening of the phenomenon is precisely what allows Heidegger to proceed beyond beings to Being. Marion cites Heidegger's lecture once again: "that which, in the most proper sense, remains *hidden* . . . is not just this being or that, but rather the *Being* of beings" (BT 59).[35] For "Being does not open like beings are uncovered, if only because its opening precedes uncoveredness and renders it possible." Consequently, the gaze of evidence, which takes measure of the given by fully re-presenting it as an object before consciousness or within the immanent stream of consciousness, is only capable of uncovering mere beings, not Being as such. Therefore, Marion concludes, while Husserl's reduction opens only to beings (objects, or flat phenomena), Heidegger's radicalization of the reduction enables us to read Being itself "starting from/on the surface of beings [*am Seienden soll alesen werden*]."[36]

> For Husserl, phenomenological reduction . . . is the method of leading phenomenological vision from the natural attitude of the human being . . . back to the transcendental life of consciousness and its noetic-neomatic experiences, in which objects are constituted as correlates of consciousness. For us [on the contrary], phenomenological reduction means leading phenomenological vision back from the apprehension of a being . . . to the understanding of the Being of this being (projecting upon the mode of its unconcealedness).[37]

Heidegger's radicalized version of the phenomenological reduction sneaks behind objectivity and opens up to the Being of beings, which Husserl's reduction had outright excluded.[38]

5. IDOL AND ICON

Thus far, I have discussed only the first two stages in Marion's proposed three-stage radicalization of the phenomenological reduction. According to Marion's schema, Husserl's reduction marks the beginning of the end of metaphysical thinking (epitomized by the principle of sufficient reason) by extending the scope of intuition and minimizing the pre-conditions that the subject imposes upon the given. However, Husserl's concern with epistemological questions and his privileging of theoretical consciousness betrayed a subtle, yet fatal, allegiance to the metaphysical (epistemological) theory of objectivity which prevented the given to appear as such. Heidegger's project, on the other hand, involved a still greater radicalization of the reduction, namely, the existential reduction (to Being as such), in which the given was neither relegated to the sphere of objectivity (ontic being) nor limited to the horizon of an epistemological subject.

I now turn to the third and final act in this elaborate play, that is, the third and final radicalization of the phenomenological reduction, the reduction to pure givenness. One cannot help but wonder what, in the first instance, authorizes this further elaboration or the reduction. What makes it possible, let alone desirable? What are the shortcomings of Heidegger's existential reduction? In fact, we shall see that Marion's motivation for proposing a third form of the reduction cannot be fully understood outside of the broader quasi-theological project which he initiated in *Idol and Distance* and which came to a head in his well-known work *God Without Being*. Even if the goal of overcoming metaphysics in the name of givenness remains intelligible, and perhaps justifiable, in view of certain developments within the phenomenological movement, Marion's initial desire to abandoning Heidegger's Being in the name of that which is beyond (or even without) Being seems to have been prompted by strictly theological concerns. His reduction is undertaken not in the name of philosophy, but first and foremost in the name of love, charity, gift, revelation—each in its carefully qualified Judeo-Christian acceptation. Thus, in order to make sense of the third reduction (the so-called reduction to pure givenness), we must turn our attention to the theological project of *God Without Being*, a project which no doubt sought the support of a phenomenology, but which nevertheless preceded Marion's philosophical schematization of the three reductions found in *Reduction and Givenness* and *Being Given*.

God Without Being begins by outlining what Marion refers to as a "comparative phenomenology of the idol and the icon."[39] According to Marion, idol and icon are not two types of beings—not two types of objects or works of art—but rather two different ways of signaling the divine (GWB 9). Since, in both cases, "the divine comes into play here only with the support of visibility" it stands to reason that the difference between the idol and the icon will have to do with their respective "modes of visibility" (GWB, 9).[40] The idolatry of the idol, then, does not lie "in" the physical object *per se*, but in the vision of subject which stands before it: "The gaze makes the idol, not the idol the gaze."

The phenomenologist's interests in the idol has less to do with the fashioning of idols (i.e., the idol's physical features or aesthetic formation) than with the way in which idols relate to vision, to the gaze or aim of the human subject—for it is this relation to human vision that sets the idol and the icon apart. Their distinction is not, properly speaking, a problem for the art historian, who traces the developments of aesthetic forms preserved in material objects, but for the phenomenologist, who examines the various modalities of the "intentional" relations between a gaze and its "object," between noesis and noema, between a conceptual aim and its type of intuitive fulfillment.[41] This does not mean, of course, that artistic production has no bearing whatsoever on such a phenomenological analysis—in fact, we shall soon discover that, according to Marion, the very possibility of fixing an idolatrous experience within an artistic (and therefore material) object points to the specific kind of intentional relation belonging to the idol (GWB 15). But the idolatrous function far surpasses the life of objects. For the type of idolatry that interests Marion most is conceptual rather than aesthetic.

The opening analysis of the relation of the idol to vision presupposes (without ever explicitly referring to) certain basic concepts borrowed from Husserlian phenomenology. Our reading of *God Without Being*, therefore, must remain attentive to the Husserlian themes lying just beneath the surface of Marion's text—the first and most influential of which concerns the distinction between intention and fulfillment. We have already touched upon this distinction earlier, when we discussed Husserl's description of the perception of a cube. This experience was said to involve the intention (or concept) of a six-sided object, on the one hand, and the intuition (i.e., the perceptual givenness) of as many as three of the cube's sides. Such an experience, then, involves a certain degree of fulfillment—it partially fills or satisfies the subject's aim or intention. However, on Husserl's account, the intention can never be completely filled, since perception always (by definition) involves a shortage or deficit owing to the eidetic structure of physical objects. In the case of the perception of a cube, for instance, only three of its sides can be given at any single time. Total fulfillment, for Husserl, remains a merely regulative ideal, one which could never be actually achieved in perceptual experience.[42]

Marion's formulation of the idol, however, demands that such fulfillment be given in actuality. It is made possible, however, only because the gaze (read: intention) itself determines and delimits the object of its intention. "The gaze makes the idol, not the idol the gaze—which means that the idol with its visibility *fills the intention of the gaze*, which wants nothing other than to see. The gaze precedes the idol because an aim precedes and gives rise to that at which it aims" (GWB, 10–11, my italics). The idol offers the perfect fulfillment of an intentional aim—there is a certain isomorphism between the conscious intention and what the idol offers or 'gives' to be seen. In other words, the gaze is perfectly satiated by what is given to be seen in the idol. With the idol, there is neither a surplus nor a shortcoming of intuition vis-à-vis the intention, but rather a kind of equilibrium or agreement (*adequatio*) between them. "[I]n the idol, the divine actually comes into the visibility for which human gazes watch: but this advent is measured by what the scope of particular human eyes can support, by what each aim can require of visibility in order to admit itself fulfilled" (GWB 14).

If, however, the idol is defined as that which gives precisely what the gaze expects to find, then the given is determined *in advance* by the scope of this expectation. "That god whose space of manifestation is measured by what portion of it a gaze can bear—[is] precisely, an idol. [. . .] Thus, the idol consigns the divine to the measure of a human gaze" (GWB 14). This explains why, according to Marion, the idol is capable of being "consigned" to the material domain of the plastic arts in the first place. The artist is able to fix in stone, carve from wood, or render with pigment only that which he or she is first of all capable of conceiving. The finished product reflects the limited scope of this artist's gaze: "Because the idol allows the divine to occur only in man's measure, man can consign the idolatrous experience to art and thus keep it accessible" (GWB 15). Moreover, the symmetry characteristic of the idolatrous gaze also accounts for "the ease with which we desert idolatry"—that is, the ease with which we abandon the idols of the past (or the idols of so-called primitive cultures, for that matter). Though we may have an aesthetic appreciation for the artistic representations found in ancient ruins or on display in museums, these idols-of-old no longer seem to possess the life that they presumably once had. Though they can have a historical significance, which we may immediately recognize and appreciate, they no longer 'fill our eyes' so to speak. Simply put, our conception of divinity—whatever that may be—certainly no longer corresponds to the image captured in stone. One is dazzled by the idol only so long as one possesses an "aim whose expectation could let itself be fulfilled and hence frozen" by it (GWB 15).

This does not mean that we 'moderns' have "overcome" idolatry altogether; rather, the site of idolatry has simply shifted from the aesthetic domain to the conceptual domain, where the intentional relation between the gaze, on the one hand, and the idea in which the divine is fixed, on the other, continues to display a marked symmetry. "If we occidentals, dated (and endowed) by the completion of metaphysics, lack the aesthetic means to grasp the idol, others remain or even open up for us. Thus the concept" (GWB 16). The idolatry-function continues to operate wherever the symmetry between our gaze and our conceptual determination of "God" persists—wherever the divine is consigned to the concept we make of it.

It is not surprising that Marion likens this symmetrical relationship between the gaze and the idol (whether aesthetic or conceptual) to a mirror, in which the reflected image (in this case, the idol) is determined by that which it reflects (namely, the gaze). "The idol thus acts as a mirror, not as a portrait: a mirror that reflects the gaze's image, or more exactly, the image of its aim and of the scope of that aim" (GWB 12). Like a mirror, "the idol returns the gaze to itself" (ibid.). Whereas a portrait holds the potential to expand the scope of one's gaze by transporting the gaze beyond the image and towards that which is imaged by the image (in the way, for instance, that a sign carries us toward what is signified), the mirror confines the scope of the gaze since it merely reflects the gaze back onto itself.

If this were all that Marion had to say about the idol, the necessity (let alone the novelty) of his particular phenomenological approach would remain questionable. For what would this supply that was not already articulated by all those who have regarded the divine as a mere projection, construction, or reflection of humanity? What would a phenomenology of the idol add to, say, Feuerbach's judgment in *The Essence of Christianity* that "man is the original of his idol"? (GWB 16). In fact, the real contribution of Marion's analysis does not consist in his discovery of the idol's so-called mirror function (i.e., the manner in which the idol reduces the divine to the limitations of the human gaze); rather, the real contribution of his analysis has to do with what he refers to as the "invisibility" of this mirror function (i.e., why and how the mirror function remains obfuscated by the idol itself). In fact, such an account would seem to be absolutely essential for any theory—Feuerbach's to be sure, but also Freud's—that regards the divine as a projection of human consciousness. After all, what could account for the emergence of the idol in the first place, if the idolater him- or herself were to recognize in it nothing more than a reflection of his or her own gaze? Why would the idol continue to captivate and dazzle this gaze?

Here is where Marion's phenomenological analysis proves to be most instructive: he seeks to demonstrate that although the gaze is "reflected" in the idol, the gaze nevertheless does not recognize this reflection as the reflection *of itself*. What is at issue, then, is not only the mirror function, but the apparent *invisibility* of this mirror function. Marion describes the situation in the following terms:

> The idol, as a function of the gaze, reflects the gaze's scope. *But the idol does not at once manifest its role and status as mirror*. For the idol, precisely because

it fixes upon itself the light and the scope of the gaze, shines immediately with a brilliance by definition equal (at least) to what this gaze can see; since the idol fills the gaze, it saturates it with visibility, hence dazzles it; *the mirror function obscures itself precisely by virtue of the spectacle function*. The idol masks the mirror because it fills the gaze. (GWB, 12)

The idol exploits what one might call (though Marion does not) the narcissistic potentialities of the gaze itself—for like Narcissus, the human gaze remains dazzled by its own image. The gaze remains incapable of recognizing itself in (or *as*) the idol for the very reason that it remains mesmerized by its own image, its own reflection. This fixation prevents or blocks any recognition of the idol's reflective character.

Consequently, the idol is said to "stop the gaze" precisely because it satiates the gaze. As Marion writes, "we could not do better than to say, to stop a gaze, allow it to rest (itself) in/on an idol, when it can no longer pass beyond. In this stop, the gaze ceases to overshoot and transpierce itself, hence it ceases to transpierce visible things, in order to pause in the splendor of one of them [. . .] The gaze lets itself be filled" and "stopped," and the "idol concretized that stop" (GWB 11). In other words, the idol not only *reflects* the image of the gaze, it also *limits*, or more accurately, *de-limits* the scope of the gaze. In addition to being a reflection of the human gaze (a point already emphasized by the likes of Feuerbach), the idol also *delimits* the gaze and thereby prevents it from envisioning the divine as such. As this equilibrium between the idol and the gaze immediately suggests, the idol offers a certain confirmation of the scope of the gaze. Thus, while the gaze measures and delimits the scope of the idol, the reverse is equally true: the idol in turn measures and restricts the gaze. "[M]ore than just any spectacle," the gaze discovers in the idol "its own limit and proper place." Moreover, though the mirror remains invisible, it is nevertheless seen. In fact, Marion insists that in the case of the idol, *nothing but* the mirror is seen. The idolatrous reflection is said to be invisible, not because it is *not* seen, but rather because "the brilliance of its light" limits our aim and prevents us from recognizing that which is *genuinely invisible* (GWB 13).

Marion's complex line of argumentation here warrants our most scrupulous attention, as it offers a first sketch of what he means (or rather does *not* mean) by revelation. "[T]he idol offers the gaze its earth [or ground]—the first earth upon which it can rest. In the idol the gaze is buried. The idol would be disqualified thus, vis-à-vis a *revelation*, not at all because it would offer the gaze an illegitimate spectacle, but first because it suggests to the gaze where to rest (itself)" (GWB 13). The idol is said to exclude (or "disqualify") revelation, precisely because it serves to divvy up the invisible into the visible, on the one hand, and the "*invisable*," on the other. In this regard, the idol dupes us in two ways: First, it dupes us into regarding (and thereby reducing) the invisible as (or in terms of) the visible. The idol conceals the invisible *as such* precisely because it claims or pretends to make the so-called invisible appear within the space opened up by its own gaze, its own horizon. In short, it reduces the invisible to what appears, to what is immanent. Secondly, and correlatively, the idol conceals the invisible *as such* by restricting our aim to that which is subject to visibility. In order to articulate this point, Marion coins a new term, namely, the *invisable*, whose deliberate association with the French verb *viser* ("to aim at") suggests something like: 'that which cannot be aimed at,' or simply the 'un-aimable.' "With the idol, the invisible mirror admits no beyond because the gaze cannot raise the sight of its aim" (GWB 13). By restricting our aim, the idol provokes what might best be described as a hubris of vision—a blissful naïveté which convinces itself that nothing lies beyond its grasp, beyond what is already in grasp. Here, again, we might invoke the image of Narcissus, whose fixation with what is seen (namely, his own reflection) prevents him from *trans*fixing it—from piercing or "transpiercing" it. Fixation blocks transfixion. That is to say, the fixation with the icon prevents the gaze from seeing more, from taking its eyes off of the image in order to see *more*, in order to see what lies *beyond* it, in order to see something truly other. It is this fixation which prevents that which is truly beyond sight (the invisible as such) from being recognized or, rather, from being respected in its alterity: "With the idol, the invisible mirror admits no beyond, because that gaze cannot raise the sight of its aim" (GWB 13). By rendering the invisible *invisable*, the idol prevents one from envisioning (or aiming at) the invisible *as such*: "the aim no longer aims beyond, but rebounds upon a mirror [. . .] towards itself" (GWB 26). Thus, to sum up Marion's twofold argument, it could be said that in the first instance, the idol simply reduces the invisible to the visible, while in the second instance, the idol reduces the invisible to the *invisable*. As Marion observes, "That the invisible should remain invisible or that it should become visible amounts to the same thing, namely, to the idol, whose precise function consists in dividing the invisible into one part that is reduced to the visible and one part that is obfuscated as *invisable*" (GWB 17–18).

As we might expect, Marion defines the icon in strict opposition to the idol, whereby the former exhibits a precise inversion of the essential moments of the latter.[43] However, the complexity of his characterization of the idol (i.e., as an invisible mirror) does not permit him to characterize this opposition in terms of some straightforward reversal. We must, once again, pay careful attention to the phenomenological details of his analysis.

Marion begins with the formula found in Colossians 1:15, according to which Christ is said to be the "icon of the invisible God."[44] The icon is thereby associated primarily with the invisible, rather than with the visible.

However, like the idol, it, too, must find support within the sphere of the visible—for it, too, consists of wood and paint. The difference, of course, has to do with the manner in which the invisible and visible are brought into relation (or, as we shall see in the case of the icon, into a relation-without-relation, to borrow an expression from Levinas). Marion begins by drawing the following contrast: "Whereas the idol results from the gaze that aims at it, the icon summons sight in letting the visible [. . .] be saturated little by little with the invisible" (GWB 17). This suggestion immediately begs the question: How is the invisible supposed to enter into (let alone "saturate") the icon without reducing the invisible to the visible and, therefore, without committing idolatry in the strictest sense, that is, in the sense which Marion himself gives it?

Marion does not shy away from this aporia, which, in fact, sets in motion his new style of theological reflection. The first thing to be noted here is that Marion employs not one, but two senses of the invisible, and that the invisibility pertaining to the icon should therefore not be confused with the impoverished kind of invisibility which results from the stilted gaze of the idol. Why? Because in the case of the idol, the invisibility of the so-called invisible was either (a) entirely abolished by being reduced to the domain of visibility or (b) it arose from a deficiency on the side of the aim of the gaze, rather than from the invisible as such (in other words, it was invisible only insofar as "it was omitted by the aim [*invisable*]") (GWB 17). In either case, the supposed invisibility did not issue from the invisible as such. "The icon, on the contrary, attempts to render visible the invisible as such, hence to allow that the visible not cease to refer to an other than itself, without, however, that other ever being reproduced in the visible" (GWB 18).

It is only by appealing to the conciliar definition of the icon—which confirms the "theological status of the icon" on the basis of a notion of the *hupostasis* rather than *ousia*—that Marion is finally able to justify this most audacious (even paradoxical) of theses: namely, that the icon renders visible the invisible as such, though without reducing the invisible to the visible (GWB 18). According to the definition established at the Second Council of Nicea, the veneration of icons, properly understood, is not directed toward a "substantial presence" (which is reserved only for the Eucharist) but rather toward a "hypostasis of the one who is inscribed in it."[45] The crucial point here is that *hupostasis*—which, Marion emphasizes, the Latin Fathers translate as *persona*—is not deployed in terms of a substantial presence [*ousia*], but in terms of a *face* (GWB 18): "[. . .] the *persona* attested its presence only by that which itself most properly characterized it, the aim of the intention (*stokhasma*) that a gaze sets in operation. The icon lays out the material of wood and paint in such a way that there appears in them the intention of a transpiercing gaze emanating from them" (GWB 19).

Thus, "with a confounding phenomenological precision" the icon inverts the essential moments of the idol (GWB 21). This gaze no longer belongs to the subject—from which it had previously proceeded from and rebounded upon—but belongs instead to the icon itself: "If man, by his gaze, renders the idol possible, in reverent contemplation of the icon, on the contrary, the gaze of the invisible, in person, aims at man" (GWB 18). The face shows itself by concealing itself—it does not bring the invisible into the domain of the visible, but rather it allows the visible (face) to indicate or reveal a depth (the intention or gaze of the other) which is invisible as such, which can never be made visible. Thus, the relation between the visible and invisible in the icon is marked by a paradoxical and wholly inverse proportionality: the more that the face reveals the gaze of the other (the more that the visible and invisible are brought into unity), the more that the invisible is respected as such and held at an *absolute* distance from the visible.[46] This complex conceptual montage, whereby the icon is first defined in terms of *hypostasis*, then translated as *persona*, and finally interpreted as *face*, allows Marion to escape from the paralyzing dichotomy that would force him to choose between mere *presence* (in which the invisible is reduced to the visible) and mere *absence* (in which the invisible is dismissed as *invisable*, as that which is omitted from our aim).[47]

6. FIRST CONCEPTUAL IDOL: ONTO-THEOLOGY

Having articulated a precise phenomenological distinction between the idol and the icon at the level of the aesthetic object, Marion proceeds to the level of the concept, where it becomes a question of the thought rather than the material representation of God. It is not hard to envision what he might mean by a conceptual equivalent of the aesthetic idol. In fact, Marion's first thesis, simply put, is that "every conceptual discourse on God"—whether it be theological or a-theological (such as Nietzsche's)[48]—involves a certain degree of idolatry, since in such discourses the divine would be measured by concepts that are constructed by and thus limited to the scope of the philosopher's gaze (GWB 33). It is, however, much more difficult to imagine just what Marion might mean by a conceptual icon. How could God be signified by a concept without being strangled by a conceptual grasp? How could one envision a non-idolatrous conceptual discourse on God?

Marion's problematic, in fact, bears a striking resemblance to the one pursued by Heidegger in his lecture course on "The Introduction to the Phenomenology of Religion," where it was a matter of working out the appropriate manner of treating a subject (in that case, the early Christian eschatological experience expressed in Paul's *Epistles*) which defied conceptual determination in the classical sense. For Heidegger, the problem, as well as the solution—i.e., the so-called formal indication which, as we noted in chapter 2, he would never fully work out—could only be understood in relation to a classical, indeed metaphysical, theory of the concept. Though Marion does not invoke a method of formal indication, he does employ this general strategy of pushing forward by means of turning his reader's attention backward (a strategy most appropriate for radical phenomenology). Just as Marion had argued that the significance of phenomenology could only be measured against the backdrop of metaphysics, so it is the case with the conceptual icon. We can only come to understand what a conceptual icon might entail if we are first of all keenly attuned to the conceptual idolatry constitutive of metaphysical thinking. The implication here seems to be that by providing a rigorous definition of metaphysics' most determinative conceptual idol (i.e., onto-theology), we thereby indicate the limits or boundaries of conceptual idolatry as a whole and, therefore, catch sight of a space beyond those limits in which a non-idolatrous form of philosophical thought may finally become possible (and, indeed, *conceivable*).

It is no surprise, then, that in his initial gesture toward a non-idolatrous, yet philosophically rigorous (dare we say conceptual?) discourse on God, Marion makes an explicit appeal to Heideggerian thought—albeit not to Heidegger's theory of the formal indication, but to his formulation of the ontological difference and his diagnosis of the onto-theo-logical constitution of metaphysics. "We also admit that ontological difference is operative in metaphysical thought only in the forgetful figure of a thought of Being (thought summoned to and by Being) that, each time, keeps ontological difference unthought as such" (GWB 34). Thus, even while posing the question "*ti to on?*" (what is Being?), metaphysics fails to think of Being as such. In its forgetfulness of ontological difference (the difference between beings, or ontic entities, and Being as such), the question about Being is mistaken for a question about a particular being (an entity)—namely, that being which could secure or serve as a foundation for all other beings. Thus (mis)understood, the question concerning Being finds its answer or resolution in the formulation of an *ens supremum*, which is "itself understood and posited starting from the requirement, decisive for being, of the foundation" (GWB 34). Hence Heidegger's claim that "[t]he onto-theological constitution of metaphysics stems from the prevalence of that difference which keeps Being as the found, and beings as what is grounded and what gives account, apart from and related to each other."[49] Marion also admits along with Heidegger that, in modernity, the *ens supremum* receives its most decisive definition with the *causa sui*—variously expressed in Descartes, Spinoza, Leibniz, and, Marion notes, "even Hegel" (GWB 35). The concept of God that emerges within modern philosophy evidently "arises less from God himself than from metaphysics"—from its forgetfulness of Being as such, and of ontological difference (GWB 34).

But this concept of "God" is no longer charged with a vague or intangible criticism (namely, that it is limited to the conceptual aim or gaze of the philosopher). On the contrary, Marion has, with the help of Heidegger, determined this idolatrous concept in a decisive manner: "the conceptual idol has a site, metaphysics [i.e., insofar as this mode of thought is characterized by a forgetfulness of the ontological difference]; a function, the theo-logy in onto-theology [i.e., insofar as it constitutes the being par excellence which founds all other beings]; and a definition, *causa sui* [i.e., insofar as this being is finally deployed in terms of causal efficiency]" (GWB 36). With this precise determination in view, we have been brought (or so it seems) directly before the borderline that demarcates an idolatrous thought of "God" from a (potentially) non-idolatrous thought of God.

> [B]y thinking "God" as an efficiency so absolutely and universally foundational that it can be conceived only starting from the foundation, and hence finally as the withdrawal of the foundation into itself, metaphysics indeed constructs for itself an apprehension of the transcendence of God, but under the figure simply of efficiency, of the cause, and of the foundation. Such an apprehension can claim legitimacy only on condition of also recognizing its limit. Heidegger draws out this limit very exactly: 'Man can neither pray nor sacrifice to this God. Before the *causa sui*, man can neither fall to his knees in awe nor can he play music and dance before this god.' (GWB 35)[50]

Heidegger provides Marion with the first approach, the first attempt to pass beyond this limit and to engage a genuine thought of God beyond being—being, that is, as an entity or mere concept. It is in this context that Heidegger's talk of a godless-thinking must be understood. By eliminating all reference to "God," godless-thinking actually draws us closer to the divine than any metaphysical thought ever could. What is at stake here has nothing at all to do with atheism, which remains thoroughly metaphysical. Marion notes that every attempt to prove or *disprove* God's existence begins and ends with a concept, which is only subsequently (in a move which is constitutive of every kind of conceptual idolatry) equated with "God."

> Every proof, in fact, demonstrative as it may appear, can lead only to the concept; it remains for it then to go beyond itself, so to speak, and to identify this concept with God himself. Saint Thomas implements such an identification by an "*id quod omnes nominunt*," repeated at the end of each of his *viae* (*Summa theologica* Ia, q. 2, a. 3), as Aristotle concluded the demonstration of Metaphysics (A:7) by *touto gar ho theos* "for this is the god" (1:072b29-30), and as, above all, Leibniz ended at the principle of reason asking, "See at present if that which we have just discovered must not be called God." Proof uses

positively what conceptual atheism uses negatively: in both cases, equivalence to a concept transforms God into "God" [. . .]. (GWB 32–33)

The same goes for Nietzsche's proclamation of the "death of God," which, according to Marion, puts to rest only the "moral concept of God" (*à la* Kant) and not God in and of itself. From the perspective of a thinking (such as Heidegger's) that remains attuned to the ontological difference, traditional talk of the existence or non-existence of God appears naïve, confused, and imprecise since existence is already inevitably misinterpreted in terms of the objective world, that is to say, as one or another ontic entity (be it present-at-hand or ready-to-hand). It would, therefore, appear that by retrieving the question of Being as such from its metaphysical oblivion, Heidegger has brought to a close the idolatrous conception of "God" as supreme (ontic) being, preparing the way for a genuine thought of God—minus the quotation marks.

Here, at this precise point in *God Without Being*, we encounter the *theo-logical* equivalent (and indeed precursor) to what Marion will later describe in *Reduction and Givenness* as a *philosophical* radicalization (or "step back") whereby Heidegger surpasses Husserl's earlier attempt at overcoming metaphysics. But it is here and only here, in this properly *theo*-logical milieu, that we can begin to see how and why Marion's analysis requires an *even more radical step back* than the one supplied by Heidegger's ontology. We now turn to Marion's justification for the further step back, this second radicalization.

7. SECOND CONCEPTUAL IDOL: ONTOLOGICAL DIFFERENCE

So far, Marion's reading of Heidegger suggests that the horizon of Being—understood no longer as an ontic entity, but as Being as such—opens up a new space, a new frontier for the philosophical thought of God beyond mere being, and thus beyond conceptual idolatry. Or so it would seem. In truth, Marion's understanding of the relationship between Heideggerian ontology and conceptual idolatry is vastly more complicated.

> Does the overcoming of idolatry summon us to retrocede out of metaphysics, in the sense that *Sein und Zeit* attempts a step back toward Being as such by the meditation of its essential temporality? Does retroceding from metaphysics, supposing already that in doing so there arrives the thought devoted to Being as Being, suffice to free God from idolatry—for does idolatry come to completion with the *causa sui*, or, on the contrary, does the idolatry of the *causa sui* not

refer, as an indication only, to another idolatry, more discrete, more pressing, and therefore all the more threatening? (GWB 37)

"[T]he problematic of idolatry, far from falling here into disuse [that is to say, far from being surmounted], finds the true terrain of radical discussion when it encounters the attempt of a thought of Being as Being" (GWB 37). Instead of being surmounted once and for all in Heidegger, idolatry is simply reduplicated at a more radical, more obscure level (GWB 38). Idolatry, according to Marion, no longer makes its appearance at the already-surpassed level of onto-theology, where God is given the metaphysical definition of *causa sui*, but at the level of the ontological difference itself, where it finds its ultimate site, its "true terrain."

On what grounds does Marion make such a claim? In fact, we have already encountered the fundamental reasons for this assertion in Chapter 2 when we examined Heidegger's conception of the relationship between revelation and the dimension of Being. Though Heidegger is careful to keep God *as such* free from ontology, he nevertheless claims that God's *revelation* is contained or conditioned by "the dimension of Being," by "revealability," by the existential structures of Dasein. God may be above and beyond all matters of Being and ontology, but if God is to be revealed to Dasein, this revelation (*Offenbarung*) must conform to the ontological conditions of experience, that is, to revealability (*Offenbarkeit*). Marion's break with Heidegger therefore concerns, above all, the nature or status of God's *revelation*—the manner in which God is *given*. Whereas Heidegger subjects God's givenness to the ontological difference (which, he claims, conditions every form of givenness, including God's), Marion suggests that the imposition of the ontological difference represents a new, more subtle, and thus all the more dangerous form of conceptual idolatry—one that confines revelation to the horizon of Being. Marion's main point of contention regarding Heidegger has to do specifically with *revelation*. If onto-theology involved an idolatrous concept of "God," ontological difference lends itself to an idolatrous conception of revelation. This would already explain why Marion's attempt to radicalize and thereby surpass Heideggerian phenomenology will require him to make an appeal to the category of revelation, to a revelation that is no longer caught in the balance of the ontological difference.

We must once again proceed with caution, so as not to conflate the problems associated with onto-theology—that is to say, problems arising from the identification of God with an ontic being (even if the highest such being)—with the demands that the ontological difference places on Heidegger's own attempt to think of God as such—that is, to think of God apart from questions of God's existence or being. And we must be equally careful not to overstate or misplace the point of divergence between Marion and Heidegger. Like

Marion himself, Heidegger had insisted that God *as such* not be confined, defined, or delimited by Being (for such a delimitation would place him right back into the onto-theological problematic). As evidence of this position, we may cite once more Heidegger's 1951 response to the question about the relation between God and Being: "I would never attempt to think the essence of God by means of Being."[51] On this point, Marion seems to be following more than departing from Heidegger's position. But Marion believes that the Heideggerian divorce between Being and God comes at too high a price: namely, at the price of excluding all talk of God *as such* from properly philosophical discourse. God could only enter into this discourse on the condition that God also enter into the game of ontological difference, that God be revealed in the light of Being and, thus, according to the fundamental ontological conditions of revealability (*Offenbarkeit*)—and this, of course, would place limits on God's self-manifestation. Thus, rather than freeing up a space for a genuine thought of God (minus the quotation marks), Heidegger's critique of onto-theology imposes a certain silence upon theology (a silence that Marion, for his part, will refuse to keep). By casting God as such outside ontological discourse, Heidegger essentially abandons *theo*-logical discourse (discourse about God as such) to the dogs, so to speak. (In fact, our reference to "dogs" is by no means accidental. For, in at least one important sense, Heidegger's treatment of God bears a striking resemblance to Hegel's dismissal of Schleiermacher's feeling of absolute dependence as a low watermark of human experience, one that is said to be shared by and most appropriate for non-rational creatures, such as dogs. God, like that feeling to which Schleiermacher had once appealed, is antithetical to and therefore excluded from conceptual discourse.[52]) This means that if the thought of God were indeed possible, it would be capable of supporting itself only by withdrawing itself from every (rational) form of discourse (philosophical discourse to be sure, but perhaps theological discourse as well). And since the ontological difference is determinative of philosophical discourse, this implies that we must forever keep silent before God.

Marion is willing to admit that Heidegger's own silence concerning God is a productive one, inasmuch as it remains a gesture of overcoming metaphysical idolatry or a mechanism for avoiding onto-theology. However, from Marion's perspective, the true task for theology is not *only* to extricate itself from metaphysical discourse through silence, but to make sense, and indeed to make good, rational (if not even *philosophical*) sense of this extrication itself. "In other words, the highest difficulty does not consist in managing to reach, with [. . .] Heidegger, a guarded silence with regard to God. The greatest difficulty doubtless consists more essentially in deciding what silence says" (GWB 54). Heidegger, on the other hand, is satisfied with casting God outside of Being. He pays "so much attention to securing the place where only silence is suitable that [he does] not yet try to determine the stakes and the nature of this silence" (GWB 54).

On Marion's account, it appears as if two different senses or moments of silence are at work within Heidegger's texts. The first silence manages to rescue God from the "pious chattering" of onto-theological discourse, and thereby saves God from falling into being, into its idolatrous concept of "God" as *causa sui* or supreme being. This first silence, then, would consist of a certain reverence toward God. The second silence consists of silencing the first reverential moment of silence. This silence bars reverential silence from becoming the object of thought.[53] Marion rejects this second moment of silence—the "silence concerning silence"—in favor of a discourse *on* the first silence. In fact, he argues that the only way to "keep silent" in the first sense of the word (i.e., the only way to honor God) is to *not stop speaking about this silence*: "In order to keep silent with regard to God, one must, if not hold a discourse on God, at least hold a discourse worthy of God on our silence itself" (GWB 54).

Nevertheless, "Keeping our silence, in order precisely by this reserve to honor that which we would designate by silence—in other words, in this case, God—this would be thinkable only if God exposed himself to thought," that is, only if revelation were deployed in a manner which would not, in turn, be subject to the rule of Being, to the ontological difference (GWB 57). Heidegger seems to have excluded this very possibility. Why? Because even though he may no longer define theology in terms of a science of a purely ontic being (i.e., "God" as supreme being), he nevertheless continues to define theology as an ontic science, and, thus, as a science wholly subordinated to ontology. We have already examined the precise nature of this subordination (as a "one-way filiation" governed by the "logic of presupposition") in Chapter 2, where we examined Heidegger's 1928 lecture on "Phenomenology and Theology." We need not add anything further to that previous discussion. Nevertheless, it is interesting to note that Marion himself not only addresses this very same text, but that he focuses on the very same issue—namely the subordination of theology (as ontic science) to ontology (as fundamental analytic of Dasein).

> [I]f theology does not have "God" for its exclusive formal object [...] how [...] can theology be defined? Heidegger gives theology as such a precise and—to our knowledge—never retracted definition: "Theology [is] the interpretation of the divine word of revelation," or, which here amounts to the same thing, "interpretation of man's Being toward God." Theology therefore does not have to do with "God," in whatever sense one understands him. It has to do with the fact (*Factum/Positivität*) of faith in the Crucified, a fact that only faith receives and

conceives: it secures its scientificity only by fixing itself on the positive fact of faith, namely, the relation of the believer to the Crucified. (GWB 65)

Marion does not fail to recognize the repercussions of Heidegger's definition: Whereas fundamental ontology concerns the basic existential structures of Dasein, theology, as the science of faith, concerns itself with only one particular, ontic "way" of Dasein. Since the "invariant of *Dasein* appears more essential to man than the ontic variant introduced by faith," "man can eventually become a believer only inasmuch as he exists first as *Dasein*" (GWB 68). Accordingly, theology can go about its business only by measuring "the disparity that its believing variant imposes on *Dasein*" (GWB 67). Marion characterizes Heidegger's attitude toward theology as follows: "Being expresses itself more essentially than any theology can ever glimpse; and for this very reason every theology remains subjected to the question of Being, as every ontic variant of *Dasein* refers back to bare *Dasein* itself" (GWB 68). Theology's illicit affair with onto-theology is broken, but only on the condition of entering into a new and entirely inequitable relationship with fundamental ontology.

Just because Heidegger has freed theology from the speculative, metaphysical science of God *as* an ontic being, *as causa sui*, and has thereby destroyed the first, onto-theological form of idolatry, this does not mean he has altogether freed the thought of God from the reign of Being as such. Even if Heidegger is willing to admit that God is not subject to ontology, to "the dimension of Being," the manner in which God becomes disclosed (or revealed) in and through faith most certainly is. In other words, God's revelation is still wholly determined by the ontological difference. Consequently, when Heidegger defines theology's *positum* as the founding disclosure of faith (i.e., revelation) rather than God as such, he does not free theology from ontology, but rather he places it squarely within ontology's jurisdiction.[54]

The appearance of this second—albeit ontological rather than onto-theological—form of idolatry forces us to wonder why Marion had sought the support of Heidegger in the first place. What could be gleaned from this idolatrous mode of thought for a non-idolatrous thought of God? Why appeal to Heidegger, if the ontological difference leads to such an impasse? What motivated Marion's decision in *God Without Being* to proceed by way of Heidegger's fundamental ontology when other more tenable paths seem to be readily available—such as, for instance, the one offered by Emmanuel Levinas, whose ethical enterprise subordinates Heideggerian ontology and the grasp of Being to our relation toward the Other, and toward the divine. Marion would, no doubt, respond by insisting upon the definitiveness of the ontological difference for (almost) all modes of thought. In a remarkable passage from his earlier work, *The Idol and Distance*, Marion argues that all previous attempts to overcome ontological difference (not only Levinas's, but also Derrida's) have yielded premature results, landing them straight back into the fold of being/Being. It is claimed, for example, that Levinas had accomplished his task by means of a "mere inversion," that is to say, by placing one's ethical and/or religious relation to an ontic *being* (i.e., the Other or the divine) *over and above* one's relation to (neuter) *Being*. However, "the condition imposed on the divine/the Other by Being does not disappear if one appeals against it only to a particular being [. . .] because one risks thus remaining, with a mere inversion, within the ontological difference, and hence within onto-theology."[55] Derrida, too, is said to remain within the ontological difference, insofar as his formulation of *différance* consists of a mere generalization of ontological difference: "To outwit Being thus would require more than the revocation of ontological difference in favor of another difference" (GWB 85).[56] In order to escape ontological difference, it is not enough to invert the opposed terms, nor is it enough to abstract or generalize the differential relation itself. On the contrary, Marion suggests that an escape becomes possible only by first digging beneath that difference.

The *radicality* of ontological difference can neither be ignored, nor passed over lightly. "Ontological difference, *almost* indispensable to all thought, presents itself thus as a *negative* propaedeutic of the unthinkable thought of God. It is the ultimate idol, the most dangerous but also the most educational and, in its own way, profitable [. . .]" (GWB 45–6). It is profitable because it marks the true limit or borderline beyond which a non-idolatrous thought of God may finally become possible. But this border can be crossed only through a further radicalization of Heidegger's already radical project.

> Or again, does not the search for the 'more divine god' oblige one, more than to go beyond onto-theo-logy, to go beyond ontological difference as well, in short no longer to attempt to think God in view of a being [i.e., onto-theo-logy], because one will have renounced, to begin with, thinking him on the basis of Being [i.e., ontological difference]? To think God without any conditions, not even that of Being, hence to think God without pretending to inscribe him or to describe him as being. (GWB 44–45)

If, by his radical style of questioning, Heidegger managed to free God from the horizon of the object (being), Marion needs to develop an all the more radical approach in order to free God from the horizon of Being. The first radicalization calls for a second, more radical radicalization.

8. REVELATION: A GIFT ANTERIOR TO BEING/BEINGS

Marion's radicalization of phenomenology requires—at least within the orbit of his theological writings—a direct appeal to biblical *revelation*. This, as we have already noted, is hardly surprising. After all, revelation itself marks the site of Marion's strongest disagreement with Heidegger, since the idolatry implied by ontological difference concerns God's revelation more than it does God as such. What is at stake is, above all, the possibility of an instance (revelation) that is anterior to ontological difference itself. This instance must neither be opposed to such difference nor subject to its operation, but must remain essentially indifferent to the difference itself. Marion highlights three biblical texts that at least allow us to attempt a formulation of such an anterior instance. It would be all too easy to lose ourselves within the lush forest of his biblical exegesis. So as not to lose the tracks of our own investigation, we will limit ourselves to but one (indeed, the first) example, Romans 4:17, where God is designated as the one "who gives life to the dead and who calls the non-beings as beings, *kalountos ta mē onta hōs onta*" (GWB 86–89). Marion's interest in this passage lies in the second designation, which apparently "redoubles" the first, but does so within a "new, even strange" philosophical lexicon. It is, then, in light of this alien, philosophical—indeed, Aristotelian—discourse that Marion risks an interpretation. The passage, he suggests, calls to mind Aristotle's rejection of the possibility of any transformation from non-being to being, on the grounds that all changes require some material substratum. According to Aristotle, the appearance of any (ostensible) absolute generation (creation *ex nihilo*) stems from our lack of knowledge concerning the substratum of the change. In short, something (being) cannot come from nothing (non-being). Or, so it stands with the philosopher. But what about the knight of faith—an Abraham or a Paul? In fact, Marion insists that it is not here a matter of conceiving of such a change, of rending this change acceptable to reason: "the [possibility of such a] transition does not depend in any way on the conception of Paul" (GWB 87).

> Furthermore, if this transition can be conceived neither by Paul, by Abraham, nor by any man whomsoever, this results from another impossibility: this transition does not arise from the (*me*) *onta* that it nevertheless affects most intimately. The *onta* do not dispose here of any "principle of change within themselves," of any intrinsic potentiality that would require or prepare its completion. The transition befalls them from the outside; the transition from nonbeing to being goes right through them, issues from this side and proceeding beyond [. . .] (GWB 87)

That this call, which "calls the nonbeings as beings" gives, produces, or brings about this transition without the assistance of "any intrinsic potentiality" on the side of the one who is called (i.e., the nonbeing or being), seems to indicate that it is deployed indifferently to the difference between being and non-being—indifferently, that is, to the "wisdom of the world," the logic of the philosopher, and, above all, the ontological difference itself. "It is important," Marion insists, "to point out here this unique attainment: biblical revelation offers, in some rare texts, the emergence of a certain indifference of being to Being; being thus makes sport of Being only in outwitting ontological difference; [revelation] outwits [ontological difference] only inasmuch as [ontological difference] is first distorted by another instance, the gift" (GWB 101).

Having taken stock of this "unique attainment," whereby the gift (*agape*) is said to outwit Being/beings through a kind of indifference to ontological difference, Marion goes one step further:

> The gift crosses Being/beings: it meets it, strikes it out with a mark [a cross nonetheless], finally opens it, as a window casement opens, on an instance that remains unspeakable according to the language of Being—supposing that another language might be conceived. To open Being/beings to the instance of a gift implies then, at the least, that the gift may decide Being/beings. In other words, the gift is not at all laid out according to Being/beings, but Being/being is given according to the gift. *The gift delivers Being/being.* (GWB 101)

Revelation (as gift) precedes, founds, delivers, brings into play both beings and Being itself. In other words, Marion's conception of the relation between the gift and Being betrays the same, essentially Heideggerian apparatus that I have called, following Derrida, a "logic of presupposition" (above, Chapter 2). That is to say, the gift's indifference to the ontological difference is itself modeled after—or at least retains the residual structure of—the indifference that Heidegger had claimed Being displays toward beings. And, moreover, the same relation of conditionality also seems to hold: the gift becomes an insurmountable condition of possibility for Being/beings, in much the same way that Being had previously conditioned all ontic beings.[57]

I will return to these issues in a moment. But, for now, it is enough to note that we have finally reached a position from which the third and last phase in Marion's threefold schematism of the phenomenological reduction begins to make sense. Marion's "step back" is modeled with astonishing precision after Heidegger's own "step back." We had seen above how, according to Marion, the first (Husserlian) reduction was confined to the horizon of the object (of beings), which was then radicalized by Heidegger, who extended its scope to the level of Being as such. Now, Marion's reduction calls for a second radicalization, by means of which it can finally reach the level of givenness as such, the gift, or revelation.

All of this clearly suggests that Marion's philosophical project hinges upon an indisputably theological (even biblical) reference. This apparent recourse to revealed theology has been the source of much of the controversy—but also much of the interest—surrounding Marion's "purely" philosophical (i.e., non-theological) work. This work, comprised of three major texts—*Reduction and Givenness*, *Being Given*, and *In Excess*, all of which succeeded *God Without Being*—had to be defended against the charge that it was based solely on theological presuppositions, which would undermine or weaken its philosophical legitimacy. Marion's strictly phenomenological project was occupied, from its very inception, with the task of dispelling the view that his new version of the phenomenological reduction might be limited to merely theological (indeed, Christian) applications. One might go as far as to say that one of Marion's primary objectives in his strictly philosophical work is to cover over the theological tracks left behind by his earlier, explicitly theological projects in *The Idol and Distance* and *God Without Being*. And, in one sense, the schematism of the three reductions, which has provided the overarching framework for my reading of Marion in this chapter, must be regarded as one such attempt. For once the basic framework has been established, the schematism allows Marion to make the case that his own reduction (i.e., the reduction to pure givenness) receives its momentum and, thus, its legitimacy from developments within the field of phenomenology itself. It is, therefore, no surprise that his opponents have sought to undermine or dismantle this basic infrastructure.[58]

However vulnerable Marion's proposed schematism may in fact be, my line of inquiry follows a different tack, one that remains in general continuity with our analysis of Heidegger's radical phenomenology in Chapter 2. We are once more confronted with the correlative problems of *contamination* and *counter-contamination*. For just as Derrida, de Vries, and other postmodern interpreters had suspected that Heidegger's existential analytic was contaminated by certain Christian motifs, Marion faces accusations from all sides regarding what appears to be an underlying theological bias or "contamination." Once again, it is not our task here to assess the legitimacy or illegitimacy of these accusations, let alone to pass judgment about the validity or invalidity of Marion's project as a whole. Instead, we are interested in bringing to the surface a tension that is inherent (though never made explicit) within Marion's texts themselves.

Interestingly, the tension in question seems to have been unwittingly inherited (as a residual by-product as it were) from that mode of thinking which Marion sought most to overcome, namely, Heideggerian ontology. Our thesis regarding Marion remains structurally analogous to the one we advanced in the preceding chapter: Like Heidegger, Marion's effort to overcome charges of theological contamination leads him to adopt a strategy whereby revelation is divested of its material content. This process of "hollowing out" revelation leads to a merely formal conception of revelation—one that is essentially devoid of any reference to the historical, linguistic, and textual richness of revelation in its religious or theological acceptations. Rather than describing this procedure in terms of a divestment or "hollowing out," Marion portrays it in terms of a purification of revelation—that is, in terms of a reduction to the "pure" call or the call as such (i.e., revelation). This alleged "purity" serves a dual purpose in Marion's work. (1) On the one hand, it serves to guarantee the integrity of his strictly phenomenological analysis, insofar as the call's indetermination rescues it from becoming identified with the call of the Father, the call of God, or any other theological assertion. The purity of the call, therefore, permits the phenomenologist to describe the structural features of revelation without presupposing the existence of a genuine event of revelation. (2) On the other hand, the purity of the call is thought to guarantee the integrity of the religious phenomenon itself, since any determination or "denomination" of the call would (Marion argues) yield to an idolatrous concept of God limited to a finite nomination. Our analysis concerns the interplay, cross-fertilization, or inter-contamination between these two functions, which we will explore in much greater depth in the following two sections (9–10). Nevertheless, in order to bring this complex interplay between philosophy and theology (or revelation and Revelation) into view, we will first need to sketch some of the most pertinent features of Marion's "strictly" philosophical account of the gift: the saturated phenomenon, the gifted (*l'adonné*), and the anonymous or "pure" call.

9. THE PHENOMENOLOGICAL "FIGURE" OF REVELATION

As we saw earlier in this chapter, Marion had claimed that the Husserlian phenomenon "suffer[s] from a deficit of intuition, and thus from a shortage of [givenness]." Intuition always needs to be supplemented by an intentional gaze that would, so to speak, fill in the gaps. Marion's single best-known contribution to phenomenological philosophy consists in the advancing of a hypothesis which Husserl seems to have overlooked:

> Having arrived at this point, we can pose the question of a strictly inverse hypothesis: In certain cases still to be defined, must we not oppose to the restricted possibility of a phenomenality that is in the end absolutely possible? To the phenomenon that is supposed to be poor in intuition can we not oppose a phenomenon that is saturated with intuition? To the phenomenon that is most often characterized by a defect of intuition . . . why would there not correspond

the possibility of a phenomenon in which intuition would give *more, indeed, immeasurably more*, than intention ever would have intended or foreseen?[59]

But, we must ask, what is the "more" to which he refers? What sort of phenomenon is it that is still to be defined? Marion's answer lies in his formulation of the so-called saturated phenomenon.[60] The saturated phenomenon is characterized by an excess of intuition which "subverts and therefore precedes every intention that it exceeds and decenters" (BG 267). It cannot be controlled or neutralized by a conscious subject, and it cannot be reduced to or preceded by any horizon—not even by the horizon of Being (Heidegger), let alone that of objectivity (Husserl). According to Marion, the very possibility of such saturation represents the "conceptual completion of the most operative definition of the phenomenon" and thus also of phenomenology, since "it alone appears as itself, of itself, and starting from itself, since it alone appears without limits of a horizon and without the reduction to an *I*."[61]

In several different texts, Marion supplies a basic table of such saturated phenomenon, which typically includes four different types, each one corresponding to, and exceeding the scope of, one of the Kantian categories of the understanding. The saturated phenomena is said to be "invisable (unforeseeable) according to quantity, unbearable according to quality, but also unconditioned (absolved from any horizon) according to relation, and irreducible to the I (incapable of being looked at) according to modality."[62] We need not occupy ourselves with the details of each. For what is most significant for our purposes here is Marion's insistence on a fifth type—namely, *revelation*—which is said to concentrate, encompass, and therefore surpass all of the preceding four types. This so-called saturation of saturation entails such a degree of givenness that it frustrates and exceeds even the four previous figures of saturation. And, yet, Marion insists it is possible to provide a strictly phenomenological articulation of it, under the rubric of the saturated phenomenon *par excellence*—revelation (BG 235).

Marion is well aware of the stakes and indeed risks of this analysis. For even his most sympathetic readers may be suspicious of this explicit (and dare we say illicit) appeal to the theological category of revelation. Seeking to avoid impending charges of theological contamination, Marion offers his readers a telling (albeit brief) *apologia* for his analysis, founded on a distinction between *r*evelation and *R*evelation—a distinction which, he says, "I will scrupulously respect [. . .] by its graphic mark" (BG 367). Phenomenology, according to Marion, is properly concerned only with *possibilities*, not *actualities*. With respect to the phenomenon of revelation, the sole task of the phenomenologist would be to account for the mere possibility of such an experience, without having to presuppose or posit its actuality. This purely phenomenological account can and indeed must be given without having to assert the actual historical existence of any particular *R*evelation. Marion claims that his only responsibility as a phenomenologist would be to "describe [*r*evelation] without supposing its actuality, and yet all the while propose a precise figure for it" (BG 235). But, whatever 'precision' his 'figure' of revelation may indeed possess, it has received only from the phenomenological tradition itself. That is to say, his definition of revelation has not been garnered from an analysis (not even from phenomenological analysis) of scripture, faith, Christian experience, etc.; rather, this supposedly 'precise figure' of revelation arises in response to a specific set of concerns that have emerged within the field of phenomenology itself.

Thus, in seeking to maintain neutrality with respect to any dogmatic or theological assumptions, Marion is compelled to drive a wedge between the description of the phenomenological "figure of revelation" (as *possibility*) and any concrete "event" of Revelation (as *actuality*). In so doing, Marion's text runs the risk of resurrecting a new form of the Heideggerian "logic of presupposition," founded once again upon the distinction between the *Offenbarung* (*R*evelation as a particular, ontic instance or actualization) and *Offenbarkeit* (revealability, or simply *r*evelation, as the transcendental ground which would necessarily determine every actual instance). That Marion at least appears to endorse Heidegger's logic of presupposition and the one-way filiation between theology as "ontic science" and philosophy as "fundamental ontology" is evidenced by his almost shocking affirmation of the Heideggerian formula, according to which the "ontic status" of revelation alone "remain[s] the business proper to revealed theology" (BG 236). But this "logic of presupposition" would reestablish a certain hierarchical relation between revelation and Revelation, and between their two corresponding disciplines, phenomenology and theology. According to this logic, Revelation would be subordinated to revelation (its condition of possibility), a subordination which Marion's theological work had explicitly sought to overturn.

Would Marion have really come this far only to once again impose upon the given the conditions of phenomenalization that he has worked so hard to eliminate? Marion would undoubtedly respond to this charge by insisting that "phenomenology yields to revealed theology" as soon as it becomes a matter of actual revelation (BG 367). However, given the nature of the relation he has just established between revelation and Revelation, it is difficult to view this insistence as anything but a last-ditch effort to preserve, demarcate, or seal off an autonomous domain for the theology of Revelation. Moreover, one might wonder whether this division of labor does not gives rise to another, perhaps even more troubling problem: If phenomenology can establish, in the absence of any particular Revelation, the conditions under which every Revelation could ever occur, then this would mean that phenomenology, as a discipline, would owe nothing to revealed theology. In other words, if phenomenology can describe the figure of revelation regardless of whether or not Revelation has actually taken place, then the phenomenology of revelation could be pursued without having to adopt (either explicitly or implicitly) any particular theological/dogmatic stance regarding the existence or non-existence of such an event—phenomenology would remain totally autonomous.

Revealed theology, on the other hand, would not come out so unscathed, since the very object of revealed theology (i.e., Revelation, as opposed to revelation) would still have to conform to the conditions laid down by phenomenological analysis. Therefore, Marion's own explicit formulation of the distinction between revelation/Revelation and phenomenology/theology raises a question about whether his phenomenological project really provides the "relief for theology" from the oppressive force of metaphysics that he claims it does,[63] or whether it merely confirms Heidegger's earlier decision to subjugate theology to the autonomous rule of phenomenology. In the end, it is difficult to ignore the fact that Marion's text perpetuates certain basic Heideggerian moves, which were initially designed to subjugate theology to a certain phenomenological "correction" or "co-direction" (see Chapter 2, Sections 12–13).

In order to appreciate the gravity of this situation, one need only to consider a single remark from Marion's text—a remark so revealing and so problematic that he, perhaps unconsciously, hid it away in a footnote:

> Phenomenology describes possibilities and never considers the phenomenon of revelation except as a possibility of phenomenality, one that it would formulate in this way: If God were to manifest himself (or manifested himself), he would use a paradox to the second degree [i.e., a saturated phenomenon *par excellence*]. Revelation (of God by himself, *theo*logical), if it takes place, will assume the phenomenal figure of the phenomenon of revelation.[64]

And, he continues: "if an actual revelation must, can, or could have been given in phenomenal apparition, it could have, can, or will be able to do so only by giving itself according to the type of the [saturated phenomenon]—such as I will describe it."[65] Does not this phenomenological "figure" of revelation, which itself prepares a site and therefore a horizon within which every event of revelation would have to come to pass, announce the reappearance of conceptual idolatry—no longer according to the object or Being, but according to the constitutive framework of givenness (albeit a givenness pushed to the limits of rational, phenomenological discourse).[66] It is, no doubt, surprising to see Marion coming so close to adopting the kind of philosophical hubris for which he had previously faulted others. And, yet, his motivations for advancing such an argument are clear: namely, it is advanced in order to circumvent the charge that his phenomenology presupposes the existence of an actual event of Revelation. By taking revelation (rather than Revelation) as his object, Marion seems to believe that his phenomenology has managed to avoid the ever looming threat of theological *contamination*.

It is not at all surprising that Marion's most vocal critics—including Janicaud and Derrida—have seized on this problem of "contamination" (though it is not always couched in the language of contamination *per se*): Does not Marion's analysis of revelation imply or presuppose an actual instance of Revelation? If that were indeed the case, Marion would be vulnerable to the same kind of critique that various deconstructionist thinkers have leveled against Heidegger's existential analytic (see Chapter 2, Section 10). We, however, are concerned with a still more complex or at least more subtle dimension of Marion's project, one that has to do less with the problem of theological contamination than with Marion's most subtle strategy for circumventing, managing, or mitigating such contamination. In the remainder of this chapter, we seek to demonstrate that Marion's project involves a process or strategy of counter-contamination (a strategy whose most formal features have already been sketched in Chapter 2, Section 11) whereby the pure, phenomenological figure of revelation (as formal possibility) exerts a certain pressure upon Revelation (as actual event)—that is to say, this figure not only describes the formal features of any possible Revelation, it imposes a certain "formalism" upon Revelation itself. This formalism, in turn, determines what can legitimately count as Revelation and what would be excluded as mere idolatry. We will see that the only kind of Revelation capable of surviving the test of idolatry is one that is entirely abstracted from its positive, linguistic, and/or textual content under the aegis of a "pure" call. Our line of investigation, then, is less concerned with the philosophical rigor or the phenomenological legitimacy of his phenomenology, than with its capacity to remain "faithful" to the religious phenomenon under examination—namely, Revelation. Our hypothesis is that the methodological exigencies of his phenomenological analysis prevent him from examining "Revelation" in the fullness of its textual-linguistic dimensions.

Again, the question which we are pursuing here resembles (and not just by chance) the one we had explored at the close of the preceding chapter on Heidegger (Chapter 2, Sections 11–13). However, the question is all the more pressing here since Marion makes *revelation*, rather than *Being*, the highest aim and final "horizon" of his philosophical project. In other words, counter-contamination, if it were found to be operative here, would pose an even greater threat for Marion, since he, more than Heidegger, is expressly concerned with preserving the integrity of the religious phenomenon of Revelation.

10. THE PURE CALL: INDETERMINATE, NAMELESS, ANONYMOUS

If we pause to look back over Marion's schematism of the three reductions, it becomes evident that his entire project is predicated upon an inverse relation between the degree of givenness and the activity of the subject: an increase in the subject's activity (whether this involves objectifying acts of intentionality, constitution, naming, etc.) results in a decrease in the degree of givenness. Thus, it comes as no surprise that his attempt to capture maximal givenness, to return to the things themselves or to the gift as it gives itself, entails a radicalization of the passivity on the part of the subject—well beyond the level of passivity envisioned by Husserl's transcendental *I* or Heidegger's thrown *Dasein*.

This is seen most clearly in the final chapter of *Being Given*, where Marion formulates the notion of the subject as a passive "receiver."[67] Unlike the metaphysical subject, "the receiver does not precede what it forms [but, rather,] it results from it" (BG 265). Marion argues that before the given gives itself, "no filter [i.e., no transcendental subject, no intentional consciousness] awaits it." He likens the receiver to a transparent screen, which remains invisible up until the very moment it is struck by a ray of light, by what it is given. But it seems to me that this metaphor of the screen fails to capture the full magnitude (and, indeed, audacity) of his theory, since, unlike the screen, the subject envisioned by Marion is not there from the beginning, awaiting a beam of light that might bring it into view for the first time. On his account, the receiver/screen does not even exist in advance of the given/light; rather, it receives itself from what it receives, from the given/light.[68]

One might question the coherence of a theory that seems to require both that the subject is entirely produced by the given and that it nevertheless offers some, albeit minimal, resistance to the given which produces it. After all, sticking to Marion's metaphor, light would remain invisible were it not to appear upon some surface, which "is an obstacle to it" and "stops it in blocking it."[69] This surface, this site of impact or deflection, must offer some degree of resistance (albeit passive resistance), and thus it must be distinguishable from the light itself. How, then, is one to understand the claim that the given/light gives or produces its own source of resistance? In other words, how is this resistance, this reception, to be conceived? Is it not reasonable to assume that the subject's reception of the given requires a more active and hermeneutical element than Marion allows? Other readers of Marion, such as Jean Greisch, Jean Grondin, and, more recently, Shane Mackinlay, have raised similar questions concerning Marion's account of saturated phenomena, insisting that the subject must actively engage in interpretation if such phenomena are ever to appear.[70] While I am in agreement with those scholars about the need for a more robust hermeneutic, I think Marion might be in even deeper trouble than they have suggested. For Marion's particular way of conceiving of givenness not only makes it impossible for him to acknowledge a more active role for the interpreting subject, or to see hermeneutic mediation as anything but derivative, it will also make it difficult for him to conceive of language as anything other than obstructive to revelation and our reception of it. I will return to these questions later on, when it comes time to examine the place of hermeneutics in Marion's most recent work. However, I want to put aside these worries for the time being, so we can focus on Marion's implicit motives for representing the relationship between passivity and givenness in this particular way in the first place. For unless we understand these underlying motives, and the pressures that have led Marion to minimize the role of (active) linguistic mediation in his phenomenology of givenness, we might fail to appreciate his more recent characterization of hermeneutics, and the persistent tension between his radical conception of revelation and Ricoeur's hermeneutical conception, which will be discussed in the following chapter.

As we have seen, Marion's presents his unique form of the phenomenological reduction as a fuller and more faithful realization of Husserl's principle of principles, as a more radical attempt to accept the given simply as it gives itself out to be. Now, by envisioning the subject as *posterior* to the given, as an entity which merely (and thus passively) receives it, Marion seems to believe that he has ruled out the possibility of the subject actively imposing its own conditions upon the given. This new conception of passive subjectivity is, according to Marion, fully realized when the subject finally becomes the recipient of saturated phenomena:

> If the receiver is determined as a thought that transforms the given into the manifest and is received from what it receives—in short, if it is born from the very arising of the phenomenon inasmuch as given, that is to say, from a given exerting the mere impact of its event—what will happen when a phenomenon given as saturated arises? (BG 266)

Marion answers his own question: "The impact will be radicalized into a call, and receiver into 'the gifted' [i.e., *l'adonné*: literally, the addict or devotee]," a subject which is said to be given over to the gift, or which lives entirely off of what is given to it (BG 266, 369).[71] As one that "receives itself entirely from what it receives" (BG 268), the gifted (*l'adonné*) certainly represents Marion's most radical conception of passive subjectivity, the most extreme posture of receptivity. However, this idea was already foreshadowed in *Reduction and Givenness*, where he regularly spoke of the interrogated subject (*l'interloqué*). And more recently, in *Givenness and Revelation*, Marion speaks of the gifted in terms of a "witness" (*un témoin*) which, unlike the I of *aletheia*, does not organize the given "according to the concept or signification that it will have assigned to it *in advance*."[72] The idea of a subject which is so passively receptive that it first comes into being through the givenness it receives runs like a current beneath the surface of nearly all of Marion's philosophical work. It finally breaks onto the surface in *Being Given*, where we discover that this radicalization of passivity on the part of the subject is accompanied by a corresponding radicalization on the part of the given, whose activity is now exercised without limit or constraint, without having to submit in advance to the subject's concepts or significations. In this way, Marion clears the path for a pure form of the call—a call which, by its very nature, remains entirely anonymous and indeterminate, since the call reaches the subject before the subject can wield any concept, horizon, or names that might serve to delimit the call, or give it a particular determination.

Marion's claim to have uncovered a "pure form" of the call has raised eyebrows in certain philosophical circles. For those who share Derrida's suspicion that Marion's entire philosophical enterprise—including the schematism of the three reductions—had been guided by a tacit theological agenda all along, it seemed natural to assume that the unnamed caller was really (or ultimately) meant to be identified with God. The fact that Marion eventually adopts the theologically loaded term "revelation" to designate the highest form of the saturated phenomenon—the saturation of saturation—only seemed to confirm that suspicion. For such critics, Marion's repeated insistence that "revelation" names "a strictly phenomenological concept," one which need not presuppose the actuality of Revelation as an event, turns out to be a rather unconvincing defense.[73] After all, phenomenological possibilities only merit philosophical attention on the supposition that they are rooted in lived human experience rather than mere flights of fancy (and even if one does deliberately takes such phantasies as one's object of investigation, as Husserl occasionally did, these are themselves rooted in actual human experience).[74] But Marion's work contains a more subtle, if not more compelling, defense against this charge than the one explicitly mounted on the basis of the possibility/actuality distinction. This defense involves folding the methodological *indecision* of the phenomenologist (who refuses to "decide if a revelation can or should ever give itself" in actuality, and thus also refuses to identify the identity of the caller) into the religious experience of Revelation itself, so that the recipient of an actual Revelation also refuses to *determine* the identity of the caller, or to *name* God. This refusal, in fact, is baked right into Marion's conception of revelation. If we are willing to take Marion at his word, then it is made quite clear that the very act of identifying God as the caller—indeed, the act of identifying or naming the caller at all—violates the requirements of his own reduction. Such identifications are precisely what both the reduction to pure givenness *and* the associated theory of the gifted were explicitly meant to rule out. Consequently, Marion's analysis lends itself to the paradoxical conclusion that even if one grants the actuality of Revelation (as concrete event, not just a formal possibility), the accusation of a theological bias (that is, the accusation that he analysis implicitly identifies God as the origin of the call) can be still be averted.

Therefore, contrary to one of the dominant criticisms of Marion,[75] I will argue that the real obstacle facing his project has less to do with the potential presence of unwarranted theological presuppositions (or *contaminations*) than with the exertion of a certain philosophical bias upon the phenomenon of Revelation as actually given. This bias leads him to privilege a certain kind of philosophical indeterminacy or neutrality, which he then transposes upon the "figure" of revelation as if it were one of its constitutive features. In other words, I claim that the indeterminacy Marion finally attributes to revelation results from a *counter-contamination*, which imposes upon the religious phenomenon aspects that arises from his commitment to an ultimately unjustified conception of philosophical rigor.[76] This, in turn, gives rise to a distorted and attenuated conception of Revelation. Importantly, this distortion is the paradoxical consequence of a procedure initially designed to address the dominate criticism of his work—that is, a procedure designed to preserve the legitimacy of his phenomenological method by staving off theological contaminations, by refusing to identify or name the caller. If I am right, then the violation committed by Marion's analysis is not that it conflates the pure call with the call of the Father, as Derrida suggests in *The Gift of Time*, nor that it identifies givenness as a gift from God, as Janicaud suggests in his essay on the *Theological Turn*. (Again, Marion explicitly and consistently prohibits such an identification.) On the contrary, the violation moves in precisely the opposite direction—it is the philosophical that taints the religious—and so, in Marion's effort to defend the methodological rigor of his analysis, he is led to misconstrue the religious phenomenon itself.

My overall aim has been to reconstruct the moves which have led Marion to this attenuated construal of Revelation. It is no accident that this reconstruction requires us to trace the line of argument that Marion will use in order to defend himself against the charge that his phenomenology constitutes a crypto-theology, which surreptitiously identifies God as the caller of the call or the giver of the gift. After all, I have contended all along that the error of counter-contamination is generally committed in the course of defending oneself against the charge of theological contamination or of holding theological biases. As an error, counter-contamination falls into the category of overcompensation. We first caught sight of this error in our reading of Heidegger in Chapter 2. Marion's analysis of the call engages, unwittingly, in a similar strategy. The call, he insists, is "pure" insofar as the caller remains undetermined; but this lack of determination is a highly ambiguous one. I want to demonstrate in greater detail how this error arises, or how and why he comes to conflate a strictly methodological procedure or requirement with a feature or structure of the phenomenon described.

From the outset of his analysis, Marion sought to avoid determining the identity of the caller on the grounds that such an identification would violate the anteriority of givenness and the call. One can already notice in *Reduction and Givenness*, where Marion introduces the idea of the *interloqué* (the precursor to the idea the gifted, or the *adonné*, which stands in place of the subject), that his insistence upon the indeterminacy of the call, his insistence that the caller *not* be identified with any of the divine names, is justified upon strictly phenomenological (rather than theological) grounds. The undecidability about the identity of the caller belongs to the phenomenological structure of *interloqué*'s experience of the call. For to evoke the name God, or any other name for that matter, would allow "one only to name the difficult, not to resolve it" (RG 202).

> The imprecision, the indecision, and indeed the confusion of the claiming instance attests much rather that in the beginning is found the pure form of the call, as such. The surprise surprises precisely because it surprises the one who knows neither its name nor its wish [. . .] I know, in the instant of the claim, neither who nor what. In fact, the indetermination of the claiming instance alone renders possible a claim which otherwise would not surprise [. . .] This a priori exerts itself all the more insofar as it is not identified [. . .] (RG 202)

The identification for which Marion has so often been criticized (i.e., the identification of God as the caller) is in fact prohibited by his own philosophical analysis. Since the gift become visible as gift only insofar as the giver him/her/itself is bracketed, the charge of crypto theology simply does not stick. The phenomenological reduction allows givenness to appear precisely because it holds in abeyance all questions regarding the status and identity of the giver. This point becomes all the more pronounced in *Being Given*: "the gift appears as such [only] when it is recovered in the reduction," which is said to involve "the bracketing of the giver [. . .] and therefore of his name." "Anonymity again, according to the reduced gift" (BG 297).

But while this move allows Marion to dodge the first bullet (that is to say, it gives him a reasonable defense against the charge of theological contamination), I claim that it has also placed him in the crossfire of yet another bullet (that of counter-contamination). The first sign of this exposure concerns the privileged position that the phenomenologist him- or herself inevitably comes to occupy vis-à-vis the phenomenon of Revelation as a result of the necessity of the reduction. While Marion had previously characterized the task of phenomenology as offering a mere description of revelation as possibility, toward the end of *Being Given* it begins to sound as if Revelation (as event) is only ever given *in actuality* to the phenomenologist, to the one who rigorously avoids naming it, the one who is willing to live with the indecision of the gift. In contrast to those who would turn away from the gift or who would assign a name in order to conceal themselves from it, the phenomenologist is willing to be surprised by the gift, willing to be struck by its inherent difficulties. So, his proposed third form of the phenomenological reduction constitutes the necessary means whereby this openness to Revelation is finally secured.

What is perhaps more surprising still is that this phenomenological-methodological imperative has a retroactive effect upon Marion's theological attitudes and commitments. For he eventually comes to articulate those attitudes and commitment in terms that are quite clearly based upon his phenomenological program, so that it appears retrospectively as if the phenomenological reduction of the giver (i.e., the prohibition of naming) does, in fact, serve the interests of his theological program as well. This becomes most evident in his creative interpretation and adoption of the tradition of mystical theology, which he regards as a third mode of theological reflection beyond the ways of *kataphasis* and *apophasis*. Katophatic theology, on his interpretation, "proceeds through a conceptual affirmation that justifies an intuition" which is thought to fill or confirm the concept (i.e., the name). Apophatic theology, on the other hand, "proceeds by negating the concept [i.e., the name] because of an insufficiency in intuition." Here, "naming appears to be impossible because to name says too much; it finds no confirmation in intuition." "But a third possibility remains"—namely, a mystical theology, in which "The intention [i.e., the name] can never reach adequation with the intuition (fulfillment), not because the latter is lacking but because it exceeds what the concept [or name] can receive, expose, and comprehend." "In this third way, no predication or naming any longer appears possible"—though no longer "because the giving intuition would be lacking" as in apophasis, "but because the excess of intuition overcomes, submerges, exceeds—in short saturates—the measure of each and every concept."[77] Mystical theology places us before a phenomenon that demands an "absence of divine names"—or, better, that demands the deployment of a certain phenomenological reduction of these names.[78] For every name would function as an idol, blocking access to the call: "In fact," Marion writes, "it is the heretics who claim to include God within presence by assigning God a proper name [. . .]."[79] In order to hear the call, one would have to shield it from every name, from every attempt to confine it to a name. Thus, it would appear that the theologian, more than the philosopher him- or herself, has a vested interest in preserving the anonymity and indeterminacy of the call by setting the phenomenological reduction to work.

If, however, the phenomenological reduction or epochē serves an ostensibly theological function—if, that is, bracketing of question of the giver (or at least the giver's name) safeguards the "purity" of the gift of Revelation—this is only because Marion's conception of Revelation seems to be conflated with a merely formal givenness and, thus, already divested of, or severed from, its material contents. This is not to say that Revelation has simply been confused with revelation, but that Revelation is itself conceived of in terms of its form rather than its content—in fact, Revelation is construed formally precisely because it refuses any determinant content.[80]

This naturally leads one to wonder whether this formalism is phenomenologically justified, whether it is warranted by the phenomenon of Revelation as it appears or merely on the basis of certain methodological considerations that would allow for its appearance. What, if anything, authorizes Marion to speak of a pure, unconditioned, and anonymous call in the first place? Is it possible that the call *as* given, *as* heard (i.e., as *actual* Revelation) could ever be pure and devoid of all content? Could it be that the supposed purity results from a sort of category mistake, whereby the formalism of the phenomenological description is transferred onto (or mistakenly attributed to) the phenomenon itself? Is it possible that Marion's insistence on the purity of the call betrays an infectious indeterminacy which passes (almost) unnoticed from the level of methodological principles to the level of the thing in question? To be sure, this question may not have occurred within the framework of an interpretation oriented solely toward the philosophical dimension of Marion's work, one that is neither aware of, nor interested in, its theological provenance. Nevertheless, the question does impose itself upon any reading that is attuned to the complex interplay between Marion's theological and philosophical projects.

In fact, Derrida and Janicaud have already raised a similar question—though, it must be said, they failed to appreciate what is most striking from the perspective of my own analysis, namely, the occurrence of counter-contamination. Janicaud, for instance, asks, "Is not this experience [of the anonymous call], slimmed down to its a priori sheathe, too pure to dare to pass itself off as phenomenological?"[81] And Derrida has wondered, "Is it possible to hear a 'pure form of the call' (and first of all must one presume such a purity? And if one does, on what basis?)."[82] The interpretation that I am advancing here might have appeared entirely inappropriate were it not for the fact that Marion's very own texts open up this very same line of questioning. For Marion betrays his own doubts and anxiety regarding the possibility of a "pure" call: "the formal definition [of the call, i.e., revelation] is not enough, for it still leaves undetermined the point where the given is *articulated* [i.e., Revelation]"; "how can [the call as such] ever offer a precise *significative* aim"; "won't the call [as such . . .] remain definitively *empty*?"; "How could an empty [that is, pure or indeterminate] call be received, that is to say, make itself heard? And if it allows no real hearing, how will one ever be able to respond to it?" (BG 283–287).

I will now turn to Marion's own attempt to resolve this difficulty in the final chapter of *Being Given* (Book V). There, Marion tries to circumvent the problem altogether by reducing what we might have imagined to be an irreducible difference, that is, by collapsing the moment of the appearance of the call into the moment of the response. His claims that the call first "shows" itself in the response (BG 285), and he illustrates this point by way of two examples, the first of which rests upon an interpretation of Caravaggio's *The Calling of St. Matthew*. Here, Christ is depicted as indiscriminately pointing toward a group of men gathered around a table, and only one of the men (Matthew) visibly responds to this gesture. Though Christ's gesture symbolizes the pure, indeterminate call—a call that in principle would concern Matthew no more than any of the other men—the viewer is able to recognize that the call is directed at Matthew in particular simply by the expression on Matthew's face and by the (disputable) fact that he is pointing to himself, as if to say, "Who? Me?" Thus, Marion argues the call is not so much seen in Christ's gesture as in Matthew's response.

However, one could argue that his analysis of *The Calling of St. Matthew* only increases the difficulties involved in accounting for the pure call. It seems, in fact, to imply that the call *as such* never even appears. After all, what would prevent us from concluding from Marion's interpretation that Matthew's face obscures the call as such, that it claims possession of the call, exerts a claim over the call, a claim that entails a naming and determination of the call *as his own*. Marion's argument seems to lend greater support to the following conclusion: namely, that the call that "gives itself phenomenologically" (that is to say, the call that *can* appear and thus enter into phenomenological discourse) is never a pure call, never the call *as such*, but merely the call *as* reflected in the face of the respondent—a call that has always already been violated by the claim of the respondent and subjugated to the conditions of the subject.

Nevertheless, this criticism alone would not prove fatal to Marion's project, since *The Calling of St. Matthew* is really only an allegory, a depiction of the call from a third-person perspective, not the call itself. There still remains the possibility that I myself might be the recipient of an anonymous call, that the pure form of the call might, as it were, appear to me *in person*. This first-person perspective, typically considered a *sine qua non* of phenomenological research, is precisely what Marion tries to achieve in his detailed description of the child and the father. He argues that if one is to appreciate the nature of the call or claim which the child makes upon the father, one must refrain from adopting a perspective that is external to the father, since that would constitute a "phenomenologically unjustifiable view." One will need to assume the "perspective of the father" himself. Having adopted this perspective, we immediately notice that even though "every child is born naturally from its mother," its relationship to the father is marked by uncertainty, since "biological paternity remains without immediate and direct proof" (BG 300). Given this uncertainty, we might wonder how and why—aside from the obvious ethical considerations, which Marion deems only of secondary importance—"the father [comes to] recognize a child who does not bear his name" as his own. Marion's answer is as follows:

> The child thus exercises an anonymous call on the father. When the father recognizes himself as father to the point of recognizing the child as his own, to the point of giving him his name, he does nothing other than, by calling him in this way, offer a response to a call. The name by which the child is called is only the father's response to a nameless call. (BG 301)

But here again, one could argue that Marion's example proves precisely the opposite of what he intends it to. If we hold rigorously to the perspective of the father (as Marion insists), then rather than demonstrating that the child exercises an anonymous call on the father, the example seems to illustrate that the child calls the father only insofar as the child already appears to be the rightful heir or "owner" of the father's name. For is it not the case that so long as the child appears nameless, his or her paternal status remains in question and the father receives no call at all? It is only when the child *appears* to the father *as his own* (i.e., as *already* in possession of the father's name) that the child exercises a call over the father. In other words, only the child who first appears (in and of itself) as the rightful inheritor of the father's name calls forth the father, soliciting his paternal response and responsibility. Even if the father responds by officially granting his name to the child, he does so only because the child already appeared (from the perspective of the father) to have a legitimate claim to it. Therefore, the call appears to be determined even before the father answers it. It is the *name* rather than the *anonymity* of the child that solicits the father's response.

One should, therefore, conclude from Marion's example that the child never exercises an anonymous call on the father. In fact, one might even begin to wonder whether an anonymous call is even possible—since "to exercise a call" is to "exercise a claim," and thus to already appear as named, or to already appear as the rightful owner of the father's name. Perhaps bearing a name (being determined by a name) constitutes a necessary condition for exercising a call. If, in the end, we are forced to question whether givenness could ever really appear *as such*, even to the gifted, this is only because

Marion's own line of investigation inadvertently imposes the question upon its readers.

Though the question is never explicitly raised by Marion, it nonetheless haunts the final sections of *Being Given*, occasionally rising to the surface. The following passage represents just one instance: "[If] it is ever necessary to give a name to the call this will not be the job of the call itself (not of the giver), but of the responsal (or the givee). The responsal recognizes what the call gives to it, and thus identifies it."[83] The ambiguity of this passage leaves the reader wondering whether the receiver "give[s] a name to the call" or whether the receiver simply recognizes (i.e., "identifies") a name that "the call gives [itself]." In either case, Marion's readers might well suspect that his project faces the following dilemma, which I will call the problem of determinateness:

a. *Either* the receiver maintains the poster of the gifted, faithfully carrying out the reduction, and thus never imposing its own conditions upon the given. In this case, the receiver (as gifted) would only receive "what the call gives to it" (BG 298). But then we will have to admit that "what the call gives" is the name itself—that the call calls out its own name. It would then follow that givenness never appears *as such*, but only as an always already determinate givenness, which is to say that there would be no such thing as an anonymous call (or a pure gift) since the caller (e.g., the child, in the above case) would always already possess a name.
b. *Or* the receiver adopts the posture of the respondent and is indeed responsible for assigning a name to an otherwise anonymous call (of the child). But then the receiver would be imposing its own conditions, its own horizon, its own name upon givenness, and therefore, once again, givenness *as such* could never appear—for the given would now be restricted to a horizon, to the conditions of an active subjective. In this case, the receiver would never be able to adopt a nameless child, to hear an anonymous call, or to receive givenness as such, but would always submit the child, the call, and the given to its own name, its own horizon, and its own subjective conditions. In this case, givenness as such would be nothing more than an unattainable ideal. As it appears, every gift would be immediately wrapped up in an economy of metaphysics.

11. TWO INDETERMINACIES

If Marion initially managed to avoid confronting the problem of determinateness head-on, I would argue that this is only because his text employs a strategy of counter-contamination which depends upon the conflation of two irreducibly different kinds of purity or indeterminacy. More specifically, we might say that his work exploits an inherent ambiguity between two distinct senses of the indeterminate. By carefully distinguishing between these two senses, I believe I can bring into sharper focus the strategy of counter-contamination which I claim operates tacitly, if not surreptitiously, throughout Marion's philosophical analysis of revelation.

On the one hand, we are confronted with what might best be described as *formal-indeterminacy*: Here something is indeterminate because it remains at the level of sheer possibility, a formal possibility, such as the phenomenological figure of revelation that Marion attempts to rigorously describe. In this case, the form is said to be indeterminate because the phenomenologist makes no decision about whether the phenomenon has actually taken place. It remains indeterminate because the phenomenologist's ability to offer a formal description will not (and indeed cannot) depend upon material contents that might accompany the phenomenon's actual event. So, the formal possibility is not dependent upon any particular event, nor is it tethered to the material content of any such an event. It is therefore characterized by its lack of content because such content is irrelevant to the form *as* mere possibility. If and when this formally indeterminate possibility receives a determinate content, then what was previously said to be merely possible is now claimed to be actual. Generally speaking, this actualization would not alter in any way the formal description of the phenomenon in question. However, when it comes to Marion's phenomenological description of the form (or figure) of revelation, this kind of indeterminacy is absolutely essential. Why? Because Marion has chosen to defend the philosophical legitimacy of his analysis upon the grounds that it holds such determination—or, more precisely, all designation or denomination—in suspense. Determining the content of the phenomenon is tantamount to forfeiting one's neutrality towards the phenomenon itself. Any such determination threatens to undermine the phenomenological rigor of the analysis, since that rigor is secured and sustained by the bracketing of the very question about the actuality of revelation.

Clearly, Marion wants to insist that his phenomenology is indeed committed to this kind of indeterminacy insofar as he claims to suspend any judgement or position regarding the actuality (or non-actuality) of what nevertheless remains possible. Again, all such positions or "positings" would belong to a theological (or anti-theological) "attitude," which would be analogous to what Husserl has called the "natural attitude," an attitude that Marion *cum* philosopher must resist in order to maintain the legitimacy of his phenomenological description of revelation's possibility. Formal-indeterminacy, then, generally has to do with structural or formal conditions of possibility. Even if, as in the case of Marion's analysis of revelation, this is presented as the formal possibility of saturating all such conditions,[84] it still represents a *mere* possibility, the actuality of which can neither be affirmed nor denied by the phenomenologist (lest he cross the threshold of theology, and purportedly violate the philosophical rigor of the analysis).[85]

On the other hand, Marion's work suggests another kind of indeterminacy, one that belongs to the content or material of the phenomenon itself. Here, the actual content remains indeterminate precisely because this content exceeds or overwhelms all signification and concepts—in short, all efforts to comprehend it, to say it, or to give it a linguistic articulation. We might call this *material-indeterminacy* since it refers to that which is materially (i.e., actually) given, but given in a way that eludes our (linguistic) understanding of it. That which is given remains indeterminate not because it is non-actual or not-yet-given—as in the case of formal-indeterminacy—but because this actuality frustrates and exceeds every attempt to pin it down, to make determinations, and to describe its contents. Whereas formal-indeterminacy clearly pertains to revelation (as possibility), material-indeterminacy belongs to Revelation (as actually given)—and, thus, it would make no sense to speak of the formal-indeterminacy of Revelation or the material-indeterminacy of revelation.[86]

Now, with these two different kinds of indeterminacy in mind, I can pose with greater clarity the question with which I began: When Marion speaks of a pure givenness or a pure call, which type of indeterminacy does he mean to invoke—formal or material? Although careful readers of Marion must insist on this question, Marion himself seems rather careful to avoid providing an answer, for the terms *purity*, *indeterminacy*, and *anonymity* are employed in an ambiguous manner throughout his philosophical oeuvre. This lack of precision often allows him to smooth over this very difference and to skirt some of the philosophical problems that arise from their conflation. Let us consider just one example:

> the call . . . would not carry any name, because it would assume them all; the anonymity would be reinforced by the very excess of the paradox, which would require an infinite naming; thus no call would offer *less* of a name than that of a phenomenon of revelation [. . .] Far from fearing that such a call should lead surreptitiously to naming a transcendent *numen* and to turning—for the worse—to "theology," it is necessary to conclude that, on the contrary, every phenomenon of revelation (as possibility) and especially a Revelation (as actuality) would imply the radical anonymity of that which calls. (BG 297)

Keeping in mind the distinction between formal- and material-indeterminacies, it seems puzzling that Marion could so easily attribute the same radical anonymity to both revelation and Revelation. That revelation (as possibility) must remain radically indeterminate can hardly be contested, since any determination or denomination would involve a theological interpretation which immediately violates the neutrality of the phenomenological description and Marion's proposed reduction. However, Marion's claim that this very same anonymity characterizes Revelation as well seems to result from a mere category mistake, whereby Revelation is counter-contaminated by its phenomenological figure, revelation.

Is the call, which Marion so carefully describes in a strictly phenomenological fashion, pure, anonymous, and, thus, indeterminate because it remains a mere possibility, a formal possibility, a phenomenological structure or "figure," a revelation as opposed to an actually given Revelation? Does Marion's description of the call entail anonymity and purity in order to maintain formal-indeterminacy? Or does Marion insist on the purity and anonymity of the call solely because the call (as actually given) eludes conceptual grasp, because of the material-indeterminacy of an actually given call?

In an amazing, almost ingenious move, Marion argues that the excessive givenness of the call (that is to say, its *material-indeterminacy*) prevents it from receiving any theological determinations and thus guarantees its *formal-indeterminacy*. Insofar as the call (as an actual event) lacks determinative content (or exceeds the subjects capacity to determine this content), the event itself allows for a strictly phenomenological description, that is, one that remains free of theological prejudices. It would therefore appear that since Revelation (as actual event) implies a certain "indeterminacy" regarding its content, the phenomenologist is permitted to assume its actuality without being drawn into any specific theological direction. According to this logic, however, Revelation becomes an object of legitimate philosophical concern only to the extent that it has been drained of its theological content and has become a so-called pure call.

But Marion goes one step further, suggesting that Revelation as event can only ever appear to one who is willing to adopt the phenomenological attitude and carry out the phenomenological reduction. For only the formal-indeterminacy established and secured via the reduction is said to allow the purity or excessive givenness (i.e., material-indeterminacy) of the gift to appear as such: "the gift appears as such [only] when it is recovered in the reduction," which is said to involve "the bracketing of the giver [. . .] and therefore of his name" (BG 297). Paradoxically, whereas the initial goal of phenomenology was simply to describe revelation (as possibility), it now seems as if Revelation (as actuality) will only ever be given to the phenomenologist herself—or to the believer who adopts the phenomenological attitude—since it is said to appear only to those who avoid naming it, avoid identifying the giver (BG 297). But one must question whether the mystical (or apophatic) theologian's refusal to assign a name in order to remain open to Revelation as it gives itself is really equivalent to the phenomenologist's refusal to make a determination regarding the actuality of revelation via the reduction. By glossing over that difference—a difference marked by the distance separating formal indeterminacy from material indeterminacy—Marion produces the illusion that he can indeed encounter Revelation itself (via the so-called third way of mystical theology) without having to transgress the methodological exigences of his phenomenology or violate the principles of his reduction to pure givenness. It would be wrong to accuse Marion of a deliberate sleight of hand, since his motives for glossing over this difference are rooted in an honest effort to preserve the philosophical rigor of his analysis. But once this difference has been noticed, his account of revelation begins to come apart at the seams.

Philosophers might once again worry about the loss of rigor or neutrality. (Is this just mystical theology masquerading as phenomenology?) But theologians also have something to lose—namely, the content of Revelation itself. In order to avoid the charge of theological contamination—of smuggling theological commitments into his phenomenological analysis—Marion has committed an equally grave error: he has allowed his portrayal of the phenomenon of Revelation to be shaped by a set of philosophical concerns about methodological rigor. If, in the end, phenomenology seems to take the place of mystical theology in Marion's philosophical work, is this not the inevitable result of having extricated Revelation from its proper textual-linguistic milieu and conflated it with a merely empty shell of itself, a pure form devoid of any determinate content or description?

12. GIVENNESS, HERMENEUTICS, AND RADICAL REVELATION

The philosophical landscape has shifted rather dramatically in the decades since the publication of *Being Given*. In the late 1990s, the greatest challenge to Marion's newfound phenomenological method came from outside theological circles. Embroiled in a series of disputes with the likes of Derrida and Janicaud, Marion found himself under pressure to justify his phenomenological approach on strictly philosophical grounds—a pressure which, according to my interpretation, ultimately led to a process of counter-contamination in his work. But more recently, as the theological turn in phenomenology has taken hold and the philosophical environment has gradually become more hospitable towards those working on religious themes, Marion has (perhaps ironically) come under attack from the opposite flank, that is to say, from fellow members of the theological turn. In particular, his phenomenological approach has been increasingly criticized for being insufficiently hermeneutical. It is worth pausing to consider this line of criticism, how Marion has responded to it, and whether that response might provide an adequate reply to the charges I have just leveled against his work.

Shane Mackinlay's *Interpreting Excess: Jean-Luc Marion, Saturated Phenomena, and Hermeneutics* offers a good starting point for this discussion, as it shows just how deeply connected concerns about the role of hermeneutics in Marion's philosophy are to the broader theological concerns about the relation between faith and revelation.[87] Mackinlay's treatment of the issue hinges on a distinction he makes between two conceptions of hermeneutics, "ontological" and "derivative." According to the former conception, which he mainly associates with Heidegger, the subject's active process of interpretation constitutes a necessary condition of possibility for the appearance of any phenomenon, such that any given phenomenon will always already be interpreted. According to the derivative conception of hermeneutics, which he attributes to Marion, any act of interpretation on the part of the subject will invariably follow upon or lag behind a prior given, such that the appearance of the given necessarily precedes the hermeneutical moment or act. A derivative hermeneutic regards interpretation as an afterthought, as an activity that works upon an already given phenomenon, rather than a necessary condition of a phenomenon's appearance. But what is really at stake in all of this? In the end, Mackinlay worries that by reducing the subject (or *l'adonné*) to a thoroughly passive receiver of the pure given, the derivative conception of hermeneutics precludes the possibility of faith playing any role in the reception of Revelation. As Mackinlay puts it:

> However, Marion's concern to prevent Revelation from being determined or constituted by any other factor leads him to circumscribe and distort the role of faith in the appearing of Revelation, restricting it to conceptual assent to Revelation *after* it has appeared. I argue that instead of limiting faith in the way, faith must also be understood in a more fundamental sense of an existential commitment that opens a hermeneutic space in which it is first possible for Revelation to appear at all.[88]

If the phenomenon appears before interpretation, this leaves little room for an active reception (or openness) on the part of the subject. And if there is no need for an active openness on the part of the subject, then there is no need for faith either.

Mackinlay's criticism of Marion comes with a caveat: he insists that Marion's own account of saturated phenomena implies a more robust role for hermeneutics (and for faith). And yet, for some reason or another, Marion is simply unwilling to acknowledge this role. That may be so. However, if my analysis of Marion is correct, then his reluctance to concede this point, his refusal to acknowledge a more active role for the subject, has less to do with theological disputes over the nature of faith than with his deep-seated concern about the philosophical rigor of his phenomenological project. After all, Marion operates on the assumption that the success of his phenomenology of givenness depends upon a radical suspension of the subject's capacity to constitute, conceptualize, or name the given, since, as we have seen, he thinks naming the call would not only violate the given, but would also undermine the rigorous neutrality of the analysis, which he has fought so hard to maintain.

Nonetheless, in his recent essay "The Hermeneutics of Givenness," Marion has addressed Mackinlay's criticism about the supposedly derivative nature of hermeneutics in his work (though it is worth noting that he never explicitly mentions Mackinlay's work). To begin with, he tries to remove some of the criticism's bite by undermining the characterization of hermeneutics on which it depends. Marion implies that the charge rests upon a confusion between Heidegger's ontological sense of interpretation—which pertains exclusively to Dasein's self-understanding in view of its own concerns and existential possibilities—and the merely derivative forms of interpretation that involve attributing "predicates" to inter-worldly subjects through the apophantic "as," as in theoretical assertions. Marion suggests that his critics have conflated the merely derivative, deficient "apophantic" form of interpretation with the necessary or existential condition of all understanding, when in fact the two are quite distinct. While the latter may be a necessary condition for the reception of the given, the former certainly is not. The implication, as I understand it, would be that the kind of hermeneutical activity which Mackinlay and company claim to be ontological is really only ontic; and, as such, it belongs to the methodology of merely regional sciences, namely, the natural, human, or social sciences (*Geisteswissenschaften*) that seek to interpret things, texts, art objects, etc. Marion implies that one would be mistaken to take this regional kind of interpretation as a necessary condition of the reception of the given as such. "Thus understood, hermeneutics [*Auslegung*] never bears *first* on a text (vision of its sense) nor even on the intra-worldly being to which the text refers, but on the understanding [*Verstehen*] opened to and by the possibility of Dasein."[89]

If Marion's critics have assumed a theory of interpretation that is too broad (since it includes merely ontic forms of interpretation within its conception of ontological hermeneutics), Marion could be accused of having adopted a theory of interpretation that is far too narrow, since he seems to exclude from the domain of genuine (non-deficient) hermeneutics everything but the *Verstehen* proper to Dasein's own self-understanding. In fact, Marion's reading of Heidegger in "The Hermeneutics of Givenness" seems to completely erase whatever conceptual distinction might be made between *Verstehen*, on the one hand, and genuine (non-deficient) forms of interpretation (*Auslegung*), on the other. As a result, Marion is left with a conception of hermeneutics that effectively collapses multiple layers or modalities of interpretation into merely two—one that is primordial or ontological (insofar as it is indistinguishable from Dasein's concernful understanding) and another that is *totally* deficient and disruptive to our understanding of the given (insofar as it is concerned with a merely theoretical interpretation of worldly objects).[90] But Heidegger himself had claimed that

> between the kind of interpretation which is still wholly wrapped up in concernful understanding and the extreme opposite case of a theoretical assertion about something present-at-hand, *there are many intermediate gradations*: assertions about the happenings in the environment, accounts of the ready-to-hand, [and] the narration of something that has befallen. We cannot trace back these 'sentences' to theoretical statements without essentially perverting their meaning. (BT 201/158, italics mine)

Having ignored these gradations, Marion is compelled to toss out *not only* the most egregious or deficient forms of interpretation (theoretical), *but all* forms of (ontic) interpretation, that is to say, all forms of interpretation which are not *immediately* reducible to the basic fore-structures of Dasein's own concernful self-understanding. But in doing so, I cannot help but worry that the baby has been thrown out with the bathwater.

I will return to this issue in greater detail in the following chapter, where Ricoeur's theory of distanciation will be examined at length, along with his arguments in favor of a more productive role for the explanatory or epistemological methods of the human sciences in relation to an ontological theory of understanding (or belonging). However, it is worth noting here that even Heidegger himself seems to admit that the apophantic "as" of interpretation can often serve as the midwife of appearances, insofar as it involves a "pointing out" (*Aufzeigen*) which allows "an entity [to] be seen from itself" (BT196/154).[91] It is reasonable to assume that this notion of interpretation might have offered resources for further fleshing out Marion's own account of the role of interpretation in our reception of the given. Why, then, is Marion so eager to dismiss forms of ontic interpretation which seem only to facilitate the appearance of the given? If we keep Marion's broader project in mind, the reason for this exclusion is not difficult to find: Heidegger goes on to associate this "pointing out" with an act of giving "something a definite character [*bestimmt*]"—which is to say, a *determinate* character (BT 196/154). And, as we have seen time and again, Marion believes that the legitimacy of his own project depends upon the radical indeterminacy of givenness, that is to say, upon the existence of (saturated) phenomena which are characterized by a resistance to any such determination. Thus, Marion regards even the least theoretical of assertions with a great deal of suspicion, since they threaten the indeterminacy of the given (even though Heidegger was himself willing to recognize them as simply *working out*, rather than *covering over*, what is given).[92] By severing all ties with these regional acts of interpretation—which are productive in spite of the fact that they cannot be immediately subsumed by the primordial "as" of *Verstehen*—Marion demonstrates that his phenomenology is indeed even more radical than Heidegger's.

In any case, this leaves Marion's ontological conception of hermeneutics very little room to breathe, since the only thing left for it to interpret will be Dasein and its own possibilities: "Hermeneutics proceeds from the sight of the interpreter on the avenue of its possibility."[93] But, in fact, Marion claims that this interpretation concerns Dasein's openness to the given in a more general sense since it establishes the setting in which the call and response structure (which I discussed at length above) unfolds:

> Indeed, if hermeneutics (of things) originates in the understanding (of itself by Dasein), this understanding always means *pre*-understanding, and therefore Dasein's opening to its possibility. [. . .] Thus between the sense of Dasein and the signification of each being, the understanding [*Verstehen*], such as it permits interpretation [*Auslegung*], plays out in the "structure of question and answer" (Gadamer). But such a "structure" does not come from nowhere: it belongs to the game of call and response, such that one glimpses how hermeneutics can hinge on the question of givenness. If indeed the reception and the identification of the given imply that this given always remains to be interpreted as a phenomenon endowed with signification, then the hermeneutical instance sets the place of the given because it sets itself there.[94]

This passage is admittedly opaque, since it does not specify what sense of interpretation it intends by "hermeneutics (of things)." Nevertheless, it does make it clear that Marion is prepared to admit a more extensive role for hermeneutics in his account of the reception of the given than some of his critics have acknowledged. And perhaps this should come as no surprise. After all, Marion had insisted upon the need for an "infinite hermeneutics" as early as *In Excess*, where he claims that the saturated phenomenon's surplus of intuition necessitates an endless response on the part of the recipient, who inevitably finds herself in an indefinite and ultimately futile struggle to capture the *infinite* given within the *finitude* of concepts that will forever prove insufficient and inadequate.[95]

Nevertheless, even if Marion claims that this infinite hermeneutics plays an essential role in our reception of saturated phenomena, it is still a derivative role in at least one important sense suggested by Mackinlay: the act of interpretation is marked by an essential "belatedness" in that it always follows rather than precedes what is given. Marion insists upon this point throughout his analysis, and he tries to clarify it in terms of a distinction between givenness and appearance. In "The Hermeneutics of Givenness," he assigns interpretation the task of managing the "gap" between what "gives itself" and "what shows itself": "For the given does not yet show itself through the simple fact that it gives itself [. . .]. Certainly, the phenomenon shows itself only if it happens as a given, but it does not suffice that it happen as a given for it to appear as showing itself, in full phenomenality."[96] In other words, hermeneutics plays the role of taking the given and transforming or "transcribing" it into an appearance, into something that shows itself to the gifted.

Two sets of questions emerge as soon as hermeneutics is assigned this remarkably enigmatic task: First, what sense can be made of a givenness that has *not yet shown itself* through the interpretation of the gifted? If phenomenology consists of a careful description of things as they are given to us—as they appear—what authorizes Marion to affirm a given before it appears? One might suppose that the given is to be inferred after the fact, on the basis of what has subsequently appeared, and thus postulated as the necessary condition of that appearance. Since such an inference would depend upon the given eventually having appeared, it could only be made retrospectively, that is, only after the given has already been transcribed into an appearance through the interpretation. In that case, we would come to know that a given had preceded the appearance, but only after the appearing of that appearance. However, on Marion's account, this is evidently *not* the case, since he repeatedly insists that the given can fail to appear when it is not properly received: "it sometimes happens that what gives itself does not succeed in showing itself."[97] But how can one be sure that something has been given when it never even appeared? In other words, what right does one have to speak of a given that is never shown? It seems to me that Marion does not sufficiently "mind the gap" between this supposed giving and showing. By asserting a givenness in the absence of appearance, a givenness that is postulated even when it remains wholly *unapparent*, Marion has taken one step too far—a step beyond the bounds of what phenomenology can allow. Thus, his account of hermeneutics draws him back into the orbit of familiar problems that have plagued his phenomenology from the beginning.

The second set of questions concerns how we are to understand the shock, force, and indeed the "violence" that is said to accompany the interpretation of the given. As I noted in my discussion of Marion's radical conception of subjectivity (see above, Section 10), the gifted is said to phenomenalize the given precisely because it presents an obstacle or barrier to it. As Marion writes,

L'adonné phenomenalizes in receiving the given, precisely because it is an obstacle to it, stops it in blocking it and fixes it in centering it. If *l'adonné* therefore receives the given, it is in receiving it with all the vigor, even violence, of a goalkeeper blocking a shot, of a defender marking, of a receiver sending back a winning return. Screen, prism, frame—*l'adonné* takes the impact of the pure, unseen given, holding back the momentum of it in order in this way to transform its longitudinal force into a slack, even, open surface.[98]

How, then, does this violence—which Marion claims is not only conducive to, but necessary for the appearance of the given insofar as it transforms the given into what is shown—differ from the kind of violence that is said to prevent the given from appearing? This question is made all the more urgent by the fact that hermeneutics seems to operate as a kind of substitute for constitution in Marion's account—when faced with a saturated phenomenon, hermeneutics "takes up again the function that constitution can no longer assume."[99] In the case of a revelation, the supreme form of the saturated phenomenon, how will this productive interpretation differ from the problematic act of imposing a naming upon the call, an act that was said to violate the reduction to pure givenness and thereby prevent the call from being heard? In short, how do productive forms of interpretation differ from unproductive acts of constitution?

Tamsin Jones lucidly articulates this problem in *A Genealogy of Marion's Philosophy of Religion*. She asks,

> how do the particularities of the individual resisting the given in reception not inscribe it in yet another subjective horizon? If it does, does this not subvert Marion's initial claim that saturated phenomena are distinguished from other phenomena insofar as they are not limited by any horizon, but show themselves as they give themselves, starting from themselves?[100]

As far as I can tell, Marion has no real answer to this question. Rather, he seems to dance around the issue, continually oscillating back and forth between two seemingly irreconcilable positions. At some points, the interpreter is construed as active: its act of interpretation involves imposing a determination (a name or concept) upon the given. These determinations reflect the "outlines of visibility" that the given receives from the gifted, so that the gifted's response actually "decides [. . .] the *content* of the call."[101] At other points, the interpreter is portrayed as entirely passive, so as to avoid construing interpretation as an imposition of the subject's own horizon upon the given. Thus, the gifted's interpretation is said to come from the given itself: the answer (i.e., the interpretation) "does not come, in the final analysis, from the interpreter but from the interpreted [. . .]."[102] Indeed, in light of Marion's novel conception of the subject as the gifted, one might go so far as to say that the interpreter itself (and not just the interpreter's interpretation) owes its existence to what is given.

Nevertheless, I would argue that this oscillation between active and passive accounts does not constitute the core problem—or, at the very least, it is not a problem unique to Marion. For every plausible account of interpretation will inevitably involve a dialectical exchange between passive and active moments, and thus a question-answer structure which, under ideal conditions, culminates in a fusion of the anticipatory (pre)suppositions of the interpreter and the content or subject matter (*die Sache*) that he or she seeks to understand. Marion's sometimes awkward indecisiveness on this point is merely a symptom of another, and in my view, deeper problem—specifically, the one I addressed above under the aegis of "the problem of determinateness" (Sections 10 and 11). Perhaps it is for this very reason that Marion's reply to previous objections about the lack of hermeneutics in his thought has not, in the end, supplied an adequate response to the issues I have raised in this chapter.

Ultimately, the difficulties facing Marion's account of revelation stem from commitments he has made as a consequence of having adopted a radical attitude toward linguistic mediation. The problem concerns his awkward coupling of two claims, which we have already considered at some length above: first, that Revelation involves a pure givenness or an anonymous call (a view which, I argued, suggests a kind of counter-contamination in his phenomenological analysis); and secondly, the claim that the gifted owes its existence to givenness itself. Once he has embraced these two claims, he finds himself boxed in, since he is left with no coherent way explaining how the linguistic resources (e.g., the endless divine names) employed in the interpretation of Revelation could ever even arise. On the one hand, Marion needs to insist that the linguistic determinations used to make sense of Revelation originate on the side of the finite subject (the gifted), rather than the given—they are like a filament that gives visible shape to the appearance of a pure (and thus shapeless) givenness. And yet, on the other hand, since Marion argues that the interpreter (as the gifted) receives itself from what is given, it would seem impossible *not* to attribute these linguistic determinations to the given itself. After all, where else could they come from?

The dilemma facing Marion's account of revelation could be easily avoided were he only willing to abandon one of the two claims. My own hypothesis is that the second of these claims is worth preserving—indeed, we will soon encounter another version of it, namely, Ricoeur's notion of the "summoned self"—but that first claim needs to be abandoned in favor of a hermeneutical attitude that regards language as playing a more productive role in the phenomenon of revelation (and not just the *interpretation* of revelation). Gadamer encapsulates this hermeneutical attitude in the following way: "that which comes into language is not something that is pregiven before language; rather, the word gives it its own determinateness."[103] On such a view, language would no longer be regarded as an inert medium which simply mediates what has *already* been given by superimposing its determinateness upon it, but rather as a genuine source revelation itself.

NOTES

1. "No misinterpretation of Revelation could surpass that of Heidegger, in this respect a paradigm of the *Aufklärung* [. . .]" Jean-Luc Marion, *Givenness and Revelation*, trans. Stephen Lewis (Oxford: Oxford University Press, 2018), 57.

2. While Marion provides convenient labels for the first (transcendental) and second (existential) versions of the reduction in *Reduction and Givenness*, he does not yet risk naming the third reduction, referring to it simply as the "third" or "last" reduction. He will, however, eventually label it as the "pure reduction" in Jean-Luc Marion, *Being Given: Toward a Phenomenology of Givenness*, trans. Jeffrey Kosky (Stanford, CA: Stanford University Press, 2002), 38. (Henceforth, BG.)

3. Ibid., 2.

4. In the vast majority of his work (up to about 2015), Marion had generally used the lower-case "revelation" to denote the phenomenological *possibility* rather than the *actuality* of revelation (which is generally indicated by way of the capitalized "Revelation"), and it is important to stress that I continue to follow that well-established convention throughout this chapter. However, on a several recent occasions, Marion has begun to use the terms *r*evelation and *R*evelation in a new, and wholly unrelated manner, in order to distinguish between trivial (or banal) forms of *r*evelation and the properly religious phenomenon of *R*evelation. This development is particularly surprising, since he seems to have previously (though never explicitly) excluded revelation (understood broadly as a doubly saturated phenomenon) from his discussion of "banal forms of saturated phenomena" (note, for instance, the lack of any mention of revelation in his essay on "The Banality of Saturation" in *The Visible and the Revealed*, 145). By acknowledging the possibility of banal forms of revelation, Marion is now able to address a criticism that has been raised by several commentators, such as Matthew Burch: namely, that revelation is totally unlike other phenomenological experiences in that it is not at all common, but rather exceedingly rare (perhaps even nonexistent), and so it is not a suitable subject of phenomenological description. Revelation, in this banal sense, is said to occur whenever a phenomenon exerts a power over or an effect upon the one who receives, resulting in an unforgettable and genuinely transformative experience. One of Marion's examples of such an experience, namely, learning how to ski, confirms that such phenomena are quite common. Nevertheless, if banal forms of revelation (small "r") are quite common, Revelation (as a religious experience) is still rather rare. By using capitalization to mark this new distinction (between banal and exceptional forms), Marion certainly runs the risk of introducing unnecessary confusion regarding the earlier possibility/

actuality distinction. In any case, the fact that he has recently extended his use of the term *revelation* to include such trivial cases as "learning how to ski" does not void his earlier, more rigorous usage, since *R*evelation (with a capital "R") still refers to an exceptional religious experience. I will continue to use the lowercase "revelation" to refer to the *possibility* of such exceptional religious experiences, rather than to the merely banal or trivial forms of revelation, which he has only recently begun to acknowledge. See Jean-Luc Marion, "Thinking Elsewhere," *Journal for Continental Philosophy of Religion* 1 (2019), 5–26.

5. Jean-Luc Marion, *Reduction and Givenness: Investigations of Husserl, Heidegger, and Phenomenology*, trans. Thomas Carlson (Evanston, IL: Northwestern University Press, 1998), 5. (Henceforth, RG.)

6. Marion portrays Kant as the poster child of metaphysics in a number of his essays. However, we could just as well have begun by examining Marion's account of the onto-theological character of metaphysics. In that case, instead of starting with Marion's claim that metaphysics requires every appearance to pass through the bars of certain subjective conditions, we might have begun with his claim that metaphysics requires every being (*das Seiende*) to be grounded in something other than itself, namely, in Being par excellence (*das Sein*). Both arguments are intended to establish the background against which the phenomenological tradition supposedly makes its great advance. See, for example, Jean-Luc Marion, "Metaphysics and Phenomenology: A Relief for Theology," *Critical Inquiry*, Summer 1994, 20, 527–91.

7. Immanuel Kant, *Critique of Pure Reason*, trans. P. Guyer and A. Wood (Cambridge: Cambridge University Press, 2002), A218/B265.

8. Jean-Luc Marion, "The Saturated Phenomena," in *Phenomenology and the "Theological Turn,"* trans. Bernard Prusak (New York: Fordham University Press, 2000), 178.

9. Ibid.

10. Ibid., 179.

11. Ibid., 179. Marion quotes Husserl, *Ideas I*, 44, paragraph 24. His translation departs from the standard English translation, which uses the phrase "presentive intuition" rather than Marion's "donating intuition" for *Anschauung*.

12. Marion, "A Relief for Theology," 580.

13. Husserl, *Ideas I*, 43.

14. Husserl, *Ideas I*, 43–44.

15. Kant, *Critique of Pure Reason*, B 151.

16. Husserl, *Ideas I*, 44.

17. Husserl develops his theory of categorial intuition in the sixth investigation of his *Logical Investigations*. Edmund Husserl, *Logical Investigations: Volume I & II*, trans. J. N. Findlay (New York: Routledge, 2001).

18. Husserl, *Logical Investigations: Volume II*, 281.

19. Ibid., 282.

20. Ibid., 306.

21. Martin Heidegger, *History of the Concept of Time: Prolegomena*, trans. Theodore Kisiel (Bloomington: Indiana University Press, 1985), 71. Marion cites the same passage in *Reduction and Givenness*, 35.

22. Heidegger, *History of the Concept of Time*, 72.

23. According to Marion, Heidegger confirms this continuity in the so-called Zahringen seminar (RG 35).

24. Whereas Heidegger focuses his attention on the fifth investigation, Derrida deals primarily with the first.

25. "Supposing that it is founded in the texts, would this distinction [between Heidegger and Derrida] not offer a conceptual range sufficient enough that the two readings, instead of being in confrontation, might be arranged more subtly? In short, if it is a matter of defining metaphysics in order to put it in question, is the characteristic of givenness equivalent to the characteristic of presence through intuition?" This last question indicates the direction Marion is heading—moving from a framework of intuition to one of givenness (RD 6).

26. Jacques Derrida, *Speech and Phenomena: And Other Essays on Husserl's Theory of Signs*, trans. David Allison (Evanston, IL: Northwestern University Press, 1973), 93.

27. Marion's equivocal use of the term "signification" seems to blur the distinction between "expression" and "indication" that proved so crucial to Derrida's own analysis. We therefore have reason to doubt whether Marion's presentation of Derrida's critique of the first investigation really measures the true weight of his argument.

28. Marion, "The Saturated Phenomenon," 180–84. A similar discussion is found in *Being Given* (BG 185), where Marion emphasizes the last clause of Husserl's principle of all principles. See Husserl, *Ideas I*, 44.

29. Marion, "The Saturated Phenomena," 194.

30. The issue is treated extensively in BG 189–99.

31. *Zur Sache des Denkens*, in *On Time and Being*, 62–63. (I quote the passage as it appears in *Reduction and Givenness*, 50.)

32. Ibid., 56.

33. Ibid., 58.

34. Heidegger, *History of the Concept of Time*, 86.

35. I have used the translation found in RG 60.

36. Theodore Kisiel translates the phrase "*am Seienden soll ablesen werden*" as "to be read off in the entity": The entire passage reads, "Being is to be read off in the entity; that is to say, what phenomenological interpretation puts into pre-view is being" (Heidegger, *History of the Concept of Time*, 306). Marion explores the difficulties of translating *abslesen* in RG 62.

37. Heidegger, *Basic Problems of Phenomenology*, 21. I cite the modified translation in RG, 64.

38. Another key problem Marion sees with Husserl's version of the reduction concerns the status of intentional consciousness which it leaves completely unquestioned. As Marion writes:

> [With the reduction] Husserl no doubt applies himself persistently to moving back from the transcendent objects to the immanent acts, by following the reverse thread of intentionality. . . . The acts act as the means by which to arrive at the immanent givenness of the lived experiences, without they themselves, as such, becoming the stake of an authentic

questioning: in short, "the kind of Being of acts is left undetermined" (RG 47). Marion's final lines are taken from Heidegger, *History of the Concept of Time*, 124.

Once again, Marion is drawing on observations made by Heidegger in 1925:

> Husserl's primary question is simply not concerned with the character of the Being of consciousness. Rather, he is guided by the following concern: How can consciousness become the possible object of an absolute science? . . . The elaboration of pure consciousness as the thematic field of phenomenology is not derived phenomenologically by going back to the things themselves but by going back to a traditional idea of philosophy. (Heidegger, *History of the Concept of Time*, 107)

(Note that I have cited the slightly modified translation that appears in RG 83–84). Husserl's goal then would be to establish a science that could guarantee the certainty of its object. His strategy is essentially Cartesian: like Descartes, Husserl regards consciousness as the object of choice for such a science since, he argues, our knowledge of consciousness is certain and absolute, unlike our knowledge of ordinary worldly objects, which is always contingent and relative. Marion argues, however, that by distinguishing consciousness from the world on purely epistemological grounds, Husserl paradoxically winds up defining the being of consciousness in terms of the being of the world. For Husserl bases his distinction on "a pair—certitude, contingency—that belongs entirely to the mode of Being which is solely that of the reality of the world" (RG 82). Intentional consciousness is itself treated, paradoxically perhaps, as a merely ontic entity, as a merely present-at-hand and ready-to-hand object. Marion remarks, "for its epistemic primacy consciousness . . . pays, so to speak, the price of an implicit but total submission to the way of Being of reality [i.e., objectivity], and therefore of the world." Husserl's preoccupation with epistemology and scientificity actually serves to conceal intentional consciousness' true way of Being—that is, what Heidegger designated as the "ontico-ontological constitution" of Dasein.

In fact, Marion claims that Heidegger's concept of Dasein completely circumvents the epistemological problems which Husserl seemed to have obsessed over. Here, the theoretical attitude is no longer privileged: "scientific research is neither the only, nor the closest possible mode of Being of [Dasein]." Rather, Dasein "relates to the world in the mode of preoccupation, which manipulates and utilizes beings as ready-to-hand, and therefore without the least disinterest" (RG 80–85). The primacy that Heidegger attributes to Dasein within the analytic of Being and Time is not due to some epistemic status or its objective certitude. Dasein, after all, has little if anything in common with Descartes's *ego cogito*—indeed, it is formulated precisely in opposition to the Cartesian subject. Dasein is not one object among others. And yet its privilege has nothing to do with affirming some privileged kind of entity whose clarity and distinctness could serve to ground our knowledge of other entities. In fact, "it does not [even] count among the real terms, nor does it admit anything real in itself, because it precedes and renders possible the mode of Being of reality," that is to say, it renders possible the mode of Being of objects or inter-worldly beings (ibid.). Thus, Marion concludes that Heidegger, unlike Husserl, is able to determine the Being of intentional consciousness precisely because he passes beyond the idea of absolute science—and the metaphysical quest for objective certainty—in order to return to the things themselves.

39. It should be noted at the outset that the following discussion employs the term "idol" as it is used in Jean-Luc Marion, *God without Being: Hors-Texte*, trans. Thomas Carlson (Chicago: The University of Chicago Press, 1991), 9. (Henceforth, GWB.) While the question of how the terms evolved over time (especially as it comes to designate one type of saturated phenomena in Marion's philosophical writings) is certainly interesting, it is not germane to my analysis here.

40. Hence, Marion's remark that "variations in the mode of visibility indicate variations in the mode of apprehension of the divine itself" may be considered the guiding axiom of this entire analysis (GWB 9).

41. This is, of course, one of the basic definitions of phenomenology. See, for example, Levinas's definition of phenomenology in *Husserl's Theory of Intuition*, a text which, more than any other, effectively introduced phenomenology into French philosophy (it first drew Sartre's attention to the work of Husserl and Heidegger). Emmanuel Levinas, *The Theory of Intuition in Husserl's Phenomenology* (second edition), trans. André Orianne (Evanston, IL: Northwestern University Press, 1995).

42. "The discussion of possible relationships of fulfillment therefore points to a goal in which increase of fulfillment terminates, in which the complete and entire intention has reached its fulfillment, and that not intermediately and partially, but ultimately and finally. The intuitive substance of this last fulfillment is the absolute sum of possible fullness; the intuitive representative is the object itself, as it is in itself. Where a presentative intention has achieved its last fulfillment, the genuine *adaequatio rei et intellectus* has been brought about. The object is actually 'present' or 'given,' and present as just what we have intended it; no partial intention remains implicit and still lacking fulfillment." Husserl, *Logical Investigation, Vol. II*, 260–61.

43. In spite of the rigor of his analysis, Marion is not consistent in his use of these two terms—and their oppositional relation eventually gives way to an unstable differentiation. This inconsistency becomes increasingly clear in his philosophical works (especially *Being Given*) where the idol is included, along with the icon, among the various types of saturated phenomena. It appears that in order to make the idol fit into this typology, Marion is forced to attribute to it many of the characteristics that his theological work had reserved only for the icon. Thus, for example, instead of stopping the gaze, the idol is thought to open the gaze to an endless series of interpretations. One cannot help but notice, then, that the idol (as well as the icon) undergoes a significant alteration between *God Without Being* and *Being Given*, in spite of Marion's claim to the contrary: "I understand the icon (as previously the idol) in conformity with its phenomenological meaning, laid out in *Dieu sans l'être*" (BG 367). The modification concerns both the structural features of the idol's description as well as the position that the idol occupies within the phenomenal order, i.e., its place vis-à-vis other kinds of saturated phenomena, including the event, the flesh, and revelation.

44. Marion supplies us with the Greek: "*eikōn tou theou tou aoratou*" (GWB 17).

45. Marion paraphrases the relevant lines from the Council of Nicea II (GWB 202).

46. Marion's earlier study, *The Idol and Distance*, explores this inverse proportionality in greater depth. The icon has less to do with abolishing the distance that

separates us from the divine or the visible from the invisible, than with recognizing, preserving, or respecting this distance. Thus, the divine "shows" itself to the precise degree that it withdraws itself. Or, to use Levinasian language, it shows itself to the degree that it absolves itself from the relation, and therefore establishes the so-called relation-without-relation which Levinas refers to as "religion" in *Totality and Infinity*. Emmanuel Levinas, *Totality and Infinity: An Essay on Exteriority*, trans. Alphonso Lingis (Pittsburgh: Duquesne University Press, 2000). Marion essentially follows suit: "The icon conceals and reveals that upon which it rests: the separation in it between the divine and its face. Visibility of the invisible, a visibility where the invisible gives itself to be seen as such, the icon reinforces the one through the other." He also speaks of "a distance that [the icon] does not abolish but reveals." See Marion, *The Idol and Distance*, 8–9.

47. It is impossible to ignore the influence of Emmanuel Levinas in these pages on the icon, in spite of Marion's almost appalling silence regarding this debt. Marion redeems himself by giving Levinas his due in the analysis of the icon in *Being Given*. There nevertheless remains a curious attempt by Marion to outbid Levinas—an attempt to pass beyond the face, and thus beyond Levinas himself. For according to Marion, the icon is still more radical than the face. The face does not constitute the icon; rather, the icon constitutes the face. In other words, the face is capable of revealing a depth deeper than vision only because it is always already an icon. It is therefore the icon that is the constitutive and definitive phenomenon, according to Marion, and not the face. See BG 232–33.

48. From Marion's perspective, the problem of God for modernity has less to do with God's negation, with atheism, than with the reemergence of idolatry at the level of the concept—we are, above all, prevented from respecting God not because God is rejected but because the conceptual idol blinds us to God (GWB 57). Hence, the substitution of the "absolute pole" for an idol. Affirmation and negation of God are essentially the same—for, in both cases, God is measured by our concept of "God," thus, by an idol. Whether we reject or affirm God, all that is concerned in this act is a mere idol—which conceals or blinds us to the absolute pole, God proper (GWB 57). This is what Marion's reading of Nietzsche seeks to demonstrate: The true significance of Nietzsche "lies not so much in proclaiming the 'death of God' as in thinking it [i.e., God's death] on the basis of the will to power" (GWB 58). This death does not properly consist of the demise of God per se, but of an entirely legitimate recognition that the operative concept of 'God'—namely, as "moral God"—represents "an effect of a (reactive) state of the will to power" (GWB 58).

Interestingly, Marion notes that the very recognition that gives death to the "moral God" by restoring the concept to its original site of production or projection (namely, to the will to power), did not prevent Nietzsche from giving birth to "new gods" from within the very same womb. That is to say, the "new gods" which Nietzsche himself proposed also "receive their justification, their existence, and their meaning from the sole will to power, of which they offer a thousand indefinitely rejected and nascent faces, a thousand idols without twilight" (GWB 58–9). What then distinguishes the moral God from the new gods if they both arise from the same source, from the will to power? For Nietzsche the answer was obvious: "Because, simply, some originate in a more active and affirmative figure of the will to power, and others in a less affirmative, more reactive figure" (GWB 59). If one may speak here of a battle of the gods, this battle would not be fought between false projections of 'God,' on the one hand, and the actual (i.e., true) underlying drives and forces which give rise to these projections, on the other. Still less would it be a battle between the idolatrous concept of "God" and the true God beyond all idolatrous concepts or representations. Rather, Nietzsche's discourse sets off a battle between idols themselves, between "dead" gods and "future" gods—a distinction which has less to do with truth and falsity than with health and sickness. For the gods of the future are no longer pathological, like gods of the past, since they involve a certain liberating affirmation of the gaze. "Between the dead and future 'gods' the distinction remains one of degree. From the point of view of the multiform will to power, the 'gods,' whatever they may be, remain idols whose validity faithfully reflects the state of the gaze that aims at them and sees in them its own affirmation or infirmity" (GWB 59).

49. Martin Heidegger, *Identity and Difference*, trans. Jan Stombaugh (Chicago: The University of Chicago Press, 2000), 71.

50. Marion draws once again from Heidegger, *Identity and Difference*, 64–65.

51. Once again, I have chosen to cite the translation found in the English version of Jean-Luc Marion's *God Without Being* by Thomas Carlson (GWB 211–12), which is itself based on the French translation provided in the "bibliographique appendice" to *Heidegger et la question de Dieu* (ed. and trans. by Jean Greisch), 334. The original reads: "Ich glaube, dass das Sein niemals als Grund und Wesen von Gott gedacht warden kann, dass aber gleichwohl de Erfahrung Gottes und seiner Offenbarkeit (sofern sie dem Menschen begegnet) in der Dimension des Seins sich ereignet [. . .]" Heidegger, *Seminare*, 436–37.

52. Needless to say, for Hegel this so-called immediate experience of absolute dependence—along with all other lesser-developed expressions of the divine, including religious *Vorstellung*—would still need to be taken up into the concept (*Begriff*) in a way that at once preserves and abolishes its essential moments. In this regard, Heidegger could not be more different from Hegel, since it is precisely the conceptual determination of "God" that Heidegger's critique of onto-theology sought to dismiss. From this perspective at least, one might say that Hegel remains the onto-theologian *par excellence* (an identification which Marion himself does not fail to make).

53. In order to make sense of these two meanings of silence, we might return once more to Marion's distinction between invisible and *invisable*: The first silence concerns the invisible as such, while the second merely concerns the *invisable*, i.e., that which is not seen because it is simply not aimed at. The second silence mistakes the former as having nothing to say, when, in fact, the first silence remains silent not because of any deficiency, but because one could never say quite enough, because no speech could live up to that which is spoken about. The second silence, then, amounts to a certain refusal to acknowledge, aim, or direct itself toward the invisible, towards that which the first silence guards in its silence. It excludes the invisible as being merely *invisable*. Heidegger is consequently drawn back into the orbit of an idolatrous thinking—idolatrous, that is, from the perspective opened by Marion's analysis.

54. In fact, Marion acknowledges that Heidegger does envision a third possibility beyond "God" as *causa sui* and God as the object of ontic, Christian faith—namely, a God that is envisioned by what we might call an unfaithful or pre-faithful, authentic Dasein (Dasein as such). But the phenomenological meaning of this God still implies an "aim," and thus an aim of Dasein. As a consequence, it, too, is conditioned by the fundamental existentials of the analytic of Dasein, which is to say that it, too, is conditioned by Being (GWB 69).

55. Marion, *The Idol and Distance*, 218–19.

56. For Marion's most detailed treatment of Derridean *différance*, see Marion, *The Idol and Distance*, 220–33. For an exemplary treatment of the relationship between Marion and Derrida on this very topic, see Roldophe Gasché, *Inventions of Difference: On Jacques Derrida* (Cambridge, MA: Harvard University Press, 1994). Gasché, whose analysis seems to give Derrida the upper hand, draws out the differences between these two figures with unusual subtlety and clarity, showing how the line of separation falls between a theological project (Marion) and a purely philosophical one (Derrida). But it also confirms a conclusion that will be addressed toward the end of this chapter: namely, that Marion's effort to overcome ontological difference involves a certain recapitulation of the Heideggerian apparatus, insofar as it appeals to a new anterior instance (the gift) which serves as a new foundation (more fundamental even than ontological difference, since it itself is said to give beings/Being), rather than problematizing foundational thinking as such (as is the case with Derrida's *différance*). Gasché, *Inventions of Difference*, 93–106, 150–70.

57. I have already discussed the nature of this conditionality in terms of a *one-way filiation* or *derivation* (issuing from Being to beings, though never in the reverse direction), which I argued, following Jacques Derrida, runs throughout *Being and Time*. See above: Chapter 2, Section 5, page 20.

58. Indeed, one of Dominique Janicaud's main lines of attack was designed to pull the rug out from beneath Marion's feet by "dismantling" the framework of the three reductions. He writes, "The purpose of this framework is to establish an appearance of formal continuity between the best known nucleus of the phenomenological method and 'the pure form of the call.'" However, Janicaud observes: "The passage from the second to the third reduction was as if hooked onto the model of the passage from the first to the second. But the trajectory of this first passage, given as a model for the second, seem[s] to us much too complex to be formalized as Marion did, thus imperiling the whole operation" (Janincaud, *The Theological Turn*, 55–56). Indeed, Marion makes no attempt to conceal the fact that the validity of his project, culminating in the reduction to pure givenness, gathers its momentum from developments that have occurred within the phenomenological tradition itself. By calling into question Marion's overall portrayal of this development, Janicaud essentially takes the wind out of his sail. Thus, the debate between Janicaud and Marion seems to hinge on the nature of the transformation that the reduction undergoes in the transition from Husserl to Heidegger—does Heidegger's deepening of the reduction represent an improvement within phenomenology as Marion wishes us to think, or does it signal Heidegger's departure from phenomenology as Janicaud seems to suggest?

59. Marion, "The Saturated Phenomenon," 195.

60. Marion initially outlines in terms of the Kantian categories: "Neither *visable* according to quantity nor bearable according to quality, but absolute according to relation . . . the saturated phenomenon is spoken of as irregardable according to modality" (BG 212). Marion coined the term "visable" in order to describe that which exceeds the gaze of intentional consciousness. Though the visable cannot be aimed at, it nevertheless does appear to consciousness and is therefore visible. The saturated phenomenon can therefore be visible, though not visable.

61. Ibid., 212–13.

62. Marion, "The Saturated Phenomenon," 211.

63. See Marion, "Relief for Theology."

64. Ibid., 367 (ft. 90).

65. Ibid., 235.

66. As we shall soon discover, the most pressing difficulty here concerns the very possibility of a phenomenology of the gift. After all, if Revelation gives its own horizon—if, that is, no horizon awaits the gift before it is given—then how could a phenomenologist go about measuring or tracing this horizon in the absence of an actual Revelation? It appears that a phenomenology of revelation would require Revelation in order to accomplish even its most basic task of delineating revelation's formal features.

67. BG, Book V, 248–320.

68. BG, Book V, Section 26, 262–270.

69. Jean-Luc Marion, *In Excess: Studies of Saturated Phenomena*, trans. Robyn Horner (New York: Fordham University Press, 2002), 50.

70. I would also add to this list Tamsin Jones's thoughtful analysis of the place of hermeneutics in Marion's thought in her book *A Genealogy of Marion's Philosophy of Religion: Apparent Darkness* (Bloomington: Indiana University Press, 2011), 115–29. Jones's criticism picks up on that of Mackinlay's, but she attempts to address some of those concerns by supplementing Marion with a reading of Gregory of Nyssa.

71. The term's relation to the reflexive verb *s'adonner* (to give oneself over) is crucial for Marion's usage, and is therefore translated as "the gifted" rather than "the addict" or "the devotee." No translation, however, could do justice to the full semantic scope of the French. See Jeffrey Kosky's footnote in BG 369, ft. 22.

72. Marion, *Givenness and Revelation*, 52.

73. See, for example, Marion, "The Saturated Phenomenon," 215, as well as BG 235.

74. Even in the case of phantasy, Husserl was concerned with *actual* instances of phantastic presentation, and specifically with how these essentially differed from instances of perceptual presentation. See, for example, Edmund Husserl's *Phantasy, Image Consciousness, and Memory (1898–1925)*, trans. John B. Brough (The Netherlands: Springer, 2005).

75. By "dominant criticism," I refer to the claim that Marion's phenomenology represents a kind of crypto-theology. As will become evident in what follows, my worries about Marion's project are quite different, though not perhaps absolutely unique. Thomas A. Carlson raises similar concerns in "Blindness and the Decision to See: On Revelation and Reception in Jean-Luc Marion," in *Counter-Experiences:*

Reading Jean-Luc Marion, ed. Kevin Hart (Notre Dame, IN: Notre Dame University Press, 2017), 153–80.

76. The conception of "rigor" which I call into question concerns Marion's desire to describe the formal possibility of revelation without presupposing an actual event of Revelation. In order to see why this conception of philosophical rigor is ultimately untenable and unjustified, we will first have to consider the hermeneutical thought of Ricoeur, to which we turn in the following chapter.

77. Marion, *In Excess*, 159.

78. Ibid., 158.

79. Ibid., 152.

80. The phenomenological figure of revelation, then, would be something like a form of this form, or a structure of this structure—in a manner similar to the way in which *Offenbarkeit* was claimed by Heidegger to be the ontological structure of *Christlichkeit*, which was itself already a formalization of *Offenbarung* (see above, Chapter 2, Section 12).

81. Janicaud, *The Theological Turn of French Phenomenology*, 63.

82. Jacques Derrida, *Given Time: I. Counterfeit Money*, trans. Peggy Kamuf (Chicago: The University of Chicago Press, 1991), 52.

83. BG 298, my italics.

84. The paradoxical idea that Revelation's condition of possibility consists in saturating or exceeding all such conditions is expressed in various texts, including, most recently, *Givenness and Revelation*, where Marion develops the idea in light of Karl Barth's remark that "It is the condition which conditions all things without itself being conditioned. This is what we are saying when we call it Revelation." See Marion, *Givenness and Revelation*, 58.

85. Some philosophers, perhaps most famously Emmanuel Falque, will insist that this "crossing of the Rubicon" in no way violates the phenomenological enterprise. See, e.g., Emmanual Falque, *Crossing the Rubicon: The Borderlands of Philosophy and Theology*, trans. Reuben Shank (New York: Fordham University Press, 2016). One question that will be pursued via a reading of Ricoeur in the next chapter has to do with whether the philosophical hermeneutics of concrete attestations of religious faith entails an illicit crossing over into theology or a commitment to the requirements of the phenomenological method itself.

86. The distinction I am trying to draw out is analogous (but *only* analogous) to the distinction between the phenomenological essence of physical objects versus that of abstract geometric entities. On the one hand, in attending to the *eidos* or essence of a given physical object (such as the cube-shaped die lying on the desk in front of me), I can observe through imaginative variations that its position, mass, material, color, and other sensible qualities may be altered under certain conditions (under different light, for instance). It nevertheless belongs to its essence and thus to its possibility *as a physical object* to have at all times, and under any condition whatsoever, a particular position, and particular sensible qualities, even though our elaboration of its essence will leave these matters undetermined. In the event that this possibility is instantiated or actualized (as it is in the case of the piece of die lying on the table before me), the particular location, along with its other sensible qualities, will and indeed *must* be

determined. In this sense, the essence of a physical object is formally but not materially indeterminate. On the other hand, things are quite different when considering the essence of abstract geometric entities, such as a cube (taken here as the abstract three-dimensional figure rather than a physical object) since it does not belong to the essence of this entity to have sensible qualities such as color, nor even the quality of localization (of occupying a particular position). It is, then, the essence of such abstract entities to be both formally *and* materially indeterminate. (For the sake of simplicity, I am leaving aside the complex issues surrounding the origins of these abstract entities, their possible genetic constitution, etc.) By analogy, we might say that Marion initially implies that the phenomenon of revelation lacks determinate content only insofar it is considered merely in terms of its possibility (or essence). This, in turn, implies that its content would be determined or specified only in the event that it was given in actuality (as an event of Revelation), as in the case of a physical object. However, in the end, Marion suggests that the actual event of Revelation is also indeterminate. And so, like our concept of mathematical or geometric entities, Marion's concept remains thoroughly abstract, even when given *in concreto*.

87. Shane Mackinlay, *Interpreting Excess: Jean-Luc Marion, Saturated Phenomena, and Hermeneutics* (New York: Fordham University Press, 2010).

88. Mackinlay, *Interpreting Excess*, 218.

89. Marion, "The Hermeneutics of Givenness," 38.

90. For a nice summary of the various types of interpretation and their relationship to understanding in *Being and Time*, see Hubert L. Dreyfus, *Being-in-the-World: A Commentary on Heidegger's* Being and Time, *Division I* (Cambridge, MA: The MIT Press, 1995), 195–214.

91. Although one must not confuse or conflate this "pointing out" (Augzeigen) with the enigmatic and presumably non-objectifying process of "formal indication" (*formale Anzeige*) discussed above (Chapter 2, Section 9), it seems likely that Heidegger wants to allow room for a productive (non-objectifying) use of concepts. This becomes especially clear in his later writings on the nature of language, a topic which we will have occasion to discuss in the concluding chapter of this book.

92. See Dreyfus's table of the modes of understanding in *Being-in-the World*, 201.

93. Marion, "The Hermeneutics of Givenness," 38.

94. Ibid., 38.

95. Marion, *In Excess*, 104–27.

96. Marion, "The Hermeneutics of Givenness," 39.

97. Ibid., 39.

98. Marion, *In Excess*, 50.

99. Marion, "The Hermeneutics of Givenness," 42.

100. Tamsin Jones, *A Genealogy of Marion's Philosophy of Religion*, 116. Jones seems to agree that Marion lacks a sufficient answer to this problem, and so she turns to Gregory of Nyssa in order to retrieve a plausible response.

101. Marion, "The Hermeneutics of Givenness," 41 (my italics).

102. Ibid., 35.

103. Gadamer, *Truth and Method*, 475.

Chapter 4

Ricoeur's Hermeneutic Phenomenology of Revelation
The World Reconfigured

> La figure a été faite sur la vérité,
> et la vérité a été reconnue sur la figure.
>
> Blaise Pascal, *Pensées*

1. INTRODUCTORY REMARKS

In this chapter, I will not attempt to offer a comprehensive analysis of Ricoeur's philosophy of religion, nor will I simply present Ricoeur's work on the subject of revelation in its own terms. In some sense, my aim is significantly less ambitious, but in another sense, it is also more critical and perhaps consequential. For my goal is to advance an interpretation of Ricoeur's conception of revelation that is both limited to and guided by the particular set of issues that have arisen within the phenomenological theories discussed in the previous two chapters. Until recently, Ricoeur's work had been largely overlooked within the secondary literature on the so-called theological turn in phenomenology, which for the most part has focused on what I have dubbed the "radical" phenomenologists to the exclusion of hermeneutically oriented ones.[1] This chapter seeks to fill that lacuna by demonstrating that Ricoeur's work may, in fact, offer a much-needed counterpoint to the current trend in the phenomenology of religion. By situating Ricoeur's approach to revelation against the backdrop of Marion's (and to some extent Heidegger's), I am able to bring into sharper focus those features of his thought that are perhaps most distinctive. These features enable him to offset and ultimately avoid some of the problems that have plagued the radical conception of revelation: the problems of formalization/attenuation, of ontic contamination and counter-contamination, etc. So the dialogue between these two strands of phenomenology is mutually beneficial, since some crucial and yet underappreciated dimensions of Ricoeur's work can only be fully appreciated when viewed in light of this juxtaposition.

At first sight, the decision to situate my analysis of Ricoeur after that of Marion may appear counterintuitive. Of course, from a strictly historical or chronological perspective, this ordering is wholly unjustified. If Marion belongs to what has been called the "second generation" of French phenomenologists, Ricoeur more properly belongs to that generation which was first responsible for introducing phenomenological discourse into French philosophical circles in the nineteen forties and early fifties. As translator of Husserl's *Ideas*, as author of some of the earliest studies of Husserl's work in French, and as an early innovator of the phenomenological method itself, Ricoeur must be placed alongside such important figures as Merleau-Ponty, Levinas, and perhaps even Sartre. In giving Ricoeur the last word, as it were, I am obviously not claiming to offer a chronological presentation of the historical development of the phenomenological movement. In truth, my decision is motivated by an entirely different type of consideration—one that has less to do with the evolution of phenomenology than it does with the deeper philosophical continuities and discontinuities that mark the complex interrelationships between these three figures: Heidegger, Marion, and Ricoeur. With respect to revelation, Marion exhibits a greater proximity to Heideggerian thought than does Ricoeur. This proximity was already made apparent toward the end of Chapter 3, where we discovered that in spite of Marion's alleged break with Heidegger over the proper relation (or *non*-relation) between revelation and the dimension of being, the latter ultimately repeats Heidegger's "radical" gesture of returning to what is primordial, originary, and pure. But the parallels between Marion and Heidegger concern more than their mutual interest in returning to an origin of one sort or another. For under the threat of ontic contamination, Marion—like Heidegger before him—wound up advancing a purely formal figure of revelation, one that is said to precede any possible description, designation, or act of naming, and one that is therefore anterior to linguistic expression and textual mediation. Heidegger claimed that the ontic orientation of faith is supposedly always already preceded by the pre-faithful being of Dasein, so that a proper understanding of the ontic content of faith can, paradoxically, only be secured by passing over that content in favor of the more formal and fundamental ontological interpretation of Dasein itself. Marion, for his part, claims that the hermeneutical moment follows a prior moment of pure givenness, and so its arrival on the scene always comes too late and its effort to name the call involves an act of "necessary impropriety."[2] The hermeneutical response is always "belated" and it "can never, even by proliferating indefinitely, do justice the anonymity of the call" that is said to precede it (BG 303).

The most striking parallel between the two figures has to do with the manner in which each of them sought to avoid ontic, regional, or "theological" presuppositions from entering into his strictly phenomenological analyses: namely, through an increasing formalization of the concept of revelation itself. However, I have argued that this figure of revelation turns out to be only as pure as it was empty. The call, in other words, remains for Marion a pure call only insofar as it resists all determination (nomination) and is therefore emptied of its determinative (ontic) content. Thus, both Heidegger and Marion are involved in a kind of protective strategy which constantly seeks to push revelation back to a more fundamental or originary site—before nomination, language, or conceptual mediation. This rather surprising affinity between the two thinkers becomes all the more pronounced when it is viewed alongside the conception of revelation that we find in Ricoeur, who characterizes revelation in terms of the transformation or divestment of the self that occurs during the course of reading or interpreting concrete texts—and, specifically, texts that are deemed sacred by a given community. According to Ricoeur, revelation involves an event that transpires before the text. In this hermeneutical context, however, the word *before* no longer refers to the quasi-temporal anteriority or *a prioricity* of a call that precedes linguistic mediation; rather it expresses the quasi-spatial relationship that a reader maintains vis-à-vis the concrete texts that he or she desires to understand—the fact that she stands in front of it. If revelation exceeds our ordinary conceptual grasp or involves a sort of transcendence, this has less to do with an indeterminacy of a prior, pre-linguistic givenness than with an over-determinacy that is rooted within *the domain of language* itself.[3]

As with Heidegger and Marion, Ricoeur's formulation of revelation cannot be understood outside of its broader philosophical context. If we are to appreciate the full significance of this formulation, we will need to pay careful attention to the ways in which Ricoeur's philosophy serves to bridge the phenomenological insights of Husserl and Heidegger with a distinct line of philosophical inquiry which arose within the romantic and neo-romantic hermeneutics of Schleiermacher and Dilthey. It is only in light of this broader philosophical trajectory that the essential difference between Ricoeur's "hermeneutical" conception of revelation and the "radical" conceptions of Heidegger and Marion can be brought into focus. My task, then, is to provide a more precise (and hopefully penetrating) account of these contrasting—if not competing—characterizations of revelation by returning to the deeper philosophical issues animating them; and these issues have fundamentally to do with the meaning and significance of phenomenology itself.

2. PHENOMENOLOGY AS THE END OF METAPHYSICS OR THE REVIVAL OF HERMENEUTICS

As I have argued before, the fate of phenomenology as a philosophical discipline and the fate of revelation as a unique kind of phenomenon are closely intertwined within Heidegger and Marion—and we can now add Ricoeur to this list as well. The correlation or interdependency between these two fates was already evident (though not always explicit) in the early Heidegger, where the return to "facticity" or "factical life" was from the start tied to an interpretation of Christian eschatological experience—an experience that Heidegger once believed provided special access to a more primordial mode of thinking than could be found within the history of Western metaphysics. The relationship between the rehabilitation of revelation, in the wake of its enlightenment critique, and the so-called end of metaphysics over the course of the twentieth century was one of mutual reciprocity. For the return to Christian revelation was just as responsible for bringing about the destruction of metaphysical thinking as that destruction was itself responsible for sanctioning a thinking of revelation beyond its ontotheological figure. This connection becomes overt in Marion. Whereas phenomenology, by means of an increasingly rigorous reformulation of the reduction, allowed for the possibility of revelation beyond its enlightenment prohibition, revelation was itself shown to constitute phenomenology's most quintessential phenomenon. Thus, according to Marion, the possibility of revelation signals nothing less than the possibility of a phenomenological form of philosophizing that finally is what it claims to be—namely, a return to things themselves, to things before metaphysical conditions are imposed upon them.

One could claim that this correlation between the possibility of revelation and the possibility of phenomenology is operative within Ricoeur's thought as well. But that claim would need to be made with the following caveat: Ricoeur's understanding of revelation implies an entirely different range of possibilities for phenomenological philosophy than is found in Marion. Therefore, with the question of revelation, nothing less than the proper interpretation of the phenomenological heritage as a whole is at stake.

I believe two dominant interpretative frameworks stand out: The first emphasizes the indispensable role of phenomenology within the overall process of overcoming metaphysics. According to this "radical" interpretation (exemplified by both Heidegger and Marion), phenomenology is perhaps best understood as a unique kind of philosophizing, one which not only arose in the midst of the decline of metaphysics, but was partly responsible for bringing about its demise—either through a retrieval of the primordial question of

Being (as in Heidegger) or by a return to a pure givenness (as in Marion). Whether metaphysics is defined by its obliviousness towards Being or by its imposition of "conditions of possibilization" upon the given, the remedy is essentially the same: phenomenology is thought to disclose a radical form of experience which enables a return to that which precedes this oblivion and exceeds these conditions.

According to the second paradigm—the one adopted by Ricoeur—phenomenology must be situated within the broader context of hermeneutical reflection that stems from, but is not limited to, century-old epistemological concerns which crystallized toward the end of the nineteenth century, especially in historiographical reflections of Wilhelm Dilthey. This connection between phenomenology and hermeneutics was, to be sure, first glimpsed by Heidegger himself. However, for reasons that will become clear later on (see below, Section 8), rather than pursuing hermeneutics for its own sake (in the way that, say, Hans-Georg Gadamer does in his *Truth and Method*), Heidegger placed hermeneutics in the service of a critique of metaphysics. For Heidegger, hermeneutics remains largely (though not always exclusively) identified with the hermeneutics of facticity, Dasein, and, ultimately, Being. The hermeneutic enterprise of late-nineteenth-century Germany is something that Heidegger simply encounters along the way, in his broader phenomenologico-ontological project.[4] Ricoeur, on the other hand, views hermeneutics less as a means to an end, than as an independent tradition worthy of our most serious attention. It represents a mode of reflection that can never be entirely exhausted or set aside, but must be carried over into the very heart of phenomenology itself.

This shift in attitude regarding the relationship between phenomenology and hermeneutics is crucial for comprehending the genuine novelty of Ricoeur's conception of revelation for two reasons. First, it leads to a conception of revelation that unites a hermeneutical theory of the text with a phenomenological theory of world (or of being-in-the-world), thereby enabling a more genuine engagement with the concrete historical, linguistic, and textual *content* of revelation. Secondly, it inverts Heidegger's manner of subordinating the ontic (or epistemological) sciences to ontological science and, consequently, circumvents the entire problematic concerning ontic contamination and counter-contamination that we have encountered in the previous two chapters. Having averted those problems, Ricoeur has cleared a path for a more fruitful dialogue between philosophy and theology. Roughly the first half of this chapter (Sections 4–7) is devoted to the first of these consequences, while the remainder of the chapter (Sections 8–10) is primarily concerned with the second.

3. PHENOMENOLOGY AND HERMENEUTICS: FROM EPISTEMOLOGY TO ONTOLOGY

By the mid-1960s Ricoeur had already begun to envision his own constructive project in terms of this shift in perspective. His peculiar "hermeneutical" brand of phenomenology is given its most explicit formulation in two essays to which I now turn, "Existence and Hermeneutics" (1965) and "The Task of Hermeneutics" (1975).

Both essays begin by redirecting the reader's attention back to what might be called the "pre-phenomenological" history of hermeneutics. In this particular context, Ricoeur speaks of "grafting" hermeneutics onto phenomenology precisely in order to highlight the fact that "the hermeneutic problem arose long before Husserl's phenomenology."[5] We must, therefore, avoid misconstruing philosophical hermeneutics as a mere "phase" within the pheneomenological movement, as if it were one turn among others. In fact, according to Ricoeur, it would make more sense to speak of a phenomenological phase within hermeneutics, since the hermeneutic problematic predates Husserlian phenomenology by several decades, if not by several centuries.[6] It is not surprising, then, that Ricoeur's discussion of the relationship between phenomenology and hermeneutics does not begin with Heidegger, nor even with Husserl, but rather with a consideration of the epistemological problems that plagued nineteenth-century hermeneutic theory and, specifically, those relating to issues within the *Geisteswissenschaft*.

According to Ricoeur, it was Dilthey (the so-called interpreter of the historical school) who first raised hermeneutics to the level of philosophical reflection (HH 48–53). Working in the wake of the great German historians of the nineteenth century, such as Ranke and Droysen, Dilthey expanded the scope of the hermeneutical reflection from the relatively narrow domain of textual interpretation to the domain of history as a whole on the basis of a strictly Kantian model (HH 48). Just as Kant had explained the epistemological condition under which knowledge of nature was made possible, Dilthey sought to explain the epistemological conditions under which knowledge of history would be possible. The task of philosophical hermeneutics as envisioned by Dilthey was to provide for the *Geisteswissenschaften* a critique of historical knowledge that would be comparable to Kant's critique of natural knowledge (CI 5). Dilthey believed that the primary challenge would be to demonstrate that hermeneutics did indeed possess a methodology that could in some sense compete with that of the natural sciences—a methodology, that is, which could be held together on the basis of a coherent theory of understanding. And this, in turn, required that the "diverse procedures of classical hermeneutics" such as classical philology and biblical exegesis be subordinated to a more general, unified theory of historical knowledge (ibid.).

The difficulties facing Dilthey's project were no doubt compounded by the fact that he was working within a post-Hegelian environment. While Hegel's idea of the diversity of historical epochs had become engrained in current thought, his particular conception of history as a coherent and rational unfolding of world-spirit (*Weltgeist*) that would culminate in and be encompassed by a single absolute spirit was almost entirely abandoned. Hegel left some hefty historiological questions in his wake: How, in the absence of absolute spirit, could it become possible to gain knowledge of previous historical epochs? How can one gain access to these past epochs if their meaning is not somehow 'taken up' or 'preserved' within our own present? How can one come to understand the coherence of history as a whole, if we ourselves are unable to leap outside of our own limited historical context or no longer willing to claim a kind of absolute knowledge? The dominant task, therefore, was to explain how the historian may indeed "transcend finitude" without making recourse to a theory of absolute spirit which would place the observer in a unique position vis-à-vis the past.[7] Dilthey's solution was essentially twofold. On the one hand, it involved a theory of psychic life. On the other hand, it involved a theory of the fixation of meaning into units, which become the site of mediation between past and present psyches.[8] Thus, Dilthey argued that "life grasps life only by the mediation of units of meaning which [are themselves capable of rising] above the historical flux" (HH 53).

Ricoeur argues that Dilthey's attempt to describe this process by means of a *Lebensphilosophie* never managed to escape the merely "regional" perspective of a psychological theory, which was erected upon an untenable, Romantic conception of genius. According to this psychological theory, the psychic life of the author is materially fixed, inscribed, or objectified in a text which, in turn, becomes the channel through which the historian becomes capable of being transported back into the mental life of its author. Nevertheless, if the task of the historical school was to understand history *as a whole* (or what Dilthey simply called a "universal history"), then this theory of psychic transportation would prove entirely insufficient, since an historical epoch (let alone history as a whole) exceeds the scope of the mental life of any single individual, genius or otherwise. Consequently, Ricoeur argues that Dilthey's claim that history can be accounted for on the basis of this hermeneutics of life [i.e., *Lebensphilosophie*] "remains incomprehensible" since "the passage from psychological to historical understanding assumes that the interconnection of works of life is no longer lived by anyone" (HH 52–3).

Dilthey set the task for philosophical hermeneutics. But his own effort to accomplish that task ended in failure, since he remained caught in the balance between two irreconcilable philosophical trajectories—forever oscillating between a desire for a general theory of historical knowledge, on the one hand, and a *Lebensphilosophie* rooted in a regional psychological paradigm, on the other.

Although Dilthey initiated the movement away from regional methodological disciplines toward a general hermeneutic theory, he lacked the resources to bring this movement to completion. In fact, Ricoeur claims that this movement could only be accomplished on the basis of a corresponding shift from epistemology to ontology. This shift, he argues, was first made possible through a phenomenological approach which managed to free historical knowledge from the particular epistemological framework operative within the natural sciences:

> After Dilthey the decisive step was not to perfect the epistemology of the human sciences but to question its fundamental postulate, namely that these sciences can compete with the sciences of nature by means of a methodology which would be their own. This presupposition, dominant in Dilthey's work, implies that hermeneutics is one variety of the theory of knowledge. [. . .] The presupposition of hermeneutics construed as epistemology is precisely what Heidegger [. . .] place[s] in question. (HH 53)

Therefore, even if Ricoeur views Heidegger's phenomenology in terms of its contributions to the problems of nineteenth-century hermeneutics, this "contribution cannot be regarded [. . .] as a pure and simple prolongation of Dilthey's enterprise; rather it must be seen as an attempt to dig beneath the epistemological enterprise itself, in order to uncover its properly ontological conditions" (HH 53). But what does Ricoeur mean by its "properly ontological conditions"? And why does hermeneutics require the resources of phenomenology in order to uncover them?

From the perspective of Husserlian phenomenology, this association between phenomenology and ontology appears rather astonishing. After all, one of phenomenology's founding gestures—the famous epoche of *Ideas I*—consists precisely in the bracketing of all questioning (or "positing") of existence. Are not all questions of being reduced in Husserlian phenomenology to questions about the sense of being? And does not Husserl even go so far as to reduce this sense of being to a mere correlate of a conscious act (that is to say, to the noematic pole of a noetic-noematic complex)? We are therefore impelled to ask how it is that phenomenology, according to Ricoeur, could ever become responsible for initiating this turn toward ontology in the first place. To be sure, Ricoeur is not blind to the strong idealistic strands within Husserl's work, running from *Ideas I* up to the *Cartesian Meditations* (CI 9). Nonetheless, he maintains that when read retrospectively—especially through a Heideggerian lens—Husserl's work, from its very inception, can be seen as contributing to the destruction of the naïve objectivism of the epistemological tradition "by designating the subject as an intentional pole directed outward, and by giving, as the correlate of this subject, not a nature but a field of meanings" (CI 8–9). This contribution to hermeneutic philosophy becomes even more pronounced in Husserl's later work, when the critique of objectivism is joined to an ontological investigation of the *Lebenswelt* which entails "a level of experience anterior to the subject-object relation" (CI 8).

> In this way, we find delimited a field of meanings anterior to the constitution of mathematized nature, such as we have represented it since Galileo, a field of meanings anterior to objectivity for a knowing subject. Before objectivity, there is operative life, which Husserl sometimes calls anonymous, not because he is returning by this detour to an impersonal Kantian subject, but because the subject which has objects is itself derived from this operative life. (CI 9)

Thus, Ricoeur suggests:

> [I]f the later Husserl points to this ontology [of operative life], it is because his [earlier] effort to reduce being failed and because, consequently, the ultimate result of phenomenology escaped the initial project. It is in spite of itself that phenomenology discovers, in place of an idealist subject locked within its system of meanings, a living being which from all time has, as the horizon of all its intentions, a world, the world. (CI 9)

Now this shift from epistemology to ontology, brought about through the confluence of Dilthey's hermeneutical project and Husserl's phenomenological analysis, will prove to be of utmost importance for Ricoeur's 'textual' conception of revelation, which is itself intimately tied to the phenomenologico-ontological formulations of "world" and "being-in-the-world."

In order to appreciate the full range of significance of this word "world," we need to turn to the work of Heidegger. For even if, as Ricoeur suggests, Husserl's genetic phenomenology paved the way for this ontological turn,[9] it was nevertheless left up to Heidegger to take the final step: to formalize Husserl's notions of world and operative life within a theory of understanding that was neither conceived in terms of a type of knowledge nor in terms of an intersubjective, trans-historical communication between two psyches, but in terms of that particular *mode of being* belonging to Dasein, or to that being for whom understanding is constitutive of its being. It is here that phenomenology's break with epistemology comes to a head. Whereas Dilthey had essentially regarded problems of historical knowledge as problems of communication—that is, problems concerning how one goes about gaining access to another's mind—Heidegger's emphasis on being-in-the-world overshadows his concern with intersubjective relationships. In other words, the problem of being-with others, that is, the problem of communication between persons (including persons belonging to different historical epochs) finds itself displaced by a theory of understanding which centers on being-in-the-world. As a result, *Being and Time*, completely severs "the question of understanding [. . .] from the problem of communication with others" (HH 55). "There is [in *Being and Time*] indeed a chapter called *Mitsein*," Ricoeur admits, "but the question of understanding does not appear in this chapter, as one would expect from a Diltheyan perspective." (HH 55). Understanding, in the primordial phenomenological sense, is not to be found in our relations with others, but in our relation to or, better still, in our situation within a world. "The first function of understanding is to orient us in a situation. So understanding is not concerned with grasping [an objective or trans-historical] fact but with apprehending a possibility of being [. . .]" (HH 56).

4. PSYCHOLOGISM, STRUCTURALISM, AND WORLD OF THE TEXT

One of Ricoeur's most significant contributions to philosophical hermeneutics was to have applied this ontological theory of understanding to the phenomenon of textual interpretation, thereby linking it back up with the properly hermeneutical and epistemological enterprise first initiated by Dilthey.[10] Doing so, however, resulted in a radical reformulation of that enterprise itself. We have already noted the shortcomings that Ricoeur associates with a purely psychologistic theory of textual mediation: the idea that textual interpretation requires a 'return to' or a 'recovery of' the mental life of its author—a recovery that is mediated by the materially fixed text—stems from epistemological presuppositions that were themselves naïvely adopted from the natural sciences. Ricoeur wants to maintain a place for Dilthey's theory the fixation of units of meaning in signs and works, but without adopting the purely psychological understanding of interpretation as the mediation between two psychic poles: i.e., the life of the reader and the life of the author. But what does a text serve to mediate between, if not the reader and author?

One way of escaping this problem would be to pass from the pyschologistic thesis of romantic hermeneutics to a structuralist thesis in which the author-pole is replaced by the immanent structure of the text itself.[11] Interpretation, according to this view, would no longer consist of the mediation between reader and author, since the function of the author is now taken over by the text itself. Interpretation would thus consist of an encounter between the reader and the structure constituted by, in, or on-the-surface-of the text. Ricoeur takes seriously this structuralist thesis, though he insists that its solution to the above problem is unsatisfactory on the grounds that it ignores the "referential function of discourse" and tears the text from what he calls the "communicative chain" which links speaking to writing and reading to hearing (FS 220). "Discourse," Ricoeur insists, "consists of the fact that someone says something to someone *about something*" (FS 220).[12] At first glance, this talk of "discourse" and the "communication" between two interlocutors seems to betray a residual commitment to Dilthey's psychologistic hermeneutics.[13] But to interpret Ricoeur in that manner would be to miss his actual point, which in fact has more to do with an ontological theory of reference than with a psychological theory of transportation between the mental lives of two interlocutors. Hence Ricoeur's emphasis—indicated by his use of italics—is placed upon the "something" about which discourse is conducted. Following Gottlobe Frege, Ricoeur claims that discourse entails both a *sense* (i.e., "the ideal object which the proposition intends" and which is therefore purely immanent in discourse) and a *reference* (i.e., "the truth value of the proposition, its claim to reach reality) (HH 140 "What Is a Text?").[14] According to Ricoeur, the structuralist thesis rests on a false premise: namely, that in becoming a text, discourse loses its referential function altogether, leaving behind nothing but a "network of relations purely internal to the text" (i.e., its *sense*) (FS 220).[15] Ricoeur insists that the transition from speech to writing does not altogether eliminate the referential function of discourse; rather, it merely prevents the discourse from deploying its referential function on the basis of an "ostensive reference," on the "here" and "now" of conversation, that is to say, on the basis of a "unique spatio-temporal network which is shared by the interlocutors" (HH 141).[16] An interpreter who busies him or herself solely with a text's *sense* to the exclusion of its *reference* is, we might say, analogous to a diner who insists on eating the menu rather than the food described therein. The hypostasization of the text does not supply a satisfactory answer to the question posed above concerning the meaning of mediation in interpretation.

In fact, the structuralist thesis multiplies rather than dissolves the difficulties expressed by our initial question regarding textual mediation. For we now face a double-sided difficulty: what does textual mediation mediate between if not the reader and the author (as in the case of Dilthey's neo-romantic hermeneutics) or the reader and the hypostasized text (as in the case of certain structuralist theories)? Ricoeur himself articulates the question in the following way: "If we can no longer define hermeneutics in terms of the search for the psychological intentions of another person which are concealed *behind* the text, and if we do not want to reduce interpretation to the dismantling of structures, then what remains to be interpreted?" (HH 141). And his solution is sought in the Heideggerian conception of the being-in-the-world: "I shall say: to interpret is to explicate the type of being-in-the-world unfolded in front of the text" (HH 141).

Ricoeur's response warrants at least two observations. First, if Ricoeur manages to resolve the problem concerning the nature of textual mediation, he does so only on the basis of a phenomenological ontology which opens up a third possibility beyond the previous two alternatives (i.e., either "psyche of the author" or "structure of the text"): namely, the possibility of a world of the text, a world which is irreducible to either the mental life of its author or to the immanent structure of the work itself.

> [T]o understand a text, we shall say, is not to find a lifeless sense which is contained therein, but to unfold the possibility of being indicated by the text. Thus we shall remain faithful to the Heideggerian notion of understanding which is essentially a projection, or to speak more dialectically and paradoxically, a projection within a prior being-thrown. (HH 56)

Ricoeur thereby avoids falling into either a *structuralist theory*, according to which the referential function of discourse simply dissolves into a hypostasized text, or a *psychological theory*, according to which interpretation consists of an encounter between author and reader that is mediated by the text. (And, it may be worth reemphasizing here that this ontological notion of world is what allowed for the de-psychologization of nineteenth-century hermeneutics.)

Secondly, if Ricoeur opposes the structuralist claim that the referential function of discourse is abolished with the transition from speech to writing, this is only because his theory of the text leads him to a much broader understanding of *reference* (broader, that is, than the one which he attributes to the structuralist, whom he leaves unnamed).[17] One might even say that the material inscription of discourse results in the abolition of a certain limited kind of reference, namely, its "ostensive reference," the immediate spatio-temporal environment shared by two interlocutors.[18] But this restriction marks only the negative side of an entirely positive phenomenon. As noted above, the reference-function in oral discourse "is determined by the ability to point to a reality common to the interlocutors" (HH 141). That this ability is in some sense obviated in the case of texts—which, in principle, can be read anywhere and anytime by anyone who is literate[19]—actually suggests that texts possess a unique referential capacity, namely, the capacity to reveal a second-order reference, i.e., a "possible" world beyond the immediate environment or the spatio-temporally "given world" of first-order reference.

5. REVELATION AND THE WORLD OF THE TEXT

One can therefore isolate two distinct, though interrelated, moments in Ricoeur's theory of textual reference. The first 'negative' moment concerns the suspension of a first-order reference:

> This abolition of the ostensive character of reference is no doubt what makes possible the phenomenon we call 'literature,' which may abolish all reference to a given reality. However, the abolition of ostensive reference is taken to its most extreme conditions only with the appearance of certain literary genres, which are generally *linked to* [. . .] *writing*. The role of most literature is, it seems, to destroy the world. (HH 141, italics mine)

This suspension or destruction of first-order reference is to some degree made inevitable by the transition from speech to writing, which effects a certain distanciation from the original spatio-temporal setting of oral discourse.

But this negative moment of suspension turns out to be the condition of possibility for unleashing a second-order reference that itself exceeds the scope of the merely ostensive reference. This marks the second 'positive' moment in Ricoeur's theory of textual reference. The negative moment gives way to a positive moment in which an entirely different kind of referent emerges—the "world" of the text. Though certain literary genres—fiction, poetry, myth, etc.—are more apt to play with and thereby draw attention to this expanded referential function than others, in principle this expansion is an essential (ontological) feature of all forms of discourse that are mediated by text. In other words, the very ability of discourse to reveal a second-order reference depends upon the particular kind of mediation proper to texts, which themselves involve a "distanciation" from the ordinary "world" of oral discourse.

And yet, Ricoeur notes:

> [T]here is no discourse so fictional that it does not connect up with reality. But such discourse refers to another level, more fundamental than that attained by the descriptive, constative, didactic discourse which we call ordinary language. My thesis here is that the abolition of a first order reference, an abolition effected by fiction and poetry [but, we must add, also by religious narratives, parables, hymns, etc.], is the condition of possibility for the freeing of a second order reference, which reaches the world not only at the level of manipulable objects, but at the level that Husserl designated by the expression *Lebenswelt* [life-world] and Heidegger by the expression 'being-in-the-world.' (HH 141)

In an important, and indeed rigorous, sense, "poetic discourse is also *about* the world"; however, it is simply "not about the manipulable objects of our everyday environment" (FS 222). The refusal to acknowledge that poetic discourse does indeed reach reality in this fundamental sense indicates the naïve adherence to a "theoretical" or "natural" attitude. It is precisely these attitudes—whose philosophical representatives are, respectively, late-nineteenth-century positivism and naturalism—that phenomenology has all along sought to challenge in the name of either a *Lebenswelt* (Husserl), a being-in-the-world (Heidegger) or a belonging-to (Gadamer). So, it is on the basis of such a phenomenology that Ricoeur is ultimately able to argue that poetic discourse, by way of textual inscription, does in fact *refer* to a world, in this more primordial and robust sense.

> It refers to our many ways of belonging to the world before we oppose ourselves to things understood as "objects" that stand before a "subject." If we have become blind to these modalities of rootedness and belonging-to (*appurtenance*) that precede the relation of a subject to objects, it is because we have, in an uncritical way, ratified a certain concept of truth, defined by adequation to real objects and submitted to a criterion of empirical verification and falsification. (FS 222)

We are finally in a position to appreciate why Ricoeur's conception of revelation remains inextricably bound to a broader hermeneutical project, which seeks to integrate a classical theory of textual mediation (*à la* Dilthey and Schleiermacher), on the one hand, with a phenomenologico-ontological theory of world or being-in-the-word (*à la* early Heidegger and late Husserl), on the other. If revelation is provisionally (though perhaps also only minimally) defined as an encounter with the divine which in some manner transcends, shatters, or pierces through the humdrum of everyday reality—through what Ricoeur might characterize as the disenchanted world of "manipulable objects" and technological mastery—then it is only natural that the text becomes the most appropriate site for such an encounter. In fact, this site has already been prepared by any number of literary genres, both religious and non-religious, which refer to *possible* worlds by simultaneously interrupting and re-envisioning *this* one. Ricoeur explicitly states that the same process is put into operation by biblical texts: "This same consideration applies to biblical texts. [. . .] God is in some manner implied by the 'issue' of these texts, by the world—the biblical world—that these texts unfold" (FS 221).

We have thus arrived at our first conclusion regarding Ricoeur's conception of revelation—namely, that it is erected upon two separate though interrelated foundations: a theory of 'text' as a (materially) fixed discourse, on the one hand, and an ontological conception of 'world,' on the other hand. These two foundations—one hermeneutical, the other phenomenological—are woven together in the hybrid theory of the "world of the text," which, in turn, provides a sort of template (or *organon*) for making sense of the phenomenon of revelation, no longer taken as the manifestation of just any possible world, but as the revelation of a particular (biblical) world.

This affiliation between revelation in its theological or religious sense and revelation in its purely literary sense (i.e., as world disclosure) gives rise to a rather formidable question—or, at least, one that cannot be easily swept aside. By rooting his conception of revelation in a theory concerning the unique referential quality of literary texts in general, has Ricoeur not destroyed any potential basis for distinguishing between sacred texts and secular texts? If every literary or poetic text possesses the power to carry us beyond the world of manipulable objects, then what is unique about biblical texts? Are not all works of great literature capable of transforming reality through the "imaginative variations" which they "carry out on the real"?[20] Or, to state the matter more directly, if every poetic text is revelatory, then what makes revelation religious? Is revelation a merely hermeneutical concept? These questions are crucial for any phenomenological project which is interested in preserving a space for religious meaning, a space for revelation *qua* revelation.

By now, this line of questioning may appear all too familiar to us. For, in fact, this challenge is analogous to the one Marion had faced in the preceding chapter. In the case of Marion, it was a matter of determining whether or not his phenomenological figure of revelation was capable of preserving any relation at all to "revelation" taken in its strictly theological (ontic) sense. What, we had asked, makes the experience of the saturated phenomenon *par excellence* a specifically religious one if its possibility could be described and accounted for without reference to religious categories? As we recall, the fact that Marion had tried to save his phenomenological figure of revelation from any ontic determinations only served to exacerbate the difficulty. His desire to maintain what he considered to be the phenomenological rigor of his analysis prevented him—at least in his "strictly philosophical" works—from relating the figure of revelation back to its actual ontic event. In the case of Ricoeur, the difficulty is analogous, though by no means identical, as it no longer concerns an *eidetic* figure of revelation (as the saturation of saturation) but a hermeneutical one (as the disclosure of a second-order reference). And, yet, in both instances it is a question of establishing or accounting for the specifically religious character of what is *taken to be* 'revelation,' of what is given the name revelation.

6. RECOGNIZING REVELATION *QUA* REVELATION: CONVICTION, BELONGING, PREJUDICE

Ricoeur was well aware of this difficulty, and his work suggests at least two ways of addressing it. The first response that I will consider involves two stages: the initial stage indicates the level at which the special or "revealed" character of the biblical canon can be justifiably recognized, namely, the level of a belonging-to, prejudice, conviction, etc.; the subsequent stage serves to disclose the philosophical/ontological *significance* of belonging-to, prejudice, conviction, etc.

To begin with, it should be recognized that Ricoeur readily acknowledges that the privilege he grants certain texts (i.e., the canonical texts of the Christian tradition) is marked by a *contingency* which cannot be eradicated through any philosophical, critical, or purely rational argument—a contingency regarding the time and place of his birth, the prejudices pertaining to his particular tradition and religious upbringing, his membership within a specific community, etc.: "I am, then, prepared to recognize the historically limited character of my situation" within a tradition, a community, etc.[21] And this situation entails recognizing the authoritative status of a specific textual corpus—namely, the Old and New Testaments.

> To my mind, it is at the level of this canonical exegesis that the theological and the philosophical begin to split apart. The closure of the canon becomes the major phenomenon that separates from the other texts those that stand as *authoritative* for communities, which, in turn, understand themselves in light of these founding texts, distinguished from all other texts, as well as from the most faithful commentaries. The nonphilosophical moment is here, in this recognition of the authority of canonical texts worthy of guiding the kerygmatic interpretations of the theologies of this profession of faith. I agree with those exegete theologians who say that these texts are said to be inspired because they stand as authoritative, not the reverse.[22]

And yet this contingency, this situatedness, this nonphilosophical recognition of certain authoritative texts, is itself given a precise philosophical meaning by Ricoeur. In other words, although no strictly philosophical argument can justify the line that Ricoeur, as a committed Christian, will insist upon drawing between authoritative and non-authoritative texts—between, for example, a biblical narrative and a Homeric epic—philosophy can nonetheless account for what might be called the phenomenon of authority as such. On this point, Ricoeur's position is clearly indebted to the "rehabilitation of authority and tradition" carried out by Gadamer's *Truth and Method*,[23] where prejudice (which always entails the recognition of some authority) is shown to follow directly from the "projective" structure of understanding itself, that is, from the fact that we always already find ourselves "thrown" within a "situation." "To acquire an awareness of a situation is, however, always a task of peculiar difficulty. The very idea of a situation means that we are not standing outside it and hence are unable to have any objective knowledge of it. We always find ourselves within a situation, and throwing light on it is a task that is never entirely finished."[24]

This situatedness, this prior belonging or being-thrown, which precedes every act of critical reflection, finds expression in a number of dialectical pairs deployed throughout Ricoeur's work, namely: belonging and distanciation; retrieval and suspicion; understanding and explanation; and so on. With respect to the specific issue of revelation, however, its most telling expression concerns the anteriority of "conviction" with respect to "critique." Ricoeur encapsulated his position during an interview in 1995:

> But I always trusted a ground of questioning that was ultimately more resistant, more profound, and that comes from farther back than critique itself. Critique is still always linked to powers that I master, whereas this *giving of meaning* seems to me, precisely, to constitute me both as a receptive subject and as a critical subject. The polarity of adherence and of critique is itself placed under the sign of this prior giving. I am, then, prepared to recognize the historically limited character of my situation.[25]

Clearly, this "prior giving"—this giving of meaning—has nothing to do with an indeterminate or excessive modality of givenness which went by the name of revelation in the work of Marion. Rather, this giving is given in the sense that language itself is given, namely as a particular, determinate, natural language into which we are always already born. "If pushed, I would agree to say that a religion is like a language into which one is born [. . .] one feels at home there, which implies a recognition that there are other languages spoken by other people."[26] "So, in a certain manner, to be a religious subject is [. . .] to have *already* entered into this vast circuit involving a founding world, mediating texts, and traditions of interpretation."[27]

If philosophy cannot justify the particular convictions that lead one to attribute a revelatory function or status to certain texts rather than others, it can nevertheless account for the ontological possibility, inevitability and even inescapability of having convictions which are themselves "deeper" than and prior to the use of any of our so-called critical faculties.[28] This does not mean that Ricoeur does not leave any room for critical analysis. On the contrary, without a moment of "distanciation" brought about by critical reflection, "we would never become conscious of belonging-to a world, a culture, a tradition" (EBI 107). But this moment of distanciation and critical reflection "is never first, never constituting—it arrives unexpectedly like a 'crisis' within an experience that bears us," an experience of conviction. "The ultimate condition of any enterprise of justification or of grounding is that it is always preceded by a relation that already carries us"—a relation of belonging-to a given tradition (EBI 107). In this sense, the question of the authoritative status of the Bible—which has to do with the manner in which the Bible speaks to those belonging-to the Christian tradition, rather than with any body of doctrines that would be imposed by the magisterium—must be located within a theory of prejudices which is attuned to the nature of historically effected consciousness (*wirkungsgeschichtliches Bewußtsein*) as described by Gadamer (EBI 75).[29]

Let us return, once more, to the question to which Ricoeur's analyses of "conviction," "authority," "prejudice," "belonging," etc., were said to offer a first response: How can one account for the peculiarity and specificity of the religious phenomenon of revelation if it is conceived of on the basis of a more general theory of the world of the text, a theory which, in principle, equally applies to non-religious poetic works?

Ricoeur's first response addressed this problem only by circumventing it altogether, that is, by simply acknowledging that his own recognition of the authoritative status of the Bible stems convictions which—given the ontological structure of understanding itself—can never be entirely eliminated or neutralized, not even through the adoption of a critical attitude. Rather than feigning to supply a "critical" justification of the special character of biblical texts, he philosophically justifies the lack of justification.[30]

7. GENERAL HERMENEUTICS AND REGIONAL HERMENEUTICS

A second and more direct response to this problem can be gleaned from Ricoeur's essay on "Philosophical Hermeneutics and Biblical Hermeneutics."[31] Here, in fact, Ricoeur addresses the very same difficulty imposed by the above question, though he frames it in slightly different terms:

The present study aims at exploring the contribution of hermeneutical philosophy to biblical exegesis.

> By posing the problem in these terms, we appear to admit that biblical hermeneutics is only one of the possible applications of hermeneutic philosophy to a given category of texts. [. . .] In this sense, biblical hermeneutics is a *regional* hermeneutics in relation to philosophical hermeneutics, considered a *general* hermeneutics. It may then appear that we are acknowledging the subordination

of biblical hermeneutics to philosophical hermeneutics by treating it as an applied hermeneutics. (TA 89)

Needless to say, Ricoeur seeks to avoid such subordination. He argues that in the course of applying philosophical hermeneutics to the biblical text, a process of inversion is set into operation. For theological hermeneutics "presents features that are so original that the relation is gradually inverted," so that it "finally subordinates philosophical hermeneutics to itself as its own organon" (TA 90). But what exactly are these original features?

One has to read carefully in order not to miss the few instances in Ricoeur's analysis where the uniqueness of the biblical text is explicitly indicated.[32] The general idea, though, is made relatively clear: the biblical texts engender an intensification of some of the basic features that philosophical hermeneutics attributes to every poetic text. Bearing in mind our previous analyses, we can observe (though Ricoeur never does so explicitly) that this intensification transpires on two fronts, each of which corresponds to one of the two moments of textual reference discussed above: the negative moment in which the fixation by writing presents a break with ordinary everyday reality, and the positive moment in which a new world is thereby opened up before the text.

With regard to the first moment, the intensification brought about within theological hermeneutics has to do with a series of duplications or multiplications of textual mediations, in which "the initial hermeneutical situation of Christian preaching" is not only bound to texts, but is bound to texts that are themselves related back to other texts. "The very originality of the [Christic] event requires that it be transmitted by means of an interpretation of preexisting significations—*already inscribed*—available within the cultural community" (TA 94). Ricoeur describes these various strata of textual mediation as follows:

> Jesus himself interpreted the Torah; St. Paul and the author of the Letter to the Hebrews interpreted the Christic event in light of the prophesies and institutes of the old covenant. More generally, a hermeneutics of the Old Testament, considered as a given set of writings, is implied by the proclamation that Jesus is the Christ. All the 'titles' that exegetes term Christological stem from a reinterpretation of the figures received from written Hebraic culture and from Hellenistic culture: King, Messiah, High Priest, suffering Servant, Logos. [. . .] In this sense, Christianity is, from the start, an exegesis. This is not all, however: the new preaching, in its turn, is not only tied to an earlier writing that it interprets. It becomes in its turn a new writing [. . .] (TA 93–94)

It is, therefore, not surprising that Ricoeur, well before Marlene Zarader, had already faulted Heidegger's interpretation of the early Christian experience for having systematically excluded what is, in fact, most essential to it—namely, its relation to the "world" disclosed by the Hebraic Old Testament.[33] This stratification implies a demand that any reading of the New Testament must itself be related back to the Hebraic scriptures which are interpreted therein. But, in the present context, the primary significance of this complex multiplication of textual mediations has more to do with the distanciation or break which it renders possible with respect to the world of everyday experience:

> We state that the world of the 'literary' text is a projected world, one that is poetically *distanced* from everyday reality. *Is this not the case par excellence of the new being projected and proposed by the Bible?* Does not this new being make its way through the world of ordinary experience, despite the closedness of this experience? Is not the power of projection belonging to this world the power to make a break and a new beginning? (TA 97, italics mine)

Every text entails a break with everyday reality and an opening beyond any ostensive reference. The shift from speech to writing, from the spoken word to its material inscription, necessitates a separation or alienation from the limited spatio-temporal conditions of its author and original audience.[34] However, this break is intensified within biblical literature, which is, so to speak, comprised of inscriptions within inscriptions, texts within texts, readings within readings.

And yet this intensification does not prevent the text from speaking to everyday reality—that is, from re-describing the world of those who listen. After all, this break constitutes only the negative side of an entirely positive movement, in which a "new being"[35] or world is disclosed. The intensification on the side of textual mediation thus leads to a correlative intensification on the side of the possible world which is opened up—that is to say, on the side of the biblical "referent." Ricoeur insists that the most unique feature of the biblical texts stems from their ultimate referent, namely, God. "One of the features that constitutes the specificity of biblical discourse is, as we know, the central place held by the referent 'God'" (TA 97). This referent "stems from the competition and convergence" among the various literary forms which comprise the biblical canon: "the forms of narration, prophecy, hymn, wisdom, and so on" (TA 97).

A central and indeed reoccurring theme within Ricoeur's religious writings has to do with the correlation between these various *forms* of discourse and their respective *contents* or "theological meanings" (TA 93). In this regard, he clearly displays a greater appreciation for the textual nuances and the literary dimensions of biblical revelation than does Marion or Heidegger. He argues, for example, that the narrative form of Exodus reveals not just any idea of

God, but a particular one: namely, God as "the great actant in a history of deliverance." This idea of God cannot be understood apart from that particular narrative structure in which it finds expression (TA 92). This suggests that the confrontation between various forms of discourse within the Bible produces a multiplicity of theological meanings which, taken together, evoke an idea of God which in principle exceeds any single one of the literary forms found within it. "The referent 'God' is not just the index of the mutual belonging together (*appartenance*) of the originary forms of the discourse of faith. It is also the index of their incompleteness. It is their common goal which escapes them" (FS 228). In this respect, we might even say that the closure of the biblical canon, the inclusion of a multiplicity of forms within one 'book,' and the polyphonic character of the biblical language entail an intensification and transformation of the referential function itself. It is, above all, on this basis that Ricoeur claims that the ostensible priority of philosophical hermeneutics over and above theological hermeneutics is destabilized and, finally, inverted.

This observation also indicates a possible response to the objection, posed above, that Ricoeur's theory of revelation is unable to account for the distinctiveness of revelation vis-à-vis other poetic discourses since both are subject to the principles articulated by a general (i.e., philosophical) hermeneutics. For on the basis of this observation, the Bible is said to constitute a unique case among poetic texts:

> It is a unique case because all its partial forms of discourse are referred to that Name which is the point of intersection and the vanishing point of all our discourse about God, the name of the unnamable. This is the paradoxical homology that the category of the world of the text establishes between revelation in the broad sense of poetic discourse and in the specifically biblical sense. (EBI 104)

What is, perhaps, most astonishing about Ricoeur's position is that he insists that the uniqueness of the Bible only comes into view when it is approached *as* a poetic text, that is to say, when it is understood according to the categories and principles articulated by general hermeneutics, such as writing, second-order reference, and, above all, the world of the text. As Ricoeur puts it, "the areligious sense of revelation [i.e., as the general type of manifestation belonging to all poetic texts] helps us to restore the concept of biblical revelation to its full dignity" (EBI 104). In particular, Ricoeur argues that these general hermeneutical principles help to dispel some common misconceptions about the nature of revelation itself.

Here, Ricoeur strikes at the very heart of what he describes as the "original nucleus of the traditional understanding of revelation," namely, the notion of revelation as divine inspiration (EBI 75). According to this understanding, scripture is said to be revealed insofar as it was whispered by God directly into the ear of its author. Revelation would, then, be bound to a theory of double authorship, according to which the voice of another (namely, God) is to be heard behind the voice of the author (say, the prophet) (EBI 76). Ricoeur strongly opposes this narrow conception of revelation. To be sure, he admits that it remains essential to one particular form of biblical discourse, namely, prophetic discourse. However, when it is extended in such a way that it is thought to be constitutive of the entire canon, our understanding of revelation "is deprived of the enrichment it might receive from those forms of discourse [such as, for instance, narrative discourse] which are less easily interpreted in terms of a voice behind a voice [. . .]" (EBI 76). The meaning of narrative discourse, according to Ricoeur, would be entirely missed if we merely focused on authorship and the author's intention, rather than on the events recounted therein.

This, in fact, is the fundamental lesson that Ricoeur draws from the emerging field of so-called narrative theology: namely, that in a certain category of biblical texts the theological meaning is determined by and, thus, inseparable from the narrative configuration of the events described within the narrative itself. A text that falls under this category is given the name "interpretative narrative" by Ricoeur for the simple reason that theological meaning does not only (nor even primarily) result from "a work of interpretation applied *to* the text, [but] already functions *in* the text" (FS 181). In other words, such narratives are, as it were, self-interpreting, though not because the narrator's voice informs the reader of the significance of the events described, but because the significance is somehow inscribed within the events themselves through the art of literary composition, or, more specifically, though the work of "emplotment."

Ricoeur's reading of the story of the empty tomb in the Gospel of Mark offers a clear example of one such "interpretive narrative." Here, as in the rest of his Gospel, Mark's Christology is said to be inseparable from the narrative structure, or, to put it the other way around, the narrative itself serves to configure and thereby elucidate a specifically Markan Christological idea—one that opposes a "Chistology of glory" in favor of a "Christology of a suffering and crucified Son of Man" (FS 198–9). Ricoeur begins his interpretation by offering the following formula: "If Jesus lives and lives elsewhere, then here there has to be an empty tomb" (FS 198). Thus, "the absence of the body of Jesus" naturally represents the "narrative trace" of the kerygmatic message—namely, the message that the Lord has risen (ibid.). In Mark's narrative, however, this resurrection takes place without any pomp or glory, without an appearance and, thus, without the security and assurance of Jesus' presence. Why this lack, this absence? Ricoeur suggests that this conspicuous absence, this "parsimony of presence," conveys a certain theological message regarding the suffering of Christ and the challenges or risks of discipleship.

If it is true that Mark here continues to oppose a Christology that would immediately lead to a Christology of glory, short-circuiting the Master's suffering and the difficulty of being a disciple, then the narrative that best interprets this theology of the suffering Son of Man is one that does without an appearance of Jesus himself to Peter and the apostles. (FS 198–9)

This parsimony of presence is magnified by other narrative features as well, features that are unique to Mark's Gospel, such as the fact that "the only ones present at the tomb are the women, no guards (as in Matthew), no disciples (as in Luke and John), and not even the figure of Jesus himself (as in Matthew and John)" (FS 198). According to Ricoeur, "even the vision of the 'young man' (*neaniskos*) does not contradict this parsimony of presence," since he is not Jesus, but only a "messenger who represents Jesus." All that remains in the "dimension of pure presence" is the voice which says, "Do not be amazed; you seek Jesus of Nazareth, who was crucified. He has risen, he is not here" (Mk. 16:16).[36] Once again, Ricoeur maintains that this narrative feature engenders a central theme of Mark's Gospel: "This negativity of presence belongs to the guiding theme of the progressive disappearance of the body throughout the passion narrative [in Mark]. A decrease in the body, an increase in the word" (FS 199). The narrative, therefore, is an expression of the manner in which the Gospel word comes to replace the bodily presence of Jesus Christ in the world.

Whether or not we find Ricoeur's interpretation of the story of the empty tomb convincing, his theory of interpretative narrative raises some serious issues. If, in fact, the narrative were self-interpreting as Ricoeur argues, then would not this self-interpretation be an absolutely definitive one—that is, one that disqualifies all previous interpretations and bars any future interpretations? One might easily mistake Ricoeur's theory of interpretive narrative as a flimsy mechanism for legitimating his interpretation over and against all others. Indeed, like every good interpreter, Ricoeur claims not to impose his own meaning on the text, but to uncover a meaning that is already present there in it. However, Ricoeur's general attitude toward biblical texts is that they offer a plurality of meanings, and thus allow for a variety of interpretations.[37] One might wonder how these so-called interpretive narratives could allow for a plurality of interpretations when they are said to embody their own self-interpretation. Here, it seems, Ricoeur tries to walk a thin line between a potentially endless plurality of interpretations, on the one hand, and a single interpretation that is contained within the structure of the narrative, on the other.

Furthermore, Ricoeur's interpretation of Mark appears, at times, to move in reverse order. That is to say, it begins by presupposing which "ideological interpretation" Mark wishes to communicate in events (namely, a "Christology of the suffering Son of Man"), and then proceeds towards a demonstration of how and why the events function to express (or "interpret" as Ricoeur puts it) this ideology. This is, to be sure, the most obvious weakness of his argument regarding the so-called self-interpretive function of certain narrative texts: in order to perceive the manner in which the narrative serves to configure and thus promote one ideological interpretation over another, we must have already decided in advance which ideology is at play within the text. Nonetheless, it is not at all clear that Ricoeur needs (or even wants) to avoid this sort of circular reasoning. After all, perhaps it is precisely this circularity that keeps the text open to further interpretation, thereby preventing it from being reduced to any single, authoritative theological meaning.

At any rate, the purpose of Ricoeur's discussion of so-called interpretive narratives is not to demonstrate that the narrator imposes an authoritative meaning or "intention" upon the events he describes. On the contrary, his point is to demonstrate that the narrative configuration is itself expressive of a theological meaning, above and beyond the imposing voice of the narrator himself.[38] Again, it is the configuration of the events themselves (which transpires at level of the text) rather than the narrator's voice (which, as it were, would remain behind the text) that determines the meaning of the kerygmatic proclamation within the narrative genre. "These are narratives in which the ideological interpretation these narratives wish to convey is not superimposed on the narrative by the narrator but is, instead, incorporated into the very strategy of the narrative" (FS 181).[39] An interpretation that focuses exclusively on the author's (or, in this case, the narrator's) intention is therefore liable to miss the real force and novelty of the narrative genre.

We can now appreciate more concretely Ricoeur's reasons for arguing that a theory that equates revelation with inspiration (that is, with a voice behind a voice) fails to account for the richness of the narrative genre. The theological meanings embodied in and generated by this biblical genre are quite literally to be found in the narrative events, not in the voice. However, Ricoeur seems to suggest that even prophetic discourse (the biblical genre which appears to emphasize the author's voice the most) calls for a conception of revelation that moves beyond a narrow theory of inspiration (as a voice behind the text). Ricoeur makes this point by way of his reading of Ezekiel, where he demonstrates (among other things) that the force of prophecy lies in the transmitted message or announcement rather than in the messenger himself. "As for the messenger himself, the heart of what is at issue is his announcement [. . .] of judgment or salvation" (TB 168). Following Claus Westermann, Ricoeur draws a distinction between the various formulas (such as 'Thus says Yhwh . . .') that are repeated by the messenger in order to justify or accredit his announcement, on the one hand, and the announcement properly speaking, on the other. The significance of the prophetic genre, according to Ricoeur, has less to do with the manner in which the prophet claims that his announcement represents the word of God than it does with the manner in which this word is addressed directly to us—the readers.

Ricoeur drives this point home through his analysis of the unique temporal mode of the prophetic genre, that is to say, its relation to time and to history. Unlike narrative discourse, which concerns a past that has already transpired, and unlike eschatological discourse, which concerns the "end times," prophetic discourse is distinguished by its concern with the present and with the threat of an imminent future.

> Narrative theology [. . .] is a theology that gives the guarantee of the founding events to the identity of the people, events that give certitude to the lived experience of a communal existence. Prophetic theology, on the contrary, proceeds from a confrontation with a history that gives rise to anxiety, inasmuch as it includes the frightening alternative of destruction or salvation. We cannot overemphasize this opposition between the mythic and legendary history of the theology of traditions and the very real history that confronts the prophet. When Ezekiel thunders against Egypt, whose aid had helped protect the people against Mesopotamian oppression, it is contemporary Egypt and not the legendary Egypt of the Exodus that he has in view. We can see in this opposition the opposition between a traditional history that yields security and an imminent, traumatic history. (TB 169)

"[H]owever 'crazy' the prophet may appear, or to put it in a more moderate way, however 'ecstatic' or 'enthusiastic,' this madness [. . .] is set within a history that is *happening now*" (TB 170, emphasis mine). In other words, it is the reader's judgment or salvation that is at stake in the prophetic announcement. The notion of inspiration as the voice of God behind the voice of the prophet becomes relatively marginal. For, in truth, the reader confronts the announcement, so to speak, head-on—that is to say, as an original encounter. It is as if the reader stands in the place of the prophet himself, re-actualizing the event of revelation in the very act of reading (TB 168). The notion of revelation as inspiration, however, serves only to conceal the profound contribution that textual mediation makes to our encounter with the prophetic word.

Ricoeur suggests, therefore, that the idea of the world of the text provided by philosophical hermeneutics offers a more productive and versatile framework for understanding the meaning of revelation than does the notion of inspiration.

> By so orienting the hermeneutical axis of my meditation toward the issue [or world] of the text, I recognize the vanity of an inquiry oriented toward the

text's author that would seek to identify God as the voice behind the narrative or prophetic voice. I am well aware that a long tradition identified revelation with inspiration, in the sense of an insufflation of meaning that made God a sort of overarching author of the texts wherein faith instructs itself. But if the word "revelation" means something, its meaning is to be sought on the side of the issue the texts tell about, as an aspect of the biblical world. (FS 221)

By approaching the subject of revelation with the resources of philosophical hermeneutics, Ricoeur not only breaks with the traditional ideas of prophecy as inspiration or insufflation—ideas which had resonated with romanticism's emphasis on genius, the interior life of the author, divination, etc.—he also breaks with any theory that would situate revelation outside language and literature, and prior to textual mediation. Revelation can no longer be confused with some psychologism or subjectivism. It cannot be equated with some secret communicated by God to the biblical authors before (or even at the time of) the act of composition. Rather, revelation is what takes place once that text has already been fixed in writing. Revelation, one might say, following Ricoeur's suggestion, occurs in front of the text, not behind or before it.

Moreover, in a provocative reversal of the standard line of reasoning—which moves from the strictly poetic definition of revelation employed within philosophical hermeneutics to its particular biblical or theological usage—Ricoeur suggests that the particular biblical meaning of revelation actually paves the way for its broader, areligious redeployment within a general or philosophical hermeneutics.

> By using the word revelation in such a nonbiblical and non-religious way, do we not abuse the word? I do not think so. Our analysis of the biblical concept of revelation has prepared for us a first degree analogical use of the term and here we are led to a second degree analogy. The first degree analogy was assured by the role of the first analogue, prophetic discourse, with its implication of another voice behind the prophet's voice. This meaning of the first analogue was communicated to all other modes of [biblical] discourse to the extent that they could be said to be inspired. (EBL 103)

Now Ricoeur argues that a second analogue presents itself here, no longer on the basis of prophetic discourse but rather on the basis of narrative discourse, "where what is said or recounted, the generative historical event, came to language through the narration" (EBL 103). This process, whereby the 'things' said come into language through a particular form of discourse, is none other than the process of revelation or manifestation (in the hermeneutical rather than psychological sense). Consequently, this analogue can, in turn, be communicated or extended to every poetic discourse in the same manner that the

Christian tradition had previously extended the first analogue (inspiration) to the entire biblical canon.

On Ricoeur's account, there exists a kind of momentum within theological hermeneutics itself which naturally tends toward its analogical redeployment within philosophical discourse. It is as if the theological idea of revelation had always harbored a universal ambition, hope, or aspiration which not only tolerates but actually invites this philosophical extension by, or through, a general hermeneutics. (And, needless to say, this hermeneutical use of revelation would neither be the first nor probably the last of such philosophical extensions. We have seen from the start of this study that twentieth-century phenomenology and, for that matter, the entire history of modern western philosophy, abounds with similar examples—from the enlightenment's so-called natural revelation, to Heidegger's *Offenbarkeit* and Marion's 'phenomenological figure of revelation.') If we allow ourselves to follow the path suggested by Ricoeur a bit further, we might go so far as to say that each of these philosophical interpretations or extensions is to some degree sanctioned by the analogical use of the term revelation within theological discourse itself. It would be as though the very idea of revelation solicits a philosophical explication that would develop the various meanings which are already, albeit implicitly, contained *ab ovo* within the theological domain.

Does this mean that the concept of revelation culminates within philosophical discourse, or, more specifically, within a general hermeneutics that would seek to extend the concept to every form of poetic discourse? Does this mean that philosophy and philosophy alone is capable of articulating the true significance of revelation? This might at first appear to be the case. After all, has Ricoeur not already suggested that "the areligious [i.e., philosophical] sense of revelation helps us to restore the concept of biblical revelation to its full dignity"? But, in reality, Ricoeur's position is more complex. As he himself notes:

> Yet, if this areligious sense of revelation has such a *corrective* value, it does not for all that include the religious meaning of revelation. There is a homology between them, but nothing allows us to derive the specific features of religious language—i.e., that its reference moves among prophesy, narrative, prescription, wisdom, and psalms, coordinating these diverse and partial forms of discourse by giving them a vanishing point and an index of incompleteness—nothing, I say, allows us to *derive* this from the general characteristics of the poetic function. (EBI 104)

The principles of philosophical hermeneutics may serve a "corrective" function with respect to biblical hermeneutics, insofar as they help to dispel certain traditional misconceptions about revelation. Nevertheless, the religious meaning of revelation cannot be fully derived from the philosophical meaning. It would be a mistake to regard the one as foundational and the other as derivative.

In fact, Ricoeur seems to be suggesting a kind of cross-fertilization between the regional hermeneutics of theology and the general hermeneutics of philosophy. This cross-fertilization stands in sharp contrast to the one-way filiation (or *derivation*) that resulted from Heidegger's logic of presupposition. We will recall from our analysis of the opening sections of *Being and Time* (above, Chapter 2, Section 5) that Heidegger's fundamental ontology deliberately ruled out this sort of two-way exchange between regional, theological hermeneutics and general, philosophical hermeneutics. On the one hand, Heidegger had insisted that ontic sciences—and this would include "theological hermeneutics" insofar as it is concerned with the understanding of one particular object or text, namely, the Bible—are preceded, founded, guided, "corrected" by the fruits of a fundamental ontology, which, in the present context, is basically synonymous with what Ricoeur calls "general hermeneutics." On the other hand, he insisted that fundamental ontology remained absolutely independent from those ontic sciences which it, in turn, serves to ground. From the Heideggerian perspective, then, general hermeneutics would serve both to ground and to correct ontic theological hermeneutics without ever borrowing from or being affected by the latter. We saw that, in Heidegger, the border between these two types of sciences can be crossed in the direction moving from ontological (fundamental) to the ontic (derived), but not in the reverse direction.

Ricoeur, in opposition to Heidegger, wants to allow movement in both directions, to the point where the line demarcating the "fundamental" from the "derived" becomes blurred. This is not to say that the two poles themselves become confused or conflated in Ricoeur's work. As one who appreciates the value of the plurality of discourses available to us, Ricoeur insists on rigorously upholding the distinction between regional hermeneutics and general hermeneutics, between the theological and the philosophical, between ontic science and ontological science, etc. But in each instance the two poles are caught up in a sort of dialectical relationship in which each sheds light upon the other—yet without absorbing, dissolving, or exhausting it. Thus, in Ricoeur, the play between the theological and the philosophical is best understood in terms of a *mutual enrichment*, rather than in terms of an *illicit contamination* as was the case in both Heidegger (where ontology was protected from ontic incursions) and Marion (where the phenomenological figure of "revelation" was rigorously distinguished from the ontic event of "Revelation").

8. "TRUNCATED" ONTOLOGY: THE LONG AND THE SHORT ROUTES

We come now to our primary argument concerning the fundamental difference between Ricoeur's hermeneutical form of phenomenology, on the one hand, and the radical form of phenomenology exhibited in the work of Marion and the early Heidegger, on the other. However, in order to register the full impact of this discovery on the problematic of revelation, we will need to return to our initial discussion of hermeneutics and the historical sciences, with which this chapter began. For it was in light of the debates surrounding the nature of historical understanding that Ricoeur had first embarked on his own path of thinking, one which explicitly broke with Heidegger's "radical" thought, which had centered on the critique of metaphysics.

We must return, specifically, to the 1965 essay on "Existence and Hermeneutics" in which Ricoeur explored the notion of existence that results from the effort to renew phenomenology through hermeneutics. While we have already discussed certain aspects of this essay, we postponed until now the analysis of one of its most crucial components, namely, the distinction that Ricoeur posits between two ways in which hermeneutics can be grafted onto the phenomenological method. He refers to these ways as the "short" or "direct route" and the "long" or "indirect route."

> The short route is the one taken by an ontology of understanding after the manner of Heidegger. I call such an ontology of the understanding a "short route" because, breaking with any discussion of method, it carries itself directly to the level of an ontology of finite being [i.e. Dasein] in order there to recover understanding, no longer as a mode of knowledge, but rather as a mode of being. (CI 6)

Ricoeur proposes to follow a "more roundabout, more arduous path" that begins with semantic and linguistic considerations, and which claims to arrive at an ontology not directly but by degrees, through a sustained dialogue with various regional, epistemological, ontic disciplines, such as history, philology, psychology, and—why not—theology.

Ricoeur's own hermeneutical project was, if not from the start then at least from the early stages of its development, conceived in opposition to the philosophical position exemplified by Heidegger's own "fundamental ontology." We must be attentive to Ricoeur's philosophical reasons for this opposition. What was it precisely about this fundamental ontology that Ricoeur rejects?

Ricoeur's response is complex and multidimensional. We must begin by noting that Ricoeur does not reject Heidegger's position altogether. Instead, he wishes to give Heidegger "full credit" for having successfully overcome his predecessors' (especially Dilthey's) narrowly epistemological conceptualization of the hermeneutical problem (CI 6). As we saw in the first half of this chapter, it was only on the basis of Heidegger's (and Husserl's) ontological conception of "world" that Ricoeur was able to formulate his own theory of the world of the text. So Ricoeur's critique of Heidegger does not involve a call to return to an exclusively epistemological framework, such as nineteenth-century psychologism or twentieth-century structuralism. Moreover, Ricoeur is not at all interested in breaking with ontology (in the manner of, say, Levinas), or passing beyond ontology (in the manner of Marion). In fact, his own route harbors an ontological aspiration of its own: "the long route which I propose also aspires to carry reflection to the level of an ontology, but it will do so by degrees, following successive investigations into semantics [. . .] and reflection" (CI 6). For Ricoeur, the question is not whether the ontological shift in hermeneutics is valid, but only whether Heidegger's *direct* approach is the most effective means for accomplishing this shift. He is not suspicious of ontology as such, but only of Heidegger's claim to have attained a unified, fundamental ontology in one fell swoop.

> The doubt I express [. . .] is concerned only with the possibility of the making of a direct ontology, free at the outset from any methodological requirements and consequently outside the circle of an interpretation whose theory this ontology formulates. But it is the *desire* for this ontology which animates our entire enterprise and which keeps it from sinking into either a linguistic philosophy like Wittgenstein's or a reflective philosophy of the Neo-Kantian sort. (CI 6–7)

Before we can appreciate Ricoeur's motives for opposing Heidegger's so-called direct ontology, we will need to determine what Ricoeur means by that phrase. To begin with, we might say that a direct ontology is one that proceeds by way of an analysis of Dasein, to the exclusion of all (other) ontic beings. We will recall that for Heidegger, Dasein was a privileged "being" on account of its "ontic-ontological" constitution—that is, on account of the fact that an "[u]nderstanding of Being is itself a definite characteristic of Dasein's Being" (BT 32/12). In contrast to every other ontic entity, it was distinguished—indeed, "ontically distinguished"—by the very fact that "Being is an issue for it" (BT 32/12). The essential character of Dasein lies "in the fact that in each case it has its Being to be, and has it as its own" (BT 32–33/12). Thus, according to Heidegger, any analysis of the Being of history would have to proceed by way of an analysis of the historicity that is proper to Dasein. That is to say, the ontological meaning of history, and thus of historical knowledge as well, cannot be gleaned from an analysis of particular historical (ontic) objects—such as texts, artifacts, ruins, etc. It can only result from the "direct" analysis of Dasein's "fundamental temporality" to which the final sections of *Being and Time* were devoted.

According to that analysis, the conception of time employed by the historical (epistemological) sciences is merely derivative in nature. More precisely, it is said to result from an inauthentic, metaphysical interpretation—or "leveling-off"—of the more authentic, more fundamental experience of temporality. In brief, temporality in its fundamental sense has less to do with the passage of time in a succession of isolated "nows," than with the manner in which Dasein takes hold of itself in its authentic (resolute) future-oriented (ecstatic) modality, exhibited by the ontological structure of Care (*Sorge*). Heidegger argues that the true meaning of history can only be glimpsed from the vantage point of an authentic Dasein, where every turning toward the past stems from a resoluteness that is itself turned toward the future (TN vol. III 74). The genuine meaning of the past always has to do with the way it is taken up or appropriated by Dasein through an act of repetition (*Weiderholung*). To treat the past *as such*, i.e., as irrevocably past[40]—as do the so-called historical sciences—is to completely misconstrue its real significance and to miss the primacy of *historicity* (as one piece within the overall process of Dasein's temporalization) over and above *historiography* (as an ontic-positive science pertaining to present-at-hand or ready-to-hand entities). Hence Heidegger's verdict regarding the merely derivative status of the kind of hermeneutics deployed by the human sciences:

> The phenomenology of Dasein is hermeneutic in the primordial signification of this word [. . .] so far as this hermeneutic works out Dasein's [historicity] ontologically as the ontical condition for the possibility of [historiography], it contains the roots of what can be called 'hermeneutic' only in a derivative sense: the methodology of those human sciences which are [historiographical] in nature. (BT 62/37–38)

The derivative nature of this hermeneutics stems from the fact that the epistemological sciences naively adopt a concept of time from either metaphysics or, more generally, from the 'fallen' discourse of *das Man*, which is itself qualified as derivative, inauthentic, etc.[41]

We are now in a position to appreciate Ricoeur's reasons for breaking with this direct route. First reason: Heidegger's approach dodges rather than addresses the most elementary problems of hermeneutics:

> With Heidegger's radical manner of questioning, the problems that initiated our investigation not only remain unresolved but are lost from sight. How, we asked, can an organon be given to exegesis, to the clear comprehension of texts? How can the historical sciences be founded in the face of the natural sciences? How can the conflict of rival interpretations be arbitrated? These problems are

not properly considered in a fundamental hermeneutics, and this by design: this hermeneutics is intended not to resolve them but to dissolve them. (CI 10)

The explanation for this evasion is quite clear, as Ricoeur observes elsewhere: "In passing from the Analytic of Dasein, which still includes the theory of understanding and interpretation, to the theory of temporality [. . .], it seems that all critical effort is spent in the work of deconstructing metaphysics" (HH 88). It is here that we see that Heidegger's "obsession" with the critique of metaphysics overtakes his concern with properly hermeneutical questions. The critical/epistemological concerns of the historical sciences find themselves replaced by an exclusive concern with dismantling the prejudices of metaphysical thinking.[42] Heidegger's direct approach does, therefore, involve a certain kind of critique, under the auspices of *Destruktion*, but it is not one that would help us understand this or that being, this or that historical moment, text, etc. It is designed only to pierce through the conceptual sedimentations of the metaphysical tradition which have served to conceal the true meaning of Being. "Heidegger has not wanted to consider any particular problem concerning the understanding of this or that [ontic] being. He wanted to retrain our eye and redirect our gaze; he wanted us to subordinate historical knowledge to ontological understanding, as the derived form of a primordial form" (CI 10). But to do so in the manner he suggests is to sever ties with every ontic-positive science.

This leads us to the second reason Ricoeur gives for breaking with Heidegger's fundamental ontology: the derivation between the various regional hermeneutics (or ontic-positive sciences) and fundamental hermeneutics is not so clear cut. In fact, Heidegger's own work seems to attest to the fact that this derivation works in both directions. Ricoeur's most articulate justification for this claim is found in the third volume of *Time and Narrative*, where he demonstrates that Heidegger's very own explication of fundamental temporality actually depends upon certain root metaphors which are borrowed from the ordinary concept of time. Even though it is said to be "derived," the historiographical concept of time "adds to that of temporality, on the existential level itself, those features signified by the words 'stretching along,' 'movement,' and 'self-constancy'" (TN vol. III 73). This suggests, according to Ricoeur, a certain "enrichment of the primordial by the derivative"—that is to say, a two-way derivation right at the core of a text devoted to the demonstration of a one-way derivation (ibid.). "This is less of a one-way derivation than Heidegger seems to announce" (ibid.). But Ricoeur goes even further to suggest that, in the end, the epistemological sciences disclose a "plurality of temporalities," each of which is in some sense equally valid in and of itself (think, for instance, of "quantum time, thermodynamic time, the time of galactic transformations, or that of the evolution of species") (ibid., 91). Each contributes to our sense of time and displays a certain richness which cannot be accounted for by means of the process of leveling off described by Heidegger.

So, what does all of this mean for our own understanding of Ricoeur's proposed "long route"? And what is its significance with regard to the problem of revelation? Let us address the first question before turning, finally, to the second: Whereas Heidegger's ontological project entailed a "logic of presupposition" according to which phenomenology *as* "ontology" would remain wholly independent from each and every "ontico-positive science" (including theology), Ricoeur insists on maintaining a creative tension between ontology and the so-called ontico-positive sciences. In lieu of a unified ontology, Ricoeur advances what he referred to in 1965 as a "truncated ontology," one that is constantly enriched, sustained, and potentially challenged by the "regional ontologies" proposed by each of the epistemological sciences. Being itself resists all attempts at formalization, unification, totalization—there is no single, solid ground beneath this plethora of regional ontologies upon which a fundamental ontology could be constructed. Thus, Ricoeur's ontology begins and ends with the interpretation of ontic beings, and above all with language. We can never get beyond interpretation; we can never do phenomenology in the absence of hermeneutics—and thus in the absence of the conflicts between rival interpretations. Does this mean that we will never arrive at a unified ontology, one that could do without epistemology or that could unite the various "realisms" operative at the level of ontic science? Ricoeur, it seems, wants to preserve the possibility of such an ontology, but only as a limiting idea, in the strict Kantian sense of this term. That is to say, it is an ideal that guides thought towards its goal: "ontology is indeed the promised land for a philosophy that begins with language and reflection; but, like Moses, the speaking and reflecting subject can only glimpse this land before dying" (CI 24).[43]

If, as Ricoeur suggests, these strictly regional, epistemological, or ontic sciences can be shown to "enrich" rather than threaten or "contaminate" the fundamentality of ontological sciences, then the problem of ontic contamination, which was shown to plague the phenomenological projects of both Heidegger and Marion, will have been avoided from the start. In other words, if Ricoeur's phenomenology of revelation is in fact bound to a theory of the text that not only permits but even facilitates a productive dialectic between ontology and epistemology, then he will have already sidestepped one of the primary difficulties confronting the radical phenomenologists' formulations of revelation.

It has to be admitted, and indeed lamented, that this particular thesis is never explicitly worked out in Ricoeur's writings. He never articulates the advantages of his hermeneutical formulation of revelation vis-à-vis other phenomenological formulations, perhaps because his religious writings were typically addressed to theological rather than philosophical audiences. This omission is, however, to be expected for at least two additional reasons: First, because the play between the ontological and the epistemological (or ontical) is so fundamental to Ricoeur's thinking that it often operates without mention and beneath the radar. Secondly, this omission is not at all surprising since the problem to which it seems to promise a solution is one that only comes into focus once Ricoeur's treatment of revelation is placed alongside those of radical phenomenologists, such as Marion. But this confrontation never really took place during Ricoeur's lifetime. On the one hand, Ricoeur seldom ever addressed the work of the younger "theologically" inclined phenomenologist. On the other hand, proponents of the theological turn in recent phenomenology have generally failed to give Ricoeur's religious thought the attention it clearly deserves.[44] The purpose of my own reading of his work is to draw out the hitherto overlooked implications of Ricoeur's so-called long route for a phenomenological understanding of revelation.

There is indeed a second, more obvious way in which Ricoeur's proposed "long route" opens onto the problem of revelation. This has to do with the manner in which this indirect route is tied to a particular notion of "reflection," a term of art that Ricoeur borrows from the work of Jean Nabert (CI 17).[45] Paraphrasing Nabert's view, Ricoeur states that "reflection is nothing other than the appropriation of our act of existing by means of a critique applied to the works and acts which are the signs of this act of existing" (CI 17). Reflection moves in precisely the opposite direction than does Heidegger's fundamental ontology—it moves from the ontic (which for Heidegger was derivative) towards the ontological (or primordial), in clear violation of Heidegger's so-called logic of presupposition (see above, Chapter 2, Section 4). The justification for this reversal is clear: Since Heidegger's direct route failed "to show in what sense historical understanding, properly speaking, is derived from this primordial understanding," Ricoeur argues that it makes more sense "to begin with the derived forms of understanding" themselves. "This implies that the point of departure be taken on the same level on which understanding operates, that is, on the level of language" (CI 10). If, as Ricoeur suggests, we cannot proceed directly to the level of a fundamental ontology, this leaves only one option: we must begin with the interpretation of language, that is, with texts, symbols, documents, signs of a particular tradition, a particular language, a particular discourse.

This leads to a further insight regarding the so-called indirect route: in abandoning the project of fundamental ontology for a long and arduous analysis of linguistic signs and symbols, Ricoeur also abandons the pretensions of a consciousness that claims to be able to establish or constitute itself *by itself*. The first abandonment *corresponds*, so to speak, to an abandonment or divestment (*dessaisissement*) of the self in the face of the texts in which it interprets itself. Thus, "the subject that interprets himself while interpreting signs is no longer the [self-positing] *cogito*: rather, he is a being who discovers, by the exegesis of his own life, that he is placed in being before he places and possesses himself" (CI 11). But what is perhaps most surprising is that already in this essay from 1965—an essay which, moreover, was neither devoted to the philosophy of religion nor addressed to a theological audience—Ricoeur seems to indicate the distinctiveness, if not the uniqueness, of religious language: "by understanding himself in and through the signs of the sacred, man performs the most radical abandonment of himself that it is possible to imagine" (CI 22). He goes on to specify that "this dispossession [brought about through the engagement with religious language] exceeds that occasioned by psychoanalysis and Hegelian phenomenology" (the other two hermeneutical perspectives discussed in the essay) (CI 22). It is in the act of interpreting *religious* texts, in exposing oneself to the world of such texts, that one is most fully constituted by that to which one is handed over and abandoned. It is worth noting the remarkable similarity between Ricoeur's theory of self-divestment (*dessaisissement*) and Marion's theory of the gifted (*l'adonné*). Both theories involve a conception of self that is explicitly opposed the self-positing autonomy of the Cartesian subject, or *cogito*. Nonetheless, as one might expect, the two theories part company when it comes to issue of the self's relationship to language. Whereas Marion had claimed that the gifted receives itself from a pure (pre-linguistic) givenness, Ricoeur argues that the "summoned subject" receives itself from the concrete symbols, metaphors, and narratives embodied within texts.[46] For Marion, language and concepts are viewed as a kind of filament that the gifted imposes upon the infinite and excessive given in the process of phenomenalizing (or interpreting) it (see above, Chapter 3, Section 10). But on Ricoeur's account, the given is always already linguistic in character—the myths, symbols, and narratives are precisely what constitutes the summoned self in the first place.

With this, my two principal theses regarding Ricoeur's hermeneutical conception of revelation finally connect with one another (Chapter 4, Section 2). My first thesis is that (a) Ricoeur's notion of revelation—as the revelation of the world of the text—was woven together from a hermeneutic theory of textual mediation and a phenomenological theory of world or being-in-the-world. My second thesis is that (b) Ricoeur's thought necessitates a reversal of the relationship between the ontic and the ontological, whereby the ontic was shown to enrich rather than contaminate the ontological. We can now observe that this reversal also leads us back to the world of the religious text, as a privileged ground or source of enrichment for phenomenological discourse itself. Ricoeur's work therefore suggests a complete reevaluation of the proper relationship between the religious discourse and the phenomenological enterprise, one that allows, and even encourages, a kind of reciprocity between these two spheres of discourse—one religious, the other philosophical.

It must be admitted that this conclusion has been reached only through considerable interpretive effort on my part—an effort which not only attempts to tie various and often isolated strands of Ricoeur's thought into an integral whole, but one that seeks in his work a response to a specific set of problems that emerged within my previous analyses of radical phenomenology, in Chapters 2 and 3. It is therefore incumbent upon me to test this reading against certain problematic instances within Ricoeur's *oeuvre*, instances where he himself attempts to prevent religious discourse from infiltrating his phenomenological discourse (after all, such attempts seem to contradict the attitude of mutual reciprocity between philosophy and theology which I claim to have spotted in Ricoeur's own analysis). Perhaps the most obvious and well-known instance is found in his second-to-last major work, *Oneself as Another*, to which I now turn.

9. RELIGIOUS DISCOURSE AND PHILOSOPHICAL DISCOURSE

When Ricoeur published his Gifford Lectures (originally delivered in Edinburgh in 1986) under the title *Oneself as Another*,[47] he opted to exclude the pair of lectures with which he concluded the series due to their explicit reference to biblical texts. In contrast to the preceding nine lectures which "assume the bracketing, conscious and resolute, of the convictions that bind me to biblical faith," the final two lectures were animated by the "culturally contingent symbolic network" woven within the Judeo-Christian Scriptures (OA 23–4). This decision clearly runs counter to an intellectual project which has elsewhere recognized the value of culturally contingent symbols for philosophical reflection. Ricoeur provides a litany of justifications for his decision, as if to acknowledge the unexpected nature of this move. His chief concern, he claims, was to separate the kerygmatic dimension to which the last two studies make an appeal from the purely argumentative dimension of the first nine studies. He writes:

> I do not claim that at the deep level of motivations these convictions remain without any effect on the interest I take in this or that problem, [or] even in the overall problematic of the self. But I think I have presented to my readers arguments alone, which do not assume any commitment from the reader to reject, accept or suspend anything with regard to biblical faith. (OA 24)

One must bear in mind that at the time of *Oneself as Another*'s publication, the debate over the so-called theological turn in phenomenology was already brewing in France. The asceticism of Ricoeur's philosophical approach—which he goes so far as to call "agnostic"—was, no doubt, intended to preempt any accusation that his philosophical study harbors ontotheological amalgamations or conceals cryptotheolgical assertions. In this particular instance, Ricoeur's attitude regarding the relationship between theological and phenomenological discourses resembles the one adopted by Marion when he moved from his theologically oriented works to his "strictly philosophical" trilogy. But Ricoeur himself expresses some uneasiness about his decision to omit these concluding studies. In a remarkable statement, which attests to the intellectual honesty that is one of the hallmarks of his work, he admits that his decision may have been "debatable and even perhaps regrettable" (OA 24).

Indeed, Ricoeur's earlier work presents us with several good reasons for rejecting this sort of quick and easy, cut-and-dry demarcation between the philosophical and the religious—a demarcation that perhaps reflects the cultural and institutional structure of French and American academia, more than it does the temperament of Ricoeur's thought taken as a whole. It is therefore hardly surprising that during an interview conducted in 1995 Ricoeur admitted the following:

> I perhaps had other reasons to protect myself from the intrusions from the overly direct, too immediate infiltrations of the religious in the philosophical; these were cultural reasons, I would even say institutional reasons. It was very important to me to be recognized as a professor of philosophy, teaching philosophy in a public institution and speaking the common language, hence assuming the mental reservations this entailed, even if it meant that I would periodically be accused of being a theologian in disguise who philosophizes, or a philosopher who makes the religious sphere think or be thought. I take on all the difficulties of this situation, including the suspicion that, in actual fact, I would never be able to maintain this duality in watertight compartments.[48]

If I call into question the particular kind of philosophical autonomy that he claims for his analysis of conscience in the final pages of *Oneself as Another*, my aim is not to police the border between the religious and the properly philosophical. Rather, I want to suggest that this kind of demarcation or compartmentalization goes against the grain of Ricoeur's own philosophical project, which on the whole offers a much more complex and nuanced conception of the interrelationships between the two domains. For, as we have already glimpsed, Ricoeur's work—particularly during the period spanning from the *Symbolism of Evil* to *The Rule of Metaphor*—opened up a space for a philosophical thinking that would be both autonomous (perhaps even "agnostic") and, yet, one that would nevertheless be animated by poetic forms of discourse—and this would include, above all, "religious discourse" (understood not as the highly abstract or second-order discourse of speculative theologians, but as the mythical and symbolic expressions embodied in the texts of particular confessing communities).

10. CONSCIENCE AS PURE CALL OR DETERMINED CALL

In order to bring the differences between the radical and hermeneutical approaches to revelation into still sharper focus, it will be useful to examine Ricoeur's analysis of the phenomenon of conscience—and, specifically, the "call" or "voice" of conscience. The few paragraphs devoted to this phenomenon in *Oneself as Another* come at the tail end of his treatment of the dialectical relationship between the Same and the Other as it pertains to the work's overall problematic of selfhood as *ipseity* (OA 341–355). Two moments of analysis can be distinguished in Ricoeur's text. The first is a moment of suspicion directed against the "moral vision of the world" which incorrectly interprets conscience in terms of a false alternative—good and bad conscience—and thereby conceals its true capacity for discovery. It is only by way of this detour through suspicion that conscience can be related to the central phenomenon of attestation, which emerges most notably in Heidegger's *Being and Time*, where conscience (*Gewissen*) becomes associated with the attestation of self.

Here we reach the second moment of the analysis, which again relies heavily on *Being and Time*. Heidegger first put his finger on the peculiar modality of otherness that belongs to conscience when he invoked the metaphor of the voice. Conscience consists of a call (*Ruf*) or appeal (*Anruf*) which—unlike Plato's dialogue of the soul with itself—is characterized by a sort of dissymmetry, and indeed verticality by which the soul is affected. Herein lies the enigma of the phenomenon of conscience: its interiority is equaled only by its verticality: its call issues both from within me and from beyond and above me. Ricoeur writes, "Far from being foreign to the constitution of selfhood, this otherness is closely related to its emergence, inasmuch as, under the impetus of conscience, the self is made capable of taking hold of itself in the anonymity of the 'they' [*das Man*]" (AO 342). But, Ricoeur adds, what or who exactly this other *is* cannot be determined by philosophy. Is it another person whom I can look in the face, or my ancestors for whom there is no representation—or is it God? "With this aporia of the Other, philosophical discourse comes to an end" and, we might add, theological discourse begins (OA 355).

The phenomenon of conscience, more than any other, is said to straddle both sides of the philosophy-theology divide. Thus, the phenomenological investigation of conscience which crowns *Oneself as Another* is taken up and extended in a hermeneutical mode within the lectures that he decided to cut from that text.[49] That this phenomenon warrants both phenomenological and hermeneutical approaches can be explained by the fact that it is at once an "inalienable structure of existence" as well as the organ of the reception of the Christian kerygma. Hence the possibility of distinguishing the "neutral character" of conscience from its "religious" or theological interpretations (FS 271). Interestingly, Ricoeur points out that Saint Paul was the first to catch sight of this connection between "a nonspecifically religious phenomenon (or, at least, a nonspecifically Christian phenomenon), which he called *suneidesis*—knowledge shared with oneself—and the kerygma about Christ that he interpreted in terms of 'justification by faith'" (FS 271). Conscience, for Paul, acts as a sort of anthropological presupposition without which justification by faith would be impossible. Having a conscience—that is to say, possessing the autonomy implied by this inner-dialogue with oneself—does not of course amount to being saved. Ricoeur stresses that "Christian faith does not simply consist in proclaiming, along with Rousseau's Savoyard Vicar, that it is God who speaks in our conscience"—this would be to misconstrue the endless process of interpretation that serves to mediate between the verdict of conscience and the symbolic space opened and delimited by the biblical canon (FS 274–75). In some ways, then, the provocative question about God at the end of *Oneself as Another* was potentially misleading, since Ricoeur himself bars any straightforward identification between God and the call of conscience even at the level of a theology.

However, the point that needs to be stressed here is that Ricoeur (at least in the context of the Gifford Lectures) claims that conscience as an existential structure constitutes the ontological condition of possibility for the specifically Christian phenomenon of 'justification by faith.' Does this not imply that Ricoeur has himself adopted what Derrida, in reference to Heidegger, called a "logic of presupposition," according to which the theological interpretation of conscience would be subordinated to a meaning which it already presupposes, as its condition of possibility? Does Ricoeur not seem to suggest here that the supposedly impermeable border that rigorously separates the properly ontological from the merely ontical or regional interpretations must never be crossed—or at least not by the philosopher, and certainly not by the author of *Oneself as Another*? This line of argumentation would hardly be surprising were it not for the fact that Ricoeur's very own hermeneutic phenomenology was initially formulated in order to combat precisely this manner of thinking.

Now, this obvious discrepancy seems to suggest that the philosophical agnosticism of Ricoeur's phenomenology of conscience in *Oneself as Another* is purchased at too high a price: namely, at the price of having to adopt a "logic of presupposition" which ultimately conceals what we might call the true order of discovery—that is, the sequence in which the phenomena in question are encountered by the philosopher, or by the reflecting subject. In fact, upon closer inspection, Ricoeur's very own analysis suggests (though never explicitly states) the uncomfortable fact that before the philosopher arrives at the existential structure of the call of conscience, he or she first encounters a particular determination of this call. This explains the qualification that Ricoeur makes parenthetically in the statement about *suneidesis*, which we just cited above. "*Suneidesis*," he writes, is a "nonspecifically religious phenomenon"—but then he adds in parenthesis: "or, at least, a nonspecifically *Christian* phenomenon" (FS 271). And again, when Ricoeur claims that conscience belongs to all humans, he is nevertheless compelled to specify that it belongs to all humans—"pagan or not, Greek or Jew" (FS 272).

These specifications imply that although conscience is a universal feature of human experience, it is never experienced universally, it is never experience as such—that is to say, it is only ever encountered in a particular fashion, as a determinate call. Though it is a feature shared by all, it nevertheless belongs to each in a particular way: it belongs to pagans *as* pagans, Jews *as* Jews, Christians *as* Christians, etc. It is not as if conscience *first* appears in its general or universal (i.e., ontological) form, which is *then* given a particularly Christian (i.e., ontic) interpretation. Rather, the call of conscience is always already a determined call—determined as either Christian, pagan, Jew, or Greek. Christian conversion, in a Pauline sense, would not involve adopting an interpretation of conscience for the first time; but would involve shifting from one interpretive framework (be it pagan, Greek, or Jewish) to another (this time Christian) interpretive framework. The shift is not from a universal, fundamental structure (which Heidegger had designated by the term "pre-Christian") to a particular instance; rather it would involve a shift from one particular determination to another.

Thus, while on the face of it Ricoeur seems to buy into Heidegger's logic of presupposition—especially when he speaks of conscience as an inalienable structure of human existence—his analysis actually suggests a break with this kind of thinking. When Heidegger speaks of the pre-Christian interpretation of conscience, he is referring to its universal ontological structure—a kind of condition of possibility for having a conscience at all. For Ricoeur, on the other hand, a pre-Christian conscience would be a particular kind of conscience, a pagan conscience or a Jewish conscience, for example. The phenomenon of conscience never appears as such, in its pure form or raw immediacy. The call of conscience is always a mediated call—mediated by a particular vocabulary, whether it is theological or not. The ontologico-phenomenological interpretation of conscience (that is to say, its inalienable structure) is not present at the origin, at the beginning, but rather it is achieved only at the end of a comparative analysis of a series of determinate consciences.

Ricoeur drove this point home a few years later, in a colloquium paper which he delivered on the subject of "Experience and Language in Religious Discourse."[50] There, in a manner which seems to be more consistent with the overall trajectory of his work, he argues that "We cannot even be sure that the universal character of the call/response structure can be attested independently of the different historical actualizations in which this structure is incarnated."[51] With this declaration, the logic of presupposition gives way to what we might call a logic of post-supposition—and the true order of discovery is finally made explicit. Since conscience is "nowhere visible in its naked immediacy," phenomenology cannot precede directly to its existential/ontological meaning. Rather, it must first pass through a hermeneutical detour of the concrete historical (and dare we say *ontic*) representations in which it is initially expressed. Or, as Ricoeur puts the matter, it must "run the gauntlet of a hermeneutic and more precisely of a *textual* and *scriptural* hermeneutic."[52]

Does this mean that the phenomenology of conscience remains forever tainted by certain theological prejudices? Or worse, that it represents a crypto-theology masquerading as phenomenology?

From the perspective of radical phenomenology this would certainly appear to be the case. Nevertheless, between a strictly philosophical discourse that would be hermetically sealed off from the field of religious representations and a theological discourse that would only serve to develop the kerygma according to its own internal criterion of coherence, Ricoeur's indirect route seems to open up a third possibility—namely, a "philosophical hermeneutics of religion" in which the ontical richness of religious representation becomes a source from which philosophical reflection can draw. These representations would serve to deepen and expand the scope of philosophical reflection without threatening its autonomy as a separate and essentially non-theological discourse. Ricoeur points to two important predecessors of this type of approach, drawn from the history of German idealism: namely, Hegel's *Berlin Lectures on the Phenomenology of Religion* and Kant's *Religion within the Limits of Reason Alone*. These examples are admittedly flawed. After all, Kant ultimately excludes the positive character of the religious from his philosophy, and Hegel finally claims that religious representations (*Vorstellung*) are entirely exhausted by the philosophical concept (*Begriff*). But in both instances there was at least a tentative move toward acknowledging ways in which concrete forms of religious language might serve to enrich philosophical discourse, and for that reason Ricoeur can justifiably point to them as precursor to his "philosophical hermeneutics of religion."

In the remainder of this chapter, I try to situate Ricoeur's philosophical hermeneutics of religion within the framework of his broader philosophical project—and, in particular, his work on metaphorical discourse—in the hope of gaining a better understanding of its aims.

11. THE PHILOSOPHICAL HERMENEUTICS OF RELIGION AS A COMPOSITE DISCOURSE

I will begin by venturing a hypothesis: namely, that Ricoeur envision the philosophical hermeneutics of religion as a kind "composite discourse," as this term is understood in the eighth study of *The Rule of Metaphor*. In a subsection entitled "The Intersection of the Spheres of Discourse," Ricoeur argues that metaphorical and speculative modes of discourse can and do maintain a relation of interdependence without collapsing into a unity. According to Ricoeur, the "semantic dynamism of the metaphorical utterance" creates new meaning by functioning on two referential levels at once. By provoking a suspension of literal reference, a metaphorical utterance opens onto a second-order reference, which would otherwise exceed the grasp of the lexicon restricted to its "proper" usage.[53] However, owing to the split reference or double meaning of the metaphorical utterance—its openness to both literal *and* figurative interpretations—the metaphor does not disclose any determinate meaning, but only a sketch, image, or a schematic representation of its semantic aim. (Though it is important to note that this semantic aim already implies an ontological significance—for, as Ricoeur puts it, "Something must *be* for something to be *said*") (RM 304). Metaphor therefore consists of "an experience seeking to be expressed" (RM 303). In another context, Ricoeur says that symbolic language is already "en route toward explication . . . the *mythos* is on the way toward *logos*" (CI 427). And this reveals the real significance of his well-worn axiom that "the symbol gives rise to thought."[54] This axiom not only says that philosophical thought is sustained by mytho-poetic discourse—it also says that thought fulfills an aim that is already present at the mytho-poetic level. The symbol invites thought, provokes it, awakens it.

But even though the metaphor's "semantic shock produces a conceptual need, [it does not] as yet produce any knowledge by means of concepts" (RM 296). Thus, it falls to speculative discourse to develop this semantic aim by transposing it into "a network of meanings of the same order in accordance with the constitutive laws of the logical space itself" (RM 301). "Because it forms a system," Ricoeur claims that the conceptual order manages to "free itself from the play of double meaning and hence from the semantic dynamism characteristic of the metaphorical order" (RM 302). Thus, "on the one hand, speculative discourse has its condition of *possibility* in the semantic dynamism of metaphorical utterance, and, on the other hand, speculative discourse has its *necessity* in itself, in putting the resources of conceptual articulation to work" (RM 296). The shift from the metaphorical to the speculative entails a transfer from the dynamism of representation to the determinateness of the concept—from *imaginatio* to *intellectio*. On these grounds, Ricoeur argues (*contra* Heidegger and ostensibly Derrida, too) that the two orders maintain their respective autonomy in spite of this carefully qualified interdependence.

Having identified the difference between these two registers of discourse, Ricoeur raises a question which will have serious consequences for his philosophical hermeneutics of religion: "[D]oes this discontinuity of semantic modalities imply that the conceptual order abolishes or destroys the metaphorical order?" (RM 302). By raising the metaphor's nascent semantic intention to the level of conceptual clarity, has speculative discourse not rendered the metaphor obsolete, in the manner, say, of a Hegelian *Aufhebung*? Does the speculative concept exhaust the metaphor's initial upsurge of meaning? Ricoeur offers the following response: "My inclination is to see the universe of discourse as a universe kept in motion by an interplay of attractions and repulsions that ceaselessly promote the interaction and intersection of domains whose organizing nuclei are off-centered in relation to one another" (RM 302). Ricoeur envisions this space of attraction and repulsion, this field of endless play, as the proper site of hermeneutical thought. Thus, he suggests that hermeneutics represents a "composite discourse," a third register which functions "at the intersection of the two domains, metaphorical and speculative." This discipline would "seek the clarity of the concept" and at the same time "hope to preserve the dynamism of meaning that the concept holds and pins down" (RM 303). As such, it would be a discipline inspired by two irreducible yet complementary aims.

Now, it is safe to assume that the "philosophical hermeneutics of religion" falls under this rubric of "composite discourse." In this particular kind of composite discourse, the category of testimony—which consists of the historically contingent representations of religious traditions (symbols, narratives, etc.)—the category of testimony "occupy[s] a place comparable to that of poetic [i.e., metaphorical] discourse in relation to the objective aspect of philosophical discourse" (EBI 115). The philosophical hermeneutics of religion consists of "an ellipse with two foci [namely, conceptual thought and religious representation] that mediation tends to conflate but which can never be reduced to a unified central point" (EBI 143). It can never settle into a single unitary ontology (Heidegger), or a single phenomenological figure (Marion).

Thus, we can already anticipate that the conclusions reached in our above analysis of the poetic and speculative discourses equally hold for the dialectical relationship between religion and philosophy. In his essay "Toward a Hermeneutic of the Idea of Revelation," Ricoeur clarifies this dialectical relationship by appealing to paragraph 49 of Kant's *Critique of the Power of Judgment* (EBI 73). There, in order to account for aesthetic productions of genius, Kant invoked the imagination's power "to present" those ideas of reason for which we lack adequate concepts. Although the representation cannot be "completely compassed and made intelligible by language" it nevertheless "confers" on thought "the ability to think further."[55] Although the representation (*Darstellung*) "occasions more thought than can ever be comprehended in a definite concept," it succeeds in "aesthetically enlarging" the concept itself.[56] Historical revelation is said to have the same structure and to perform the same function for philosophical thought—it enriches and extends the scope of philosophical discourse through representations whose meaning can never be fully exhausted (EBI 116–17).

But this act of transposition from the poetic to the speculative, from the ontic to the ontological, from the "positive" domain of textual revelation to the "transcendental" domain of autonomous phenomenological discourse can be accomplished in many ways—explicitly, inadvertently, and on occasion, surreptitiously (as, perhaps, in the final paragraphs of *Oneself as Another*, where Ricoeur claims to bracket his religious convictions in the name of a philosophical agnosticism). I have argued in previous chapters that within a radical phenomenology which seeks to uncover the pre-linguistic or pre-textual structure of revelation, such as we see in Heidegger and Marion, this act is suppressed, though it is never entirely avoided. Like Ricoeur's, their conceptualizations of revelation were also influenced by a particular religious and indeed Christian understanding of revelation. But this influence was interpreted, by them, as an illicit theological contamination of the strictly phenomenological domain—a contamination which they sought to contain, control and finally eliminate through a series of philosophical maneuvers (i.e., counter-contaminations) which ultimately severed revelation from its cultural, historical, and linguistic contexts. I have claimed that these maneuvers ultimately alienate us from the very thing that a phenomenology of revelation was first called upon to describe.

The situation is entirely different with Ricoeur, for whom the analysis of language and texts marks the primary path of philosophical reflection. Or, at least the situation is *almost* entirely different. For there are moments in Ricoeur's work where even he seems to let the dream of a pure, unprejudiced, or 'agnostic' form of philosophizing get the best of him—moments where he claims to have fully placed his personal religious convictions in suspense, implying that a critical attitude can somehow uproot the ontological condition of belonging. However, as I noted above in Section 9, these moments are fleeting, and they appear to reflect his desire to conform to the norms of the public institution within which he worked and taught more than they do his own philosophical temperament or trajectory. When Ricoeur's decisions are determined by the exigencies of his own philosophical method—rather than by fear of criticism or by the secular norms of the academy—the transition from the "positive" domain of textual revelation to the "transcendental" domain of autonomous phenomenological discourse is embraced in the form of a wager, such as the one expressed in the final pages of *The Symbolism of Evil*: "I wager that I shall have a better understand of man and of the bond between the being of man and the being of all beings if I follow the indication of symbolic thought"—and, we might add, the indication of the biblical texts.[57] The fate of Ricoeur's philosophical hermeneutics of revelation is forever bound to the success or failure of this wager itself.

Like all wagers, Ricoeur's particular wager cannot be rationally or philosophically justified in advance. What *can* be justified, however, is the necessity of making a wager in the first instance, the necessity of beginning from some place rather than from no place at all. We have seen that Ricoeur, drawing upon the work of hermeneutical thinkers (most notably Gadamer), was able to demonstrate that all self-understanding is shaped by one's belonging to a certain tradition (above, Section 6). We are inevitably shaped by the history we inherit, by the language we speak, and by the texts we read. Given this ontological fact of human existence, it would appear that Ricoeur's so-called wager is less of a gamble than it is an acknowledgment of this irreparable debt. But, instead, he suggests that his wager consists of an active choice, one which he willingly and self-consciously affirms. If that is indeed the case, then Ricoeur's wager not only requires the passive acceptance of one's debt to tradition, language, texts, etc.; rather, it demands an active decision to allow oneself to be shaped by this *particular* tradition, this *specific* text, etc. On the one hand, Ricoeur *cum* philosopher will argue that every "poetic" text has the potential to deepen one's self-understanding and to reshape one's world. On the other hand, according to Ricoeur *cum* Christian—and that is say, according to the individual Ricoeur happened to be—the biblical canon held a unique power to transform the self in the most profound manner.

If, however, Ricoeur's hermeneutic phenomenology of revelation hinges upon this wager, upon this seemingly arbitrary decision to favor one body of texts (the biblical canon) over all others, then it appears that it must abandon any claim to provide an ultimate philosophical (or purely rational) justification. In the end, perhaps it is precisely Ricoeur's attempt to take this wager (of faith?) *as* the starting point for a *philosophical* reflection which makes his hermeneutic phenomenology of revelation at once so very intriguing and yet so very problematic.

NOTES

1. Hent de Vries, *Philosophy and the Turn to Religion* (Baltimore: Johns Hopkins University Press, 1999); Bruce Benson, ed., *Words of Life: New Theological Turns in French Phenomenology* (New York: Fordham University Press, 2010); Joeri Schrijvers, *Ontotheological Turnings?: The Decentering of the Modern Subject in Recent French Phenomenology* (New York: SUNY Press, 2012); Robyn Horner, *Rethinking God as Gift* (New York: Fordham University Press, 2001); Kevin Hart, *The Trespass of the Sign* (New York: Cambridge University Press, 1989). These are just a few examples of justifiably influential works on the theological turn, which, despite their many strengths, have largely ignored Ricoeur's contribution to the movement.

2. Marion, *In* Excess, 144.

3. Later, we will see how the inter-signification of the word "God" as it circulates within biblical texts represents one of the most intriguing examples of such over-determinacy.

4. As Gadamer observes: "Heidegger's hermeneutical phenomenology and his analysis of Dasein's historicity had as their aim renewing the question of being in general and not producing a theory of the human sciences or overcoming the aporias of historicism. These were merely particular contemporary problems in which he was able to demonstrate the consequences of his radical renewal of the question of being." Gadamer, *Truth and Method*, 258.

5. Paul Ricoeur, *The Conflict of Interpretations: Essays in Hermeneutics*, trans. and ed. D. Ihde (Evanston, IL: Northwestern University Press, 1974), 3. (Hereafter, CI.)

6. Whether one regards the hermeneutical problem as decades or centuries old will depend on whether one views Schleiermacher's project as a continuation of medieval biblical exegesis, or as a radical break with it. But Ricoeur's point remains salient no matter how that question gets settled.

7. Ricoeur briefly indicates the enormity of this problem in CI 5–6.

8. See, for example, Wilhem Dilthey, *Introduction to the Human Sciences (Selected Works, Vol. 1)*, eds. R. Makkreel and F. Rodi (Princeton, NJ: Princeton University Press, 1989), 322–23.

9. Ricoeur is not all that interested in speculating about whether or not Husserl's final treatment of these themes may have been provoked by the publication of *Being and Time*, since Husserl had developed these themes much earlier on in unpublished materials. See, for instance, Paul Ricoeur, *Husserl: An Analysis of His Phenomenology*, trans. Edward G. Ballard and Lester E. Embree (Evanston, IL: Northwestern University Press, 1967).

10. Needless to say, Gadamer's *Truth and Method* is equally responsible for (re)turning Heideggerian ontology towards a problematic of the text. However, the uniqueness of Ricoeur's approach lies in his effort to resurrect the properly epistemological issues that Heideggerian and Gadamerian ontology seems to have ignored.

11. It would be wrong to assume that the structuralists' hypostasis of the text eliminates the author-pole altogether, since the author re-emerges within certain

structuralist theories, albeit no longer as a psychic force, but as a function of the text itself—i.e., the text's author-function.

12. As noted in our introduction, Ricoeur's notion of discourse is consequently much more aligned with a Gadamerian view of language—which consists of a three-way relation between two conversation partners and the thing about which they converse—than it is with a Levinasian view of language, which accentuates the binary dimension of discourse as the exposure of one face to another.

13. The fact that this formulation of discourse includes an explicit reference to both an author and a reader (i.e., the two "someones") makes it easy to mistake Ricoeur's position as a as revamped psychology. But the emphasis here is not on the psyche of the author or reader (i.e., the "someone") but on that which is spoken of in discourse itself (i.e., the "something").

14. See Gottlobe Frege, "On Sense and Reference," in *Meaning and Reference* (Oxford: Oxford University Press, 1994).

15. It is important to note that Ricoeur's critique of structuralism's underlying *theoretical* premises does not detract from his estimation of its *methodological* merits. In fact, Ricoeur's ontological project preserves an essential role for epistemological forms of analysis, including structuralist analysis. (Ricoeur states in an interview with Richard Kearney that he is entirely uninterested in Lévi-Strauss's metaphysics of the nothing; and, yet, he maintains the value of Lévi-Strauss's analyses themselves. See Richard Kearney, *Debates in Continental Philosophy* (New York: Fordham University Press, 2004), 107–18. I would go so far as to suggest that in Ricoeur's oeuvre structuralism maintains a privileged position among the various regional disciplines, insofar as it involves something like the twentieth-century equivalent to the classical hermeneutical notion of "fixation by writing" (even though the genealogies of the two disciplines hardly intersect).

At any rate, Ricoeur does not reject structuralist analysis per se—and, again, he insists that structuralist analysis must be vigorously distinguished from a structuralist 'metaphysics'—he simply regards the methodical suspension of the referential function as a temporary stage in the larger interpretive process, which he calls the "hermeneutical arc." This stage is justifiably concerned with the economy of signifiers within a closed system (such as text or myth). But, according to Ricoeur, this purely analytic stage must ultimately give way to an act of understanding or appropriation, in which the referential function is, as it were, once again vindicated. Interpretation means nothing if not an act of appropriation in which "something" is finally understood.

16. In conversation, "reference is determined by the ability to point to a reality common to the interlocutors" (HH 141). Though this is no longer the case with a text—which can in principle be read by anyone, anywhere, anytime—the text may still preserve a reference. This reference must simply be defined in terms that transcend spatio-temporal determinations. This point will be addressed in greater detail below, when we turn our attention toward the significance that this broader theory of reference holds for Ricoeur's hermeneutical theory of revelation.

17. In the context of this problematic, at least, Ricoeur does not name his hypothetical structuralist interlocutor, Lévi-Strauss remained his most common structuralist sparing partner throughout the sixties and seventies.

18. In this technical sense, the word "ostensive"—which derives from the past participle of the Latin *ostendere*, "to show"—has less to do with what is merely apparent or superficial, than with an ability to define one's meaning by pointing to an exemplary or paradigmatic referent—an ability that is clearly confined to the natural conditions of oral communication. Wittgenstein, for instance, has precisely this use of the term in mind when he problematizes the manner in which it is commonly believed that one comes to learn the language of a foreign country, namely, by watching its inhabitants point to the 'things' about which they speak (Husserl, *Philosophical Investigations*, §32). It seems to me, however, that Ricoeur's argument makes more sense if we extend the scope of 'things' beyond merely spatial, physical objects, so as to include the ideas, concepts, etc. that are common to a particular culture or linguistic community.

19. Ricoeur observes that "with writing [. . .] there is no longer a situation common to the writer and the reader, and the concrete conditions of the act of pointing no longer exist" (HH 141).

20. See "The Hermeneutical Function of Distanciation," (HH 142).

21. Paul Ricoeur, *Critique and Conviction: Conversations with François Azouvi and Marc de Launay*, trans. K. Blamey (Oxford: Polity Press-Blackwell, 1998), 146.

22. Ibid., 143.

23. Gadamer, *Truth and Method*, 271–85.

24. Ibid., 301. Gadamer notes that the "structure of the concept of situations" was previously illuminated by Karl Jaspers, a philosopher whose influence upon Ricoeur's thinking not only preceded but in some respects outweighed that of Gadamer.

25. Ricoeur, *Critique and Conviction*, 146.

26. Ibid., 145.

27. Ibid., 145.

28. Neither the critical methods employed by the natural and social sciences, nor the critical attitude of the enlightenment project upon which these are based, can eliminate the role that prejudice or conviction plays in guiding our thought. However, the realization of the necessity of certain governing prejudices has nothing at all to do with skepticism or relativism; rather, it follows from the very nature of understanding itself, which always proceeds by way of pre-understanding. Prejudices play a necessary and productive role in understanding. This is why, for example, the ontological analysis of the phenomenon of prejudice precedes any epistemological analysis in Gadamer's *Truth and Method*. The rehabilitation of prejudice can and must remain prior to and thus independent of the attempt to distinguish between true and false prejudices, legitimate and illegitimate prejudices, enabling and disabling prejudices—for such distinctions can only become meaningful with respect to particular traditions, and are thus governed by particular readings of particular texts. In fact, even here at this level the criteria would have to be more ontological than epistemological. For, according to both Ricoeur and Gadamer, a legitimate prejudice would ultimately be one that serves to open up the world or matter of the text, one that exposes the reader to a world which, in turn, effectively reconstitutes his or her own self-understanding.

29. The problem of distinguishing between the authoritative status of religious texts vis-à-vis non-religious texts could be said to hinge upon the meaning of a "classic," as

articulated in *Truth and Method*. For the classic, like the sacred canonical text, exhibits a certain timelessness or "contemporaneity" whereby it is said to belong to our world as much as we, through the act of reading, belong to its world (Gadamer, *Truth and Method*, 290). Gadamer often emphasized the "secular" works of classical antiquity, rather than sacred ones, Ricoeur shares Gadamer's general view of what counts as a classic and why. One crucial difference, however, should be noted: Ricoeur would reject Gadamer's claim that the classical text "resists historical criticism," in favor of a theory that incorporates all forms of criticism within a broader hermeneutical arch which integrates explanatory procedures with appropriative understanding (Gadamer, *Truth and Method*, 287). Thus, Ricoeur will appeal to critical (epistemological) modes of analysis even—and indeed, especially—in the case of reading sacred texts. See, for example, "Philosophical Hermeneutics and Biblical Hermeneutics," in Paul Ricoeur, *From Text to Action: Essays in Hermeneutics II*, trans. K. Blamey and J. Thompson (London: The Athlone Press, 1991), 89–104. (Hereafter, TA.)

30. This idea will be made clearer later on, when we examine Ricoeur's critique of the subject's claim to constitute itself without recourse to an interpretation of signs, symbols, texts, etc. (see below, Section 8).

31. TA 89–104.

32. There are, in fact, only two instances where he *explicitly* indicates the unique character of the biblical text (TA 96, 98).

33. See above, Chapter 2, Section 11.

34. We must keep in mind the importance of the "externality of a work." "Being written down as scripture removes it from the finite horizon of its authors and its first audience." This displacement is, moreover, the condition of possibility for what we might call the universalization of its message—its ability to reach readers who no longer share its author's spatial-temporal (or even cultural) environment. Its materiality or externality is tantamount to its ability to be rendered contemporaneous and thus meaningful beyond the conditions of its initial reception. See Paul Ricoeur, *Essays on Biblical Interpretation*, ed. Mudge (Philadelphia: Fortress Press, 1980), 103 (Henceforth, EBI).

35. Ricoeur holds that the "new being" disclosed by the Christian Bible is the kingdom of God, salvation, rebirth, etc.

36. Here we cite the translation of Mark as it appears in FS 199.

37. See, for example, his remarks regarding the history of the interpretation of Ezekiel. There he insists that his "contribution is meant to be a plea in favor of the plurivocity" of the text (TB 165).

38. Once again, authorship or authorial intention is not the issue—or at least not the most important issue. Thus, the suture that the historical-critical method discovers between one periscope and another does not necessarily disturb the underlying coherence between the narrative and its theological meaning.

39. Here, again, we see Ricoeur struggling to walk a thin line between a single meaning immanent within a text and the author's intention. The difficulty of this struggle is betrayed in his rather awkward attribution of agency to the narrative itself: "the ideological interpretations these narratives *wish* to convey" (FS 181, italics

mine). In the absence of authorial intention, intentions (in this case, even "wishes") are attributed directly to the text itself!

40. Here we would need to distinguish between what Heidegger refers to as the past as "no longer" (*Vergangenheit*)—which is a non-retrievable past—and the past as "having-been" (*Gewesenheit*), which still preserves the possibility of being extended toward a future and thus integrated into the overall process of temporalization which is constitutive for Dasein.

41. Of course, these are by no means synonyms. However, the important point, as Ricoeur observes, is that Heidegger's "argumentation directed against ordinary time makes no concessions. Its ambition is no less than a genesis without remainder of the concept of time as it is employed in all the sciences starting from fundamental ontology" (TN 86).

42. The matter is much too complicated for us to give it the attention that it nevertheless deserves. In a dense passage, Ricoeur sums up his reasons for claiming that Heideggerian hermeneutics cannot prepare the way for a genuine engagement with the human sciences: "[S]ince hermeneutics has become [in *Being and Time*] the hermeneutics of being—of the meaning of being—the anticipatory structure appropriate to the question of the meaning of being is given by the history of metaphysics, which thus takes the place of prejudice. Henceforth, the hermeneutics of being deploys all of its critical resources in the debate with classical and medieval substance, with Cartesian and Kantian cogito. The confrontation with the metaphysical tradition of the West takes the place of a critique of prejudices. In other words, from a Heideggerian perspective, the only internal critique that can be conceived as an integral part of the enterprise of disclosure is the deconstruction of metaphysics; and a properly epistemological critique can be resumed only indirectly, insofar as metaphysical residues can be found at work in the sciences which claim to be empirical. But this critique of prejudices which originate in metaphysics cannot take the place of a real confrontation with the human sciences, with their methodology and with their epistemological presuppositions. The obsessive concern with radicality thus blocks the return route from general hermeneutics towards regional hermeneutics: towards philology, history, depth-psychology, etc." (HH 89).

43. "The ontology proposed here is in no way separable from interpretation; it is caught inside the circle formed by the conjunction of the work of interpretation and the interpreted being. It is thus not a triumphant ontology at all; it is not even a science since it is unable to avoid the risk of interpretation; it cannot even escape the internal warfare that the various hermeneutics indulge in among themselves" (CI 23).

44. Though, it must be said, there are some recent exceptions, most notably the work of Emmanuel Falque.

45. See, in particular, Nabert's work, *Désir de Dieu* (Paris: Aubier-Montaigne, 1966), 265–80.

46. Decades later, Ricoeur expands upon this idea in the final portion of his Gifford Lectures. See "The Summoned Subject in the School of the Narratives of the Prophetic Vocation" in FS 262–278.

47. Paul Ricoeur, *Oneself as Another*, trans. K. Blamey (Chicago: The University of Chicago Press, 1992). (Hereafter, OA).

48. Ricoeur, *Critique and Conviction*, 150.

49. The most significant of these lectures (at least for our purposes here) was later published separately under the title "The Summoned Subject in the School of the Narratives of the Prophetic Vocation" in FS 262–278.

50. Paul Ricoeur, "Experience and Language in Religious Discourse," in *Phenomenology and the "Theological Turn": The French Debate*, trans. B. Prusak (New York: Fordham University, 2000).

51. Ibid., 130.

52. Ibid.

53. Paul Ricoeur, *The Rule of Metaphor: Multi-Disciplinary Studies of the Creation of Meaning in Language*, trans. R. Czerny and K. McLaughlin (London and Henley: Routledge and Kegan Paul, 1978), 299. (Henceforth RM.)

54. Paul Ricoeur, *The Symbolism of Evil*, trans. Emerson Buchanan (Boston: Beacon Press, 1967), 347–57.

55. Immanuel Kant, *Critique of the Power of Judgment*, trans. P. Guyer and A. Wood (Cambridge: Cambridge University Press, 2002), 192–93 (translation modified).

56. Ibid.

57. Ricoeur, *The Symbolism of Evil*, 355.

Conclusion
Language, Reception, Contingency

> Can a historical point of departure be given for an eternal consciousness?
>
> Søren Kierkegaard, *Philosophical Fragments*

> 'A chance transformed into destiny by a continuous choice': my Christianity.
>
> Paul Ricoeur, *Living Up to Death*

Throughout this work, I have claimed that phenomenologists have generally approached revelation in two distinct ways, that these ways reflect a fundamental division within the phenomenological movement itself (namely, between its radical and hermeneutical strands), and that this division concerns, above all, divergent attitudes toward language and linguistic mediation. Within the radical strand, which originated with early Heidegger and is further developed by Marion, the preoccupation with maintaining philosophical rigor has (mistakenly, I think) led phenomenology to purge revelation of its material, linguistic content, leaving behind a mere figure of revelation—one that, while undoubtedly "pure" (insofar as it remains uncontaminated by theological presuppositions), is also, and for that very reason, equally empty. By seeking to avoid the charge of crypto-theology, radical phenomenologists have situated the event of revelation *before* (i.e., anterior to) linguistic mediation and "theological" determination. As a consequence, their work might very well assume the mantle "first philosophy," in the strict Husserlian sense. However, this philosophical rigor is purchased at the price of a complete attenuation of revelation itself, resulting in a failure to adequately address the content of the very phenomenon they sought to describe. In contrast to the radical phenomenology of early Heidegger and Marion, I have insisted that the hermeneutical phenomenology of Ricoeur allows for a more robust engagement with the content of revelation—with the symbols, metaphors, narratives, and, in short, the *texts*, which, historically, constitute the core of revelation within the Judeo-Christian tradition. For Ricoeur, revelation entails a reconfiguration of the self that results from exposing oneself to the world of the text, from standing *before* the text. But this approach also comes at a price. Since his strand of phenomenology is predicated upon a hermeneutic wager which involves privileging a certain text (or set of texts) over others, it can no longer claim to operate from a place of absolute neutrality, as a "presuppositionless science." And so, it must renounce the pretensions of first philosophy altogether.

It seems that we have arrived at a kind of impasse. For it appears that *either* the phenomenology of revelation maintains a commitment philosophical rigor, but, as a consequence, must sacrifice the material richness of the phenomenon it seeks to describe, *or* it attempts to engage the phenomenon in its fullness, but must then renounce its claims to philosophical reason and transparency. In other words, it seems as if we face the burden of an unbearable choice. Reason *or* revelation.

But have we really traveled this far only to wind up where we first began, once again staring out across an unbridgeable divide—across the "ugly, broad ditch" that appeared to Lessing and his contemporaries as marking an insurmountable gap between reason and revelation, between so-called eternal truths and those that are merely contingent? Is there really no way of preventing the two approaches to revelation from hardening into an intolerable antinomy? Is there no way of softening their outer edges just enough so that we might begin to mold them into a single, coherent form? I want to conclude by attempting to soften those edges, by considering some aspects of their respective views which help to dull the otherwise sharp distinction between the radical and hermeneutical characterizations of revelation. And in doing so, I also hope to gesture in a direction that might eventually allow us to bridge the gap between reason and revelation itself.

From Marion's project, we can preserve an idea that he shares with most theological conceptions of revelation[1]—namely, the idea that revelation does not originate from the self, as if it were entirely the result of our own human initiative, but rather that it comes from outside of us, that it is received as a *gift* from beyond and from above. Questions concerning the capacities for and conditions of *receptivity* are certainly important; but in order for something to be received, it must first of all be given. Thus, the phenomenological account of revelation will have to preserve the idea of the gift and its 'verticality.' What must be rejected in Marion's work is the idea that this gift is *materially indeterminate*, that Revelation as an *actually* given phenomenon involves a wholly anonymous call.[2] If anything has been learned from Ricoeur's hermeneutical phenomenology, it is this: far from undermining its revelatory status, the *textual* determinations of revelation (its concrete symbolic, metaphorical, and narrative forms) are precisely what contribute to its revelatory potentiality—that is to say, it is on account of its concrete linguistic or literary texture that revelation holds the power to transform and renew the self, to open the self up to new "worlds" or, to put it in the terms of biblical tradition itself, to the "kingdom of God."

Acknowledging the determinate nature of revelation by no means requires a complete rejection of Marion's radical project. In fact, in at least one crucial sense this acknowledgement would mark a logical extension, and perhaps even a radicalization, of Marion's basic principle that the human subject cannot impose his or her subjective conditions upon the gift of revelation. I would only add the following proviso to Marion's principle: from the fact that the human subject cannot impose its own conditions upon revelation, one need not conclude that revelation is free of all determination. For the possibility remains that the call is *already* named, that revelation is *already* determined—albeit not by subjective conditions, but by the *historical, cultural*, and *textual* conditions through which the call reaches us. Thus, it might make more sense to say that these conditions are imposed upon the human subject by revelation than to say that the human subject imposes them upon revelation (though this reversal can also be misleading for reasons that will become clear in a moment).

Ricoeur supplied us with a compelling example of this phenomenon when he demonstrated how the fragmentary nature of the Hebrew Scriptures exercises a polyphonic or triadic call (corresponding to Torah, Prophets, and Wisdom literature) which, in turn, results in a fragmentary subject. The subject who exposes herself to this text is in some sense produced, determined, and reconfigured as a "fragmented self" by the polyphonic nature of the call.[3] I would suggest that, far from being opposed to Marion's thinking, this theory of revelation can actually help underwrite his radical conception of the subject as "the gifted" (*l'adonné*), i.e., as the one who not only gives itself over to the given, but whose very existence is constituted by the gift it receives.

As it stands, however, I fear that Marion's notion of the gifted rests upon a basic misconception about the nature of language, for it assumes that all predication or nomination necessarily entail objectification and, therefore, that the act of nomination is more or less indistinguishable from the act of imposing the limitations of a theoretical concept upon intuition. And for that very reason, Marion has argued in his theological writings that the Name that calls us is not really a name at all—and certainly not a proper name—as it remains unutterable, unsayable, and in any case beyond what any concept could ever contain. But if the Name that calls remains so abstract, anonymous, and indeterminate that it precludes the very possibility of a proper response, then it is hard to imagine how it could ever have a decisive and determining effect upon the gifted. For such an impact would, it seems, leave us as unaffected as we are speechless. Moreover, one might also wonder what kind of language could ever be heard but never spoken. It seems to me that hearing and saying are two indissoluble phenomena, that the possibility of hearing a language and, thus, of receiving the call of revelation, implies the possibility of appropriately and intelligibly responding to it. I believe Marion's claim that the gifted's response invariably proves insufficient—and that its hermeneutical effort is marked by a "necessary impropriety"—stems from his broader failure to appreciate the fundamentally non-objectifying potentiality inherent in language itself.

In order to clear up these related issues, it will be useful to turn once more to Heidegger—though not to the still youthful author of *Being and Time*, but rather to the late Heidegger, whose understanding of language had evolved considerably since the publication of his *magnum opus*. In 1964, nearly four decades after delivering his lecture on "Phenomenology and Theology," Heidegger found himself engaging with group of theologians once again; this time, in the form of a letter that would serve as the basis for a discussion at Drew University (a discussion Heidegger was unable to attend in person). On this occasion, he was no longer concerned with theology *per se*, but rather with the potentiality of language for non-technological and non-objectifying modes of thought in general. His sights were set upon what he regarded as the "uncritically accepted opinion that all thinking, as representing, and all speaking, as vocalization, are already 'objectifying.'"[4] Heidegger observed:

> When in a tacit saying [*Sagen*] we are enthralled with the lucid red of the rose and muse on the redness of the rose, then this redness is neither an object nor a thing nor something standing over against us [. . .] All the same we think it and tell it by *naming* it. There is accordingly a thinking and saying that in no manner objectifies or places things over against us.[5]

Naming, according to Heidegger, does not involve the subject's violent imposition of an alien concept upon the given in order to objectify it, rather naming is the very means whereby the given is received by the subject *as it appears*. "Is not speaking, in what is most proper to it, a saying, a manifold showing of that which hearing, i.e., an obedient heed of what appears, lets be said?"[6] Speaking, in other words, goes hand in hand with hearing. It is the expression of our most profound capacity to hear, to receive, and to think that which is given.

But what is it that one hears in the call? If we follow Heidegger's line of thought, then we must conclude that the call calls out in the very same language that one speaks.[7] This might sound dubious or even paradoxical. After all, if the call speaks one's own language then how could we even account for the possibility of the verticality of the call (the idea that the call of revelation represents the voice of another, over and above me, rather than my own)? In order to answer this worry, we will need to attend to the mysterious nature of language itself. Heidegger warns us that confusion on this issue arises whenever we erroneously take artificial, objectifying languages (those which are invented only under unique circumstances and for the purpose of establishing a scientific or technological mastery of the world) as the basis of a general interpretation of the essence of language. After all, these artificial languages are not primary but merely derivative, in that they are constructed "in reference to and from out of an already spoken language." But, Heidegger asks, "Is language at all within the human being's power of disposal? [. . .] Is the human being that being that has language in its possession? Or is it language that 'has' human beings, insofar as they belong to, pay heed to language, which first opens up the world to them and at the same time thereby their dwelling in the world?"[8]

Language, in other words, "is not a work of human beings: language speaks. Humans speak only insofar as they co-respond to language."[9] It is on account of the mysterious way in which one's own being is constituted by the non-objectifying language that one speaks (or, better, that speaks *through* oneself), that one can be assured that one's answer to the call is anything but insufficient or improper. For the words (and the names) with which one replies (or answers) the call are the very same words that one has already received—words in virtue of which one first comes to dwell in the world. In responding to the determined call, the gifted has no more imposed her own words upon the given, than she has chosen her own mother tongue. This fact also explains the verticality of the call as well. For even the early Heidegger—the author of *Being and Time*—recognized that "The call comes from me," in the sense that it speaks the language that is my own, "and yet [it also comes] *from beyond me and over me*," insofar as this language is one that I have myself *received*, not invented, and thus one that constitutes me more than I do it.

A phenomenology that is willing to come to grips with this mysterious nature of language can no longer speak of a pure, anonymous Revelation, but only of particular historically, textually, and linguistically determinate Revelations. This observation about language will also release a radical phenomenology of revelation (such as Marion's) from the requirement of having to establish a single, absolute phenomenological structure of revelation (revealability, or *Offenbarkeit*), since it would open up the possibility of engaging in a phenomenology of revelation in one or another of its historical instantiations. As Ricoeur's project suggests, no account of the structure of revelation— or of the call/response structure—could be attested to independently of a historically given Revelation which incarnates it.[10] Stripped of its pretensions to have uncovered the formal conditions of possibility of revelation through a supposedly pure eidetic analysis, phenomenology would need to work from the ground up—starting from and thus presupposing an actual (i.e., historical) Revelation. The insertion of a hermeneutical moment into the heart of a radical phenomenology of revelation would mean that the philosopher (as much as the theologian) would have to come to terms with the fact that he or she lacks an ahistorical or *a priori* foundation upon which his or her analysis of revelation could be grounded. In short, a phenomenology of revelation would have to recognize the historical contingency of its own discourse.

Does this mean that contingency prevails, and that revelation remains inevitably stranded on one side of Lessing's ditch, as that which is "merely" historical, as opposed to the eternal truths of reason? Perhaps. But only if we chose to ignore an essential feature of language itself. As I noted a moment ago, all technical or scientific forms of language intended to establish univocity and objectivity are themselves derivative, since their very construction presupposes one's prior belonging to a (natural) language. Now, the fact that one happens to speak this (natural) language rather than another is in some sense contingent (since one might have been born elsewhere, under different circumstances or at a different time). Nevertheless, the *fact* that one must speak some particular language (or languages) rather than another is a *necessary* feature of human existence—it is a condition of our inhabiting a world in the first place.

Ricoeur found himself reflecting upon this "necessary fact" toward the end of his own life: "I cannot choose my ancestors, or my contemporaries. There is, in my origins, a chance element, if I look at things from the outside." If, however, "I consider them from within," then it appears as "an irreducible situational fact. So I am my birth and heritage."[11] This situational dimension of myself "is not limited to feelings, emotions and passions, in short to the irrational side of my convictions, opposed to the rational side of my arguments; it includes everything I place under the heading of heritage, birth, culture."[12] Thus, the urge for rational, speculative, or conceptual understanding characteristic of the philosophical tradition is as much a part of Ricoeur's linguistic inheritance as is the calling to biblical faith. "The polarity of adherence [to a religious tradition] and of [philosophical] critique is itself placed under the sign of this prior giving": in other words, the tension between reason and revelation is itself subsumed within "the fullness of language" that we inherit, and it is from this fullness of language that philosophical reflection begins.[13]

In the end, the phenomenology of revelation is perhaps best seen as an attempt to respond to the solicitations implicit within a complex linguistic heritage which encompasses, in a mutually productive tension, both critique and conviction, reason, and revelation. Ricoeur articulated his response to this necessarily contingent dimension of his own existence with the following formula: "A chance transformed into destiny by a continuous choice."

> By this word destiny I do not indicate any imposition, any unbearable burden, any misfortune, but the very status of a conviction, about which I can say: well, here I stand. [. . .] It is this destiny whose hermeneutic status I am seeking to express. I will risk characterizing this "here I stand"—another formula for a destiny into which chance gets transformed—by the paradox of a relative absolute.[14]

It is only by passing through this paradox that one can begin to bridge reason and revelation, the historical and the eternal. To reason in the face of revelation, to accept the paradox of a relative absolute, is to assume the endless task of owning up to the contingency of one's own past—a past inherited in the form of a language, a world received through words always already addressed to oneself.

NOTES

1. See above, Chapter 1, Section 1.
2. See above, Chapter 3, Section 11.
3. Ricoeur, "Experience and Language," 143, 145.
4. Martin Heidegger, "'The Problem of a Nonobjectifying Thinking and Speaking in Today's Theology'—Some pointers to Its Major Aspects," in *The Religious*, ed. John Caputo (Malden, MA: Blackwell Publishers, 2002). This letter was eventually published as an appendix to his lecture on "Phenomenology and Theology," despite the fact that it was penned roughly thirty-six years later (PT 62).
5. Heidegger, "The Problem of a Nonobjectifying Speaking and Thinking in Today's Theology," 61–62 (italics mine).
6. Ibid., 64.
7. While one should not overlook differences between the earlier and later Heideggers, on this question concerning the content of the call, there are at least two points continuity: First, the call of conscience does not speak in objectifying language (it "asserts nothing, gives no information about world-events"). It is on account of this aspect of the call that early Heidegger concludes in *Being and Time* that the call strictly says *nothing*. Secondly, and this is the critical point of intersection, the call is in some sense addressed both to me *and* by me—thus, confirming the point I have made with respect to the later Heidegger, namely, that the call speaks Dasein's own language (BT 318–322).
8. Heidegger, "The Problem of a Nonobjectifying Speaking and Thinking in Today's Theology," 62.
9. Ibid., 61.

10. Ibid.
11. Paul Ricoeur, *Living Up to Death*, trans. David Pellauer (Chicago: The University of Chicago Press, 2009), 62.
12. Ibid., 63.
13. Ricoeur, *Critique and Conviction*, 146.
14. Ibid., 64–65.

Epilogue
In the Beginning Was the Word

> Description is revelation. It is not
> The thing described, nor a false facsimile. [. . .]
> As text we should be born that we might read,
> More explicit than the experience of sun
> And moon, the book of reconciliation,
> Book of a concept only possible
> In description, canon central in itself,
> The thesis of the plentifullest John. [. . .]
> Thus the theory of description matters most.
> It is the theory of the word for those
> For whom the word is the making of the world,
> The buzzing world and lisping firmament.
>
> Wallace Stevens, "Description Without Place"

A "description without place" is a description of a world beyond *this* place, beyond the *hic et nunc*, beyond the "thing described," the humdrum reality of manipulable objects. Perhaps revelation is just such a description, and all such descriptions revelations. But these descriptions "without place" would not, for all of that, be beyond words, beyond the domain of language and text. For the world that revelation would open—at least for those prepared to "read" it—is "buzzing" and "lisping" with language; it is a world made by the living word itself. "It is," as Stevens writes, "a world of words to the end of it."

What could such a world be if not a world of the text? It would not amount to a "false facsimile" of our own, nor a mere phantasy, nor a projection of ourselves; rather it would involve a reconfiguration which, lifting our sights toward the firmament of a second-order reference, brings into view new possibilities. A world of possibilities revealed by "concepts" that are "only possible / In description"—in the plentiful surplus of a language that speaks *to* us, *through* us, and *before* us.

The theory of revelation, like Stevens's "theory of description," would be nothing less than a "theory of the word for those / For whom the word is the making of the world."

Bibliography

Baillie, John. *The Idea of Revelation*. New York: Columbia University Press, 1965.
Barash, Jeffrey. *Martin Heidegger and the Problem of Historical Meaning: Revised and Expanded Edition*. New York: Fordham University Press, 2003.
Barth, Karl. "Concluding Unscientific Postscript on Schleiermacher." In *Karl Barth: Theologian of Freedom*, edited by Clifford Green, 66–90. Minneapolis: Fortress Press, 1991.
Benson, Bruce, ed. *Words of Life: New Theological Turns in French Phenomenology*. New York: Fordham University Press, 2010.
Bultmann, Rudolf. *Theology of the New Testament*. Translated by Kendrick Grobel. Waco, TX: Baylor University Press, 2007.
Buren, John van. "Martin Heidegger, Martin Luther." In *Reading Heidegger from the Start: Essays in His Earliest Thought*, edited by T. Kisiel and J. van Buren, 159–74. New York: SUNY Press, 1994.
Caputo, John. "Heidegger and Theology." In *The Cambridge Companion to Heidegger: Second Edition*, edited by Charles Guignon, 326–44. New York: Cambridge University Press, 2006.
———. *The Religious*. Malden, MA: Blackwell Publishers, 2002.
———. "Apostles of the Impossible: God and the Gift in Derrida and Marion." In *God, the Gift, and Postmodernism*, edited by John Caputo and Michael Scanlon. Bloomington: Indiana University Press, 1999.
———. *The Prayers and Tears of Jacques Derrida*. Bloomington: Indiana University Press, 1997.
Calvin, John. *Institutes of the Christian Religion*. Translated by Henry Beveridge. Grand Rapids, MI: W. M. B. Eerdmans Publishing Company, 1989.
Carlson, Thomas A. "Blindness and the Decision to See: On Revelation and Reception in Jean-Luc Marion." In *Counter-Experiences: Reading Jean-Luc Marion*, edited by Kevin Hart, 153–80. Notre Dame, IN: Notre Dame University Press, 2017.

Coogan, Michael, ed. *The New Oxford Annotated Bible: New Revised Standard Version with the Apocrypha (third addition)*. New York: Oxford University Press, 2001.

Courtine, Jean-Francois. "Introduction: Phenomenology and Hermeneutics of Religion." In *Phenomenology and the "Theological Turn."* Translated by Bernard Prusak. New York: Fordham University Press, 2000.

Cross, F. L., and E. A. Livingstone. *The Oxford Dictionary of the Christian Church*. London: Oxford University Press, 2005.

Derrida, Jacques. "Faith and Knowledge: The Two Sources of 'Religion' at the Limits of Reason Alone." In *Religion*, edited by J. Derrida and G. Vattimo, 1–78. Stanford, CA: Stanford University Press, 1998.

———. *The Gift of Death*. Translated by David Wills. Chicago: The University of Chicago Press, 1995.

———. *Aporias*. Translated by Thomas Dutoit. Stanford, CA: Stanford University Press, 1993.

———. *Given Time: I. Counterfeit Money*. Translated by Peggy Kamuf. Chicago: The University of Chicago Press, 1991.

———. "Violence and Metaphysics: An Essay on the Thought of Emmanuel Levinas." In *Writing and Difference*. Translated by Alan Bass. Chicago: The University of Chicago Press, 1978.

———. *Speech and Phenomena: And Other Essays on Husserl's Theory of Signs*. Translated by David Allison. Evanston, IL: Northwestern University Press, 1973.

Deninger, Johannes. "Revelation." In *The Encyclopedia of Religion*, edited by Mircea Eliade. New York: Macmillan, 1987.

Dilthey, Wilhelm. *Introduction to the Human Sciences: Selected Works, Vol. 1.*, edited by R. Makkreel and F. Rodi. Princeton, NJ: Princeton University Press, 1989.

———. *Pattern and Meaning in History*, edited by H. P. Rickman. New York: Harper Torchbooks, 1961.

Dreyfus, Hubert L. *Being-in-the-World: A Commentary on Heidegger's* Being and Time, *Division I*. Cambridge, MA: The MIT Press, 1995.

Falque, Emmanuel. *Crossing the Rubicon: The Borderlands of Philosophy and Theology*. Translated by Reuben Shank. New York: Fordham University Press, 2016.

Frege, Gottlobe. "On Sense and Reference." In *Meaning and Reference*. Oxford: Oxford University Press, 1994.

Gadamer, Hans-Georg. *Truth and Method: Second, Revised Edition*. Translated by Joel Weinsheimer and Donald G. Marshall. New York: Continuum, 1998.

———. "Letter to Dallmayr." In *Dialogue and Deconstruction: The Gadamer-Derrida Encounter*, edited by Diane P. Mchelfelder and Richard E. Palmer, 93–101. Albany, NY: SUNY Press, 1989.

———. "*Destruktion* and Deconstruction." In *Dialogue and Deconstruction: The Gadamer-Derrida Encounter*, edited by Diane P. Mchelfelder and Richard E. Palmer, 102–13. Albany, NY: SUNY Press, 1989.

———. *Philosophical Hermeneutics*. Translated and edited by David E. Linge. Berkeley: University of California Press, 1977.

Gasché, Rodolphe. *Inventions of Difference: On Jacques Derrida.* Cambridge, MA: Harvard University Press, 1994.
Gilson, Etienne. *The Christian Philosophy of St. Thomas Aquinas.* Translated by L. K. Shook. Notre Dame, IN: University of Notre Dame Press, 2006.
Grondin, Jean. "Die Wiedererweckung der Seinfrage auf dem Weg einer phänomenologisch-hermeneutischen Destruktion." In *Martin Heidegger: Sein und Zeit,* edited by Thoman Rentsch, 8–289. Berlin: Akademie Verlag, 2001.
Gschwandtner, Christina M. *Degrees of Givenness: On Saturation in Jean-Luc Marion.* Bloomington: Indiana University Press, 2014.
Hanson, J. A. "Jean-Luc Marion and the Possibility of a Postmodern Theology." In *Mars Hill Review,* Fall 1998 (12), 93–104.
Hart, Kevin, ed. *Counter-Experiences: Reading Jean-Luc Marion.* Notre Dame, IN: Notre Dame University Press, 2017.
Hart, Trevor. "Revelation." In *The Cambridge Companion to Karl Barth,* edited by John Webster, 37–56. Cambridge: Cambridge University Press, 2000.
Hegel, G. W. F. *Phenomenology of Spirit.* Translated by A. V. Miller. Oxford: Oxford University Press, 1977.
Heidegger, Martin. *The Phenomenology of Religious Life.* Translated by M. Fritsch and J. Gosetti-Ferencei. Bloomington: Indiana University Press, 2004. *Phänomenologie des Religiösen Lebens, Gesamtausgabe* vol. 60, Frankfurt: Vittorio Klostermann, 1996.
———. "Phenomenology and Theology." In *The Religious,* edited by John Caputo, 49–66. Malden, MA: Blackwell Publishers, 2002. / "Phänomenologie und Theologie" *Wegmarken, Gesamtausgabe* vol. 9, Frankfurt: Vittorio Klostermann, 1996.
———. "'The Problem of a Nonobjectifying Thinking and Speaking in Today's Theology'—Some Pointers to Its Major Aspects." In *The Religious,* edited by John Caputo, 60–66. Malden, MA: Blackwell Publishers, 2002.
———. "The Onto-theo-logical Constitution of Metaphysics." In *The Religious,* edited by John Caputo, 67–75. Malden, MA: Blackwell Publishers, 2002.
———. *Identity and Difference.* Translated by Jan Stambaugh. Chicago: The University of Chicago Press, 2000.
———. *Seminare, Gesamtausgabe* vol. 15, Frankfurt: Vittorio Klostermann, 1996.
———. "Letter on Humanism." In *Martin Heidegger: Basic Writings (Revised and Expanded Edition),* edited by D. Krell and translated by F. Capuzzi, 213–66. San Francisco: Harper San Francisco, 1993.
———. *History of the Concept of Time: Prolegomena.* Translated by Theodore Kisiel. Bloomington: Indiana University Press, 1985.
———. *Basic Problems of Phenomenology.* Translated by Albert Hofstadter. Bloomington: Indiana University Press, 1982.
———. *Being and Time.* Translated by Macquarrie and Robinson. New York: Harper & Row, 1962. / *Sein und Zeit.* Tübingen: Max Niemeyer Verlag, 1953.
Horner, Robyn. *Rethinking God as Gift: Marion, Derrida and the Limits of Phenomenology.* New York: Fordham University Press, 2001.

Husserl, Edmund. *Phantasy, Image Consciousness, and Memory (1898–1925)*. Translated by John B. Brough. The Netherlands: Springer, 2005.

———. *Logical Investigations: Volume I & II*. Translated by J. N. Findlay. New York: Routledge, 2001.

———. *Cartesian Meditations: An Introduction to Phenomenology*. Translated by Dorion Cairns. London: Kluwer Academic Publishers, 1997.

———. *Ideas Pertaining to a Pure Phenomenology and to a Phenomenological Philosophy: First Book*. Translated by F. Kersten. Boston: Kluwer Academic Publishers, 1982.

Janicaud, Dominique. *The Theological Turn of French Phenomenology*. In *Phenomenology and the "Theological Turn."* Translated by Bernard G. Prusak, 3–106. New York: Fordham University Press, 2000.

Jones, Tamsin. *A Genealogy of Marion's Philosophy of Religion*. Bloomington: Indiana University Press, 2011.

Kant, Immanuel. *Critique of Pure Reason*. Translated by P. Guyer and A. Wood. Cambridge: Cambridge University Press, 2002.

———. *Critique of the Power of Judgment*. Translated by P. Guyer & A. Wood. Cambridge: Cambridge University Press, 2002.

———. *Religion within the Boundaries of Mere Reason, and Other Writings*, edited by Allen Wood and George di Giovanni. New York: Cambridge University Press, 1998.

Kearney, Richard. *Debates in Continental Philosophy*. New York: Fordham University Press, 2004.

Kierkegaard, Søren. *Philosophical Fragments/Johannes Climacus*. Translated by Howard Hong and Edna Hong. Princeton, NJ: Princeton University Press, 1985.

Kisiel, Theodore. *The Genesis of Heidegger's 'Being and Time.'* Los Angeles: University of California Press, 1995.

———. "Heidegger (1920-21) on Becoming a Christian: A Conceptual Picture Show." In *Reading Heidegger from the Start: Essays in His Earliest Thought*, edited by T. Kisiel and J. van Buren, 174–94. New York: SUNY Press, 1994.

Kleinberg, Ethan. *Generation Existential: Heidegger's Philosophy in France 1927–1961*. New York: Cornell University Press, 2005.

Kosky, Jeffrey. "Translator's Preface: The Phenomenology of Religion: New Possibilities for Philosophy and for Religion." In *Phenomenology and the Theological Turn*, edited by Janicaud et al. New York: Fordham University Press, 2000.

Kuhn, Thomas. *Structure of Scientific Revolutions*. Chicago: University of Chicago Press, 1970.

Lacoste, Jean-Yves, ed. *Encyclopedia of Christian Theology*. New York: Routledge, 2005.

Lehmann, Karl. "Christliche Geschichtserfahrung und ontologische Frage beim jungen Heidegger." *Philosophisches Jahrbuch* 74, 1966, 126–53.

Levinas, Emmanuel. *Totality and Infinity: An Essay on Exteriority*. Translated by Alphonso Lingis. Pittsburgh: Duquesne University Press, 2000.

———. *The Theory of Intuition in Husserl's* Phenomenology: *Second Edition.* Translated by André Orianne. Evanston, IL: Northwestern University Press, 1995.
———. "Language and Proximity." In *Collected Philosophical Papers*, edited by Alphonso Lingis, 109–26. Dordrecht: Martinus Nijhoff Publishers, 1987.
Lessing, Gotthold. *Lessing's Theological Writings*. Translated by Henry Chadwick. Stanford, CA: Stanford University Press, 1957.
Mackinlay, Shane. *Interpreting Excess: Jean-Luc Marion, Saturated Phenomena, and Hermeneutics*. New York: Fordham University Press, 2010.
Marion, Jean-Luc. "The Hermeneutics of Givenness." In *The Enigma of Divine Revelation: Between Phenomenology and Comparative Theology*, edited by Marion and Jacobs-Vandegeer, 17–48. Cham, Switzerland: Springer, 2020.
———. "Thinking Elsewhere." *Journal for Continental Philosophy of Religion* 1 (2019), 5–26.
———. *Givenness and Revelation*. Translated by Stephen Lewis. Oxford: Oxford University Press, 2018.
———. *The Reason of the Gift*. Translated by Stephen Lewis. Charlottesville: University of Virginia Press, 2011.
———. *Prolegomena to Charity*. Translated by Stephen Lewis. New York: Fordham University Press, 2002.
———. *In Excess: Studies of Saturated Phenomena*. Translated by Robyn Horner. New York: Fordham University Press, 2002.
———. "The Final Appeal to the Subject." In *The Religious*, edited by John Caputo. Malden, MA: Blackwell Publishers, 2002.
———. *Being Given: Toward a Phenomenology of Givenness*. Translated by Jeffrey Kosky. Stanford, CA: Stanford University Press, 2002.
———. *The Idol and Distance: Five Studies*. Translated by Thomas Carlson. New York: Fordham University Press, 2001.
———. "The Saturated Phenomena." In *Phenomenology and the "Theological Turn."* Translated by Bernard Prusak. New York: Fordham University Press, 2000.
———. "The Other First Philosophy and the Question of Givennes." In *Critical Inquiry*. Summer 1999, 25 (4), 784–800.
———. "Sketch of a Phenomenology of Gift." In *Postmodern Philosophy and Christian Thought*, edited by Marold Westphal, 122–39. Bloomington: Indiana University Press, 1999.
———. *Reduction and Givenness: Investigations of Husserl, Heidegger, and Phenomenology*. Translated by Thomas Carlson. Evanston, IL: Northwestern University Press, 1998.
———. "Metaphysics and Phenomenology: A Relief for Theology." *Critical Inquiry*, Summer 1994, 20, 527–91.
———. *God without Being: Hors-Texte*. Translated by Thomas Carlson. Chicago: The University of Chicago Press, 1991.
Moran, Dermot. *Husserl: Founder of Phenomenology*. Malden, MA: Polity Press, 2005.
Moyn, Samuel. *Origins of the Other: Emmanuel Levinas Between Revelation and Ethics*. London: Cornell University Press, 2005.

Nabert, Jean. *Désir de Dieu*. Paris: Aubier-Montaigne, 1966.

Palmer, Richard. *Hermeneutics: Interpretation Theory in Schleiermacher, Dilthey, Heidegger, and Gadamer*. Evanston, IL: Northwestern University Press, 1969.

Pöggeler, Otto. *Martin Heidegger's Path of Thinking*. Translated by D. Magurshak and S. Barber. Atlantic Highlands, NJ: Humanities Press International, Inc., 1987.

Proudfoot, Wayne. *Religious Experience*. Berkeley: University of California Press, 1985.

Rahner, Karl, ed. *Encyclopedia of Theology*. London: Burns & Oats, 1975.

Ricoeur, P. and A. Lacocque. *Thinking Biblically: Exegetical and Hermeneutical Studies*. Translated by D. Pellauer. Chicago: The University of Chicago Press, 1998. / *Penser la Bible* (La couleur des idées). Paris: Seuil, 1998. [Co-authored by A. Lacocque.]

Ricoeur, Paul. *Living Up to Death*. Translated by David Pellauer. Chicago: The University of Chicago Press, 2009.

———. "Experience and Language in Religious Discourse." In *Phenomenology and the "Theological Turn": The French Debate*. Translated by Bernard G. Prusak, 127–46. New York: Fordham University, 2000.

———. *Critique and Conviction: Conversations with François Azouvi and Marc de Launay*. Translated by K. Blamey. Oxford: Polity Press-Blackwell, 1998. / *La critique et la conviction. Entretien avec François Azouvi et Marc de Launay*. Paris: Calmann-Lévy, 1995.

———. *Figuring the Sacred: Religion, Narrative, and Imagination*, edited by M. Wallace and translated by D. Pellauer. Minneapolis: Fortress Press, 1995.

———. "The Summoned Self." In *Figuring the Sacred: Religion, Narrative, and Imagination*, edited by M. Wallace and translated by D. Pellauer, 262–78. Minneapolis: Fortress Press, 1995.

———. *Oneself as Another*. Translation by K. Blamey. Chicago: The University of Chicago Press, 1992. / *Soi-même comme un autre* (L'ordre philosophique). Paris: Seuil, 1990.

———. *A Ricoeur Reader: Reflection and Imagination*, edited by M. Valdes. New York: Harvester-Wheatsheaf, 1991.

———. *From Text to Action. Essays in Hermeneutics II*. Translated by K. Blamey and J. Thompson. London: The Athlone Press, 1991. / *Du texte à l'action. Essais d'herméneutique. II*. (Esprit). Paris: Seuil, 1986

———. *Fallible Man*. Translated by C. Kelbley. New York: Fordham University Press, 1986. / *Philosophie de la volonté. Finitude et Culpabilité. I. L'homme faillible* (Philosophie de l'esprit). Paris: Aubier, 1960.

———. *Time and Narrative. Vol. III*. Translated by K. McLaughlin and D. Pellauer. Chicago: University of Chicago Press, 1984. / *Temps et récit. Tome III. Le temps raconté* (L'ordre philosophique). Paris: Seuil, 1985.

———. "The Status of *Vorstellung* in Hegel's Philosophy of Religion." In *Meaning, Truth and God*, edited by L. Rouner, 70–88. Notre Dame, IN: University of Notre Dame Press, 1982.

———. *Hermeneutics and the Human Sciences: Essays on Language, Action and Interpretation*, edited and translated by J. Thompson. Cambridge: Cambridge University Press, 1981.

———. *Essays on Biblical Interpretation*, edited by L. Mudge. Philadelphia: Fortress Press, 1980.

———. "Note Introductive." In *Heidegger et la Question de Dieu*, edited by R. Kearney and J. O'Leary, 17. Paris: Grasset, 1980.

———. *The Philosophy of Paul Ricoeur: An Anthology of His Work*, edited by C. Reagan and D. Stewart. Boston: Beacon Press, 1978.

———. *The Rule of Metaphor: Multi-Disciplinary Studies of the Creation of Meaning in Language*. Translated by R. Czerny and K. McLaughlin. London and Henley: Routledge and Kegan Paul, 1978. / *La métaphore vive* (L'ordre philosophique). Paris: Seuil, 1975.

———. *Freud and Philosophy: An Essay on Interpretation*. Translated by D. Savage. New Haven, CT: Yale University Press, 1977. / *De l'interpretation. Essai sur Freud* (L'oder philosophique). Paris: Seuil, 1965.

———. *Interpretation Theory: Discourse and the Surplus of Meaning*. Fort Worth: Texas Christian University Press, 1976.

———. "Philosophy and Religious Language." *The Journal of Religion* 54 (1974), No. 1, 71–85.

———. *The Conflict of Interpretations: Essays in Hermeneutics*. Translated and edited by D. Ihde. Evanston, IL: Northwestern University Press, 1974. / *Le conflict des interpretations. Essais d'herméneutique* (L'ordre philosophique). Paris: Seuil, 1969.

———. *Husserl: An Analysis of His Phenomenology*. Translated by Edward G. Ballard and Lester E. Embree. Evanston, IL: Northwestern University Press, 1967.

———. *Symbolism of Evil*. Translated by E. Buchanan. Boston: Beacon Press, 1969. / *Philosophie de la volonté. Finitude et Culpabilité. II. La symbolique de mal.* (Philosophie de l'esprit). Paris: Aubier, 1960.

Rousseau, Jean-Jacques. *Emile, or On Education*. Translated by Allan Bloom. New York: Basic Books, 1979.

Rorty, Richard. *Philosophy and the Mirror of Nature*. Princeton, NJ: Princeton University Press, 1979.

Sartre, Jean-Paul. *Existentialism and Human Emotions*. New York: Citadel Press, 1997.

Schrijvers, Joeri. *Ontotheological Turnings?: The Decentering of the Modern Subject in Recent French Phenomenology*. New York: SUNY Press, 2012.

Vedder, Ben. *Heidegger's Philosophy of Religion: From God to the Gods*. Pittsburgh: Duquesne University Press, 2007.

Vries, Hent de. *Philosophy and the Turn to Religion*. Baltimore: Johns Hopkins University Press, 1999.

Wallace, Mark. *The Second Naiveté: Barth, Ricoeur and the New Yale Theology (second edition)*. Macon, GA: Mercer University Press, 1995.

Wittgenstein, Ludwig. *Philosophical Investigations*. Translated by G. M. Anscombe. Oxford: Basil Blackwell, 1968.

Yadav, Sameer. *The Problem of Perception and the Experience of God: Toward a Theological Empiricism*. Minneapolis: Fortress Press, 2015.

Zahavi, Dan. *Husserl's Phenomenology*. Stanford, CA: Stanford University Press, 2003.

Zarader, Marlène. *The Unthought Debt: Heidegger and The Hebraic Heritage*. Translated by Bettina Bergo. Stanford, CA: Stanford University Press, 2006.

Index

abandonment, 178–79
absolute, 26, 34–36, 40–42, 56, 62, 67n4, 95, 172
   paradox of relative, 203
   See also knowledge; science
adonné, 107, 113, 114, 116, 126, 131, 179, 199
agape. *See* gift
anonymity, 116–18, 120, 123–24, 147, 182
anonymous call. *See* call
apophantic reasoning. *See* assertions
apophatic, 7, 19, 117, 125
appearance, xxvi, xxviii, 3, 9, 54, 61, 78, 86, 126, 128–32, 134n6, 166–67
Aquinas, xxi–xxii, 11, 12, 209
Aristotelian, 57–59, 98, 104
assertions, 127–29
attenuation, 16, 23, 50, 145, 197
attestation, 66, 142n85, 182
Aufgehoben, 14, 65
Aufhebung, xxiv, 14, 65, 187
Aufzeigen, 128
Auslegung, 29, 127–29
authorial intention. *See* authorship
authoritative status of text, 160–62, 168, 193n29
authorship, 151, 154–56, 166, 170, 191, 193n34

Barash, Jeffrey, 58, 72n41
Being: of entities, xxix, 2–3, 6–9, 12, 14, 21n61, 27–45, 48–49, 54–66, 68n6, 69n18, 70n21, 71nn27–28, 72n46, 78, 82–88, 96–106, 108, 134, 135n36, 136n38, 140nn54–57, 146–53, 173–74, 175–77, 189, 190n4, 194n2
   -in-the-world, 154–58, 179
   -towards-death, 2, 32, 45
   non-, 104–5
Being Given: Toward a Phenomenology of Givenness by Jeffrey Kosky (BG), 85–87, 108–16, 119–21, 124–25, 133n1, 135nn28–30, 138, 141n60, 142n73, 142n83, 147
Being and Time by Martin Heidegger (BT), 19n21, 27–29, 31–32, 34–40, 67n2, 68n7, 69n11, 69n13, 69n18, 69n20, 70n21, 70n23, 71n28, 75n75, 87, 128–29, 174–75, 203n7
belonging, 8, 58–59, 158, 160–62, 164–65, 189
bracketing questions of truth, xxvii, 3, 116–18, 122–24, 152, 180, 188
   See also truth

call

anonymity or pureness of, xii, 7,
    107, 111, 113–32, 140, 146–
    47, 198–201
  pure, xii, 107, 111, 115, 119,
    123, 124, 147
  and response, 129, 185, 201
  to revelation or faith, xii,
    13, 79, 105–7
  See also consciousness
Caputo, John, xii, xxvii, xxxiin27, 17n1,
    72n36, 76n80, 203n4
Caravaggio, 119
Cartesian, 7, 8, 136, 137, 179, 194
  See also Descartes
categorical intuition, 81–84, 135n17,
    108, 141n60
  Heideggerian, 60, 73, 78
  mistakes of, 118, 124
  See also revelation
categories, 53, 58, 80, 159, 165–66, 187
causa sui, 97–99, 101–2, 140n54
child-father relationship, 120–21
Chrétien, John-Louis, xxvii–xxix, 2
Christlichkeit, 24, 55–67, 142n80
cogito, 179, 194
composite discourse, 186–87
concrete
  experience, 36–37, 42–43, 52,
    72, 192n19
  experience of revelation, 15, 24,
    50–51, 109, 115, 142, 149
  historical content, x, xii, 45, 185
  texts and religious discourse, ix,
    xii, 4–16, 52–53, 61–62, 147,
    179, 185, 199
conditions of possibility, 5, 15, 34, 61,
    67, 123, 202
The Conflict of Interpretations: Essays
    in Hermeneutics, by Paul Ricoeur
    (CI), 150–53, 173–79, 190n5, 194n3
consciousness, xxvii–xxviii, xxxin16,
    1–3, 15, 80–81, 85–88, 90, 136–37,
    141n60, 162, 178, 181, 197; call of,
    182–84, 203n7
  See also call

constitution, 7, 112, 127, 131, 138, 179,
    183, 199, 201
  ontological or onto-theo-logical,
    31–32, 38, 65, 96, 136,
    174, 194n40
  See also Dasein; ontic
contamination, x, xii, 7, 16, 23–24,
    49–57, 62–66, 77–79, 106–18,
    122–25, 132, 145–46, 149, 172, 175,
    179, 188, 197
contingency, 136, 160, 136n8 160, 180
  of history, xxiv–xxv, xxxi,
    188, 202–3
  of truth, xxi–xxii, 198, 202–3
conviction, 160–62, 180
counter-contamination. *See*
    contamination
crypto-theology, 115–16, 142n75,
    181, 185, 197

Darstellung, 188
das Man, 7, 175, 182
Dasein, 2, 7, 25, 31–32, 38–48, 52, 56,
    60, 64–67, 67n4, 68n23, 25, 71nn27–
    28, 99–102, 112, 127–29, 136n38,
    140n54, 146, 149, 153, 173–76,
    190n4, 194n40, 203n7
  See also Being
de Vries, Hent, xxii, xxvii, 17n3, 24,
    42, 46–49, 53, 63, 71n30, 72n36,
    72n43, 73nn51–53, 74n68, 75n77,
    106, 190n1
death, 30–32
debt, 138n47, 189
deconstruction, 7, 24, 46–49, 51,
    111, 176, 194
Derrida, Jacques, xii, xxxiin19, 18n19,
    19n24, 19n32, 24, 30–34, 40, 47–52,
    69nn8–19, 72n36, 73nn47–52,
    74nn66–67, 83–85, 103–6, 111,
    114–15, 118, 125nn24–27, 135,
    140nn56–57, 142n82, 183, 187
Descartes, 15, 78, 97, 136–37
  See also Cartesian
dessaisissement. *See* divestment

destiny, 79, 197, 203
determinacy, xii, 7, 15, 50–52, 66–67, 79, 115, 120–25, 129, 143, 147, 159–61, 184–87, 198, 190n3, 191n16, 199–201
 indeterminacy, 63, 79, 115–18, 122–25, 129, 147, 198
Dilthey, Wilhelm, 44, 147–55, 158, 174, 190n8
distanciation, 59, 128, 157, 161, 164, 192
divestment, or dessaisissement, 50–51, 67n3, 107, 147, 179
divine name(s), 7, 116–17, 132
Droysen, Johann, 150

eidetic, 89, 159, 202
eidos, xxvi, 15, 143
emplotment, 166
epistemology, epistemic, xxii, xxv, xxix, 3, 6, 9, 31–32, 54, 74n69, 88, 136, 149–54, 173, 174–78, 190n10, 191n15, 192n28, 193n29, 194n42
epistles, 1, 43, 96
epoche, 118, 152
Erfahrung, 29, 73n50, 139n51
Essays on Biblical Interpretation by Paul Ricoeur (EBI), 161–62, 165–66, 171, 187–88, 193nn34–35
essentia, 39, 70n26
eucharist, 94
evidence, 3, 83–84, 87
ex nihilo, 104
excess of intuition, 108
exercising a claim, 114, 120–21, 199
existentials, 24, 32, 45–46, 50, 53, 140n54
existentiell, 60, 65–66, 67n4, 69n16

face, 18n18, 86, 95, 119, 138nn46–47, 191n12
factical, facticity, ix, xxi, 26–27, 32–33, 42–46, 53, 56, 59–65, 71n35, 72n36, 72n38, 73n48, 148–49

faith, xii, xxi, xxv, xxvii, xxxin14, xxxiin29, 1–3, 12, 14, 24–26, 44–47, 55, 58–68, 73n47, 73n52, 74n66, 75n78, 102, 104, 109–13, 121, 126–27, 138n48, 140n54, 142n85, 146, 156, 160, 165, 170, 180, 183, 189, 202
Falque, Emmanuel, xxvii, xxxn1, xxxiin29, 142n85, 194n44
father, 11, 14, 94, 107, 115, 120–21
 See also child-father relationship
Feuerbach, Ludwig, 91–92
figure of revelation, xxvi, 79, 109–11, 122, 142n80, 146–47, 159, 171, 197
Figuring the Sacred: Religion, Narrative, and Imagination, by Paul Ricoeur (FS), 75n78, 155, 158, 165–70, 183–84, 193n36, 193n39, 194n46, 195n49
finitude, 7, 130, 151
first order reference, 157
fixation, 92–93, 151, 154, 163, 170, 191
formal or formalization, xxii, 10, 15–16, 18n12, 23–24, 50–57, 62–67, 69n20, 71n35, 72n36, 73n56, 79–80, 86, 96, 102, 107, 111, 115, 118, 140, 141n66, 142n76, 142n80, 145–47, 153, 177, 202
 indeterminacy, 119, 122–25, 143
 indication (formale Anzeige), 42–43, 50, 57, 65, 71n35, 72n36, 96, 143n91
forms, ix, xxxin14, 8, 30, 72n46, 127–34, 164–66, 178, 182, 185, 191n15, 193n29, 199, 202
Frege, Gottlobe, 155, 191n14
Freud, Sigmund, 91
fulfillment, 89, 90, 137n42
 of intuition, 83, 89, 117
fundamental structures, 33, 67

gap, between reason and revelation, 86, 107, 130, 198
 See also revelation

gaze, 36, 66, 86–97, 107, 137, 138n48, 141n60, 176
  See also other
Geisteswissenschaft, 127, 150
genius, 151, 170, 188
genre, 157–58, 168–69
gift, 14, 78, 88, 105–7, 112–18, 121, 124, 130–32, 140, 141n66, 141n71, 179, 198–201
givenness, x, xii, xxviii–xxix, 5–7, 77–89, 98–99, 106–8, 111–18, 121–32, 135n25, 136n38, 140n72, 146–49, 161, 179
  pregiven, 133
  pure givenness, xxviii, 78, 86–88, 106, 115, 123–25, 131–32, 140n58, 146, 149
  See also reduction
god, xii, xxi–xxv, xxix, xxxin17, 2–4, 10–14, 19n24, 19n33, 20n36, 20n40, 20n48, 21n50, 44, 48, 58–60, 67, 73, 77–78, 88–110, 114–18, 137n39, 137n43, 138n48, 139nn51–52, 140n54, 158, 164–70, 182–83, 190n3, 193n35, 199
  of Abraham, 4, 14; death of, 98, 138–39
God without Being: Hors-Texte by Jean-Luc Marion (GWB), 89–105, 137nn39–40, 138nn44–45, 138n48 139n51, 140n53
Greisch, Jean, 113, 139n51
Grondin, Jean, 113
guilt, 65–66

Hart, Kevin, xxvii, 142n75, 190n1
Hart, Trevor, 18n11
Hebrew, 10–11, 46, 51–52, 72n46, 73n56, 74n59, 74n62, 163–64, 199
  See also Torah
Henry, Michel, xxvii–xxviii, 2
hermeneutics, ix–xii, xiiin2, xxiii, xxviii, 6–8, 10, 15–16, 23, 31–32, 37–38, 70n21, 74n69, 113, 126–33, 141n70, 142n76, 142n85, 145–89, 190n4, 191n15, 193n29, 194nn42–43, 197–98, 200–203
hermeneutical phenomenology, x, 7–9, 190, 197
infinite, 129–30
  See also suspicion
Hermeneutics and the Human Sciences, by Paul Ricoeur (HH), 74n69, 150–57, 176, 191n16, 192nn19–20, 194n42
historical school, 151
history, x–xxv, xxix–xxx, xxxin5, xxxin7, 3, 5, 9, 16, 18n11, 26, 33, 42, 45–48, 57–62, 65, 69n20, 72n41, 73n48, 74n62, 75n71, 78–79, 90, 107–9, 146, 149, 150–54, 160–62, 170–78, 185–88, 193n29, 193n38, 194n42, 198–203
hollowing out, 50–55, 79, 107
horizon, xxviii–xxix, 78, 85–88, 93, 98–99, 104–8, 110–11, 114, 121, 131–32, 141n66, 153, 193n34
Husserl, Edmund, x, xxv–xxix, xxxinn15–18, xxxiin25, 1–3, 9, 15, 17n1, 18n9, 21nn60–61, 78–90, 98, 108, 112–14, 123, 134n5, 134nn11–16, 135nn17–20, 135n26, 135n28, 136n38, 137nn141–42, 140n58, 142n74, 146–47, 150–53, 157–58, 174, 190n9, 192n18, 197

icon, 89, 93–96, 137n43, 138nn46–47
idol, 88–107, 110–11, 117, 137n39, 137n43, 138n46, 138n48, 140n53
imagination, 9, 19n30, 75n78, 81, 188
indeterminacy. See determinacy
infinite, 123, 129–30, 179
intentionality, xxviii–xxix, xxxiin25, 86, 112, 117, 136
interloqué, 114–16
intersubjective, 153–54
intuition, 3, 15, 29, 80–90, 107–8, 117, 130, 134n11, 135n17, 135n25, 137n41, 199
invisable, 93–95, 108, 140n53

invisibility, 91–92, 94
ipseity, 182

Janicaud, Dominique, xxviii, xxix, xxxiin19, xxxiinn22–26, 111, 115, 118, 125, 140n58, 142n81

kairological, 2, 43–46, 51, 62, 66
  See also kerygma
Kant, Immanuel, xi–xxiv, xxxin11, xxxin14, 18n18, 34–35, 78–81, 98, 108, 134nn6–7, 134n15, 141n60, 150, 153, 174, 177, 185, 188, 194n42, 195n55
  neo-Kantian, 17n7, 174
kataphasis, 117
Kearney, Richard, xxvii, 191
kerygma, 75n78, 160, 166–68, 180, 183–85
Kisiel, Theodore, 17n2, 17n7, 41–43, 68n5, 70n22, 71nn30–32, 72nn36–37, 72n40, 135n21, 135n36
knowledge, xi, xxi–xxiv, xxvii, xxxin7, 4, 6, 12, 20n48, 21n50, 25, 30–33, 59–61, 64, 70n22, 75, 102–4, 136, 137n38, 161, 173–76, 180, 183, 186
  absolute, xxiv, 151
  historical, 62, 150–53, 174–76
Kuhn, Thomas, 68n6

language, x–xii, 3, 6–9, 16, 18n18, 19n24, 33–34, 51–52, 74n62, 84, 105, 111–13, 133, 138n46, 143n91, 147, 157, 161, 165, 170–71, 177–81, 185–89, 191n12, 192n18, 197–203, 203n7, 205
  See also linguistics
Lebensphilosophie, 151–52
Lebenswelt, 153, 157–58
Leibniz, Gottfried, xxii, 80, 97–98
Lessing, Gotthold, xxii, xxiv, xxxn3, xxxin12, 18n11, 198, 202
Levinas, Emmanuel, 6, 17n5, 18n18, 54–55, 94, 103, 137n41, 138nn46–47, 146, 174, 191n12

life, xi, xxvi, 2, 8, 14, 24–25, 28, 32–33, 36, 41–47, 53, 56, 61–66, 71n35, 72n36, 72n38, 75n76, 87–90, 104, 148–57, 170, 179, 202
linguistics, ix–xii, 6–10, 16, 18n18, 33, 51, 77–79, 107, 111–13, 123–25, 132, 146–49, 173–74, 178–79, 188, 192n18, 197–202
  pre-linguistic, 6, 147, 179, 188
  See also revelation
Locke, John, xxiii–xxiv, xxxin8, 17n8, 153
logic of presupposition, 23, 29–33, 40–41, 47–49, 53, 105, 109, 178, 183–85
logos, 163, 186

Mackinlay, Shane, 113, 126–27, 130, 141n70, 143nn87–88
manifestation, 11, 36–37, 47–49, 59, 71n27, 90, 100, 110, 113, 159, 165, 170
Mark, Gospel of, 166–67, 193n36
material, x, 14–15, 46, 54, 77, 89–90, 95, 104, 107, 118, 122–25, 143n86, 151, 154, 158, 164, 193n34, 197–98
Matthew, 119, 167
mediation, ix–xii, 7–10, 18n18, 113, 132, 146–47, 151, 154–58, 163–64, 169–70, 179, 187, 197
Merleau-Ponty, Maurice, 146
metaphor, xx–xxi, 19, 72, 112, 176, 179, 182, 186–87, 195n53, 197–99
metaphysics, xxv–xxvii, 3–9, 12, 18nn18–19, 19n24, 19n27, 39, 42, 59, 70n28, 71–91, 96–101, 110, 121, 134n6, 135n25, 136n38, 148–49, 173–76, 191, 194n42
mystical theology, 7, 19n24, 117, 125
myth, 157, 169, 179, 182, 186, 191

Nabert, Jean, 178, 194n45
name, 7, 8, 11, 20n35, 57, 79, 84, 88, 114–27, 131–32, 146, 156, 158–59, 161, 165–66, 188, 199, 201

naming, 19, 84, 112, 115, 117, 119, 123, 125, 127, 131, 133, 146, 200
narrative, 14, 128, 157, 160, 164–71, 179, 193nn38–39, 198–99
neo-Kantian. *See* Kant
Nicea, Second Council of, 94, 138n45
Nietzsche, Friedrich, 78–79, 95, 98, 138n48
noesis, and noema, 87–89, 152
non-being. *See* being

objectivity, ix, xxix, 6, 14, 78, 84–88, 108, 136, 153, 202
Offenbarkeit, xii, 23–24, 46–55, 61, 66, 73n50, 99, 100, 109, 139n51, 142n80, 171, 201
  See also revealability
Offenbarung, xii, 23–24, 46–52, 61–67, 77, 99, 109, 142n80
  See also revelation
Oneself as Another by Paul Ricoeur (OA), 180–82
ontic, 16, 23–63, 68n6, 68n22, 70, 88, 96–105, 109, 127–29, 136, 140, 145–49, 159, 172–79, 183–88
  See also science
ontology, x, xii, 2, 16, 17n4, 18n18, 24–66, 67n3, 69n18, 69n20, 70n23, 70n25, 71n27, 74n67, 75n73, 77–78, 82, 86, 98–103, 107–9, 150–56, 172–78, 187, 190n10, 194n41, 194n43
  ontological difference, 27, 96–105, 140n56
  ontological structures, 24, 31–32, 50, 64–66, 142n80, 162, 175, 184
  See also science
onto-theology, 96–103, 139n52
  See also ontic
originary, 6, 9, 46–52, 73n48, 74n62, 81, 84, 146–47, 165
ostensive reference, 155–57, 164, 192n18
other, xi, xxi–xxii, xxv, xxvi, xxviii, 4, 9, 17n7, 29, 39, 95–97, 103, 136n38, 154–55, 166, 174, 180–83, 201

paradox, xii, xxvi, xxvii, 4, 35, 41, 55–56, 94–95, 110, 115, 123–24, 136, 142n84, 146, 156, 165, 200, 203
parousia, 2, 43–45, 72n38, 94
Pascal, Blaise, 4
passivity, 73, 81, 112–14, 126, 132, 189
past, 28–29, 30, 35, 60, 151, 169, 175, 194n40, 203
Paul, 1, 11, 26, 42–44, 66, 72n38, 74n62, 96, 104, 163, 183–84
phenomena, xi, xxvii, xxviii, xxix, 2–7, 43, 47, 58, 67n3, 68n6, 70n23, 71n35, 74n62, 75n73, 78–87, 108–13, 126–31, 133n4, 137n43, 138, 179, 184, 200
Phenomenology and Theology by Martin Heidegger (PT), 25–28, 40–41, 56–68, 75, 203n4
poetic, 9, 158–65, 170–71, 182, 186–89
polyphonic, 165, 199
positive science. *See* science
positum, 28–29, 39, 45–47, 55–61, 75n71, 102
possibility, x–xii, xxii, 4–5, 15, 19n32, 26–27, 30, 34–35, 43–53, 67, 73n48, 73n53, 74n62, 79–80, 87–88, 95–104, 108–32, 133n4, 136n38, 137n42, 141n66, 142n76, 143n86, 146, 150–59, 161–65, 174–77, 194n40, 199–205
  condition of, 18n18, 40, 46, 49, 61, 64, 105, 109, 126, 142n84, 157, 183–84, 187, 193n34
  See also being; revelation
post-metaphysical, 79
pre-christian, 24, 64–65, 184
prejudice, xxix, 8, 31, 124, 160–62, 176, 185, 188, 192n28, 194n42
pre-linguistic. *See* linguistic
pre-scientific, 28–29
present-at-hand, 27, 39, 43, 61, 98, 128, 136, 175
  See also ontic
presuppositionless, x, 198
pre-understanding, 31–32, 37, 192n28

primal Christian experience, 2, 24, 41–45, 51–53, 66
primordial, 6–9, 32–33, 40, 64–66, 128–29, 146–48, 158, 175–78
principle of all principles, 80, 86, 135n28
principle of sufficient reason, 5, 18n12, 80, 88, 98
proclamation, 25, 98, 163, 168
prophecy, 14, 163–71, 199
protective strategy, 24, 57, 67n3, 75n73, 79, 147
Proudfoot, Wayne, 67n3, 75n73
psychology, xxvii, xxiii, xxxin16, 3, 15, 30, 60–62, 75n73, 151–56, 170, 173, 191n13, 194n42; psychologism, 170

question-answer, 132
See also call; response

radicalization, or radicality, ix, 7, 19n24, 33–35, 67, 78–79, 87–88, 98, 103–6, 112–14, 194n42, 199
  of phenomenology, xxiiin2, 9, 79, 96, 106, 180, 185, 188, 197, 201
Ranke, Leopold, 150
ready-to-hand, 27, 39, 43, 98, 128, 136, 175
  See also ontic
reason, xi–xxx, xxxin7, xxxin14, 3–5, 11–13, 18n12, 20n48, 25, 39, 59, 65, 104, 188, 198, 202–3
  See also principle of sufficient reason
rebirth, 65–67, 193n35
reception, 14, 81, 112–32, 133n5, 161, 179, 183, 193n34, 198, 200–203
  See also gift; child-father-relationship
reduction, ix, xi, xxi, xxiii, xxiv, xxvi, xxviii, xxix, xxxin17, 3–4, 9, 14–16, 21n61, 32, 50–59, 67n3, 75n73, 78–131, 133n2, 136n38, 140n58, 148, 152–56, 168, 187, 202
Reduction and Givenness by Jean-Luc Marion (RG), 84–86, 116, 135n23, 136n38

reference, 64, 155–59, 164–65, 186, 191n13, 191n16, 201, 205
reflection, ix–xxiii, 1, 9, 64, 87, 92–94, 117, 149, 162, 174, 177–80, 185, 188–89, 202
representation, 81, 95, 139, 182, 185–88
response, 119–21, 126–32, 185, 199–201
  See also call
revealability, x–xii, 16, 23–24, 47–53, 61, 73n48, 73n53, 99–100, 109, 201
  See also Offenbarkeit
revelation
  actuality versus possibility of, 79, 109, 114–17, 122–25, 133n4, 143
  phenomenology of, x–xi, xxvi, xxx, 3–6, 9, 15–16, 17n4, 23, 37, 47, 54–55, 99, 108, 110, 117, 142n80, 159, 177, 189, 197–98, 202
  relation to language, x, 51, 113–14, 170, 203
  relation to reason, xxiv–xxvi, 4, 12, 25, 198, 202–3
  See also call; contamination; faith; gift; Offenbarkeit; Offenbarung
Romano, Claude, xxvii
romantic, 147, 151–55, 170
Rorty, Richard, 68
Rousseau, Jean-Jacques, xxiv, xxxin7, 183
The Rule of Metaphor: Multi-Disciplinary Studies of the Creation of Meaning in Language by Paul Ricoeur (RM), 19n17, 186–87

Sache, 132
Saint Matthew. *See* Matthew
Saint Paul. *See* Paul
Sartre, Jean-Paul, xxxiin25, 38–39, 70n24, 70n26, 137n41, 146
saturated phenomenon, 85, 107–10, 114, 129–31, 133n4, 135n28, 141nn59–62, 142n73, 159
Schleiermacher, 13–14, 21n55, 71n34, 100, 147, 158, 190n6

science
  historical, 62, 173–76
  human, 74n69, 128, 152, 175, 190n4, 194n42
  natural, 34, 150–54, 175, 192n28, 194n42
  ontic or ontic positive, 23–68, 101, 109, 172, 175–77
  regional or hermeneutical, 16, 33–35, 54, 68, 70n20, 77, 86, 127–29, 147, 151–52, 162, 172–73, 176–77, 183, 191n15, 194n42
  See also ontic; ontology
screen, 112, 131
scripture, 11–12, 13, 21n50, 51–52, 109, 156–59, 164–65, 180, 182, 186, 193n34, 199, 205
self, xxviii, xxx, 59, 75n78, 91, 116, 120, 127–29, 130–32, 141n71, 147, 167–69, 175–76, 178–85, 189, 192n28, 193n30, 198–203
  summoned self, 133, 179, 212
  See also being; Dasein; divestment; God; manifestation
sensibility, 80–81
sign, xxix, 59, 89–91, 135, 148, 154, 178–79, 190n1, 191n15, 193, 202
signification, 7, 18n18, 83–84, 114, 123, 129, 135n27, 163, 175, 190n3
silence, 100–101, 140n53
sin, 65–66
situatedness, 160–61
speech, 6–8, 11, 83, 135n26, 140, 155–57, 164
Spinoza, Baruch, 97
statements, xxv, 12–13
structuralism, 154–56, 174, 190n11, 191nn15–17
suneidesis, 75n78, 183–84
Surplus
  of intuition, 90, 130
  of meaning, xii, 9–10
suspicion, xxvii, 6, 67n3, 129, 161, 182
symbol, 178–89, 193n30, 195n54, 197–99
  See also sign

testimony, xxii, xxiv–xxv, xxxin7, 58, 187
From Text to Action by Paul Ricoeur (TA), 163–65, 193n32
textual mediation, x–xii, 9–10, 146, 154–58, 163–64, 169–70, 179
  other, xxi, xxviii, 17n5, 17n7, 95, 103, 138–39, 182
  See also gaze; self
thematization, 28–30, 56–57, 61
Thinking Biblically: Exegetical and Hermeneutical Studies by Paul Ricoeur and André LaCocque (TB), 168–69, 193n37
Thomas, xxii, 12
Time and Narrative by Paul Ricoeur (TN), 175–76, 194n41
Tindal, Matthew, xxiv
Toland, John, xxiv
Torah, 163, 199
  See also Hebrew
truth, xi, 3, 7–14, 18n11, 19nn25–26, 19nn29–31, 19n33, 26, 34, 41, 58, 71n27, 72n38, 83, 144n103, 155, 158, 192n28, 198, 202
  of reason, xxii–xxv, 11, 202
  See also bracketing questions of truth

unapparent, 87, 130
unconditioned, 108, 118

Verstehen, 127–29
visibility, 89–94, 131, 137n40, 138n46
voice, 84, 166–70, 182, 201

wager, Ricoeur's, 189, 198
witness, 114
Wittgenstein, Ludwig, 174, 192n18
world of the text, 156–59, 162, 164–65, 169, 174, 179, 205
worldview, 25–26, 36, 41, 63, 68n5

Zarader, Marléne, 24, 41, 46–55, 72n46, 73n46, 73nn55–56, 74nn59–65, 163

About the Author

Adam J. Graves received his doctorate from the University of Pennsylvania. He is currently professor of philosophy at Metropolitan State University of Denver, where he also serves as founding director of D-phi, a center for public humanities.

www.ingramcontent.com/pod-product-compliance
Lightning Source LLC
Chambersburg PA
CBHW021351300426
44114CB00012B/1183